"*Mindfulness Meditation in Psychotherapy* by St~~e~~ wise, scholarly, and practical. For anyone int~~e~~ therapy, it is a must-read. This book lies at the ~~...mindfulness~~ and psychotherapy, and clearly illustrates how mindfulness intersects with psychotherapy."

> —**Bob Stahl, PhD,** coauthor of *A Mindfulness-Based Stress Reduction Workbook, Living With Your Heart Wide Open, Calming the Rush of Panic, A Mindfulness-Based Stress Reduction Workbook for Anxiety,* and *MBSR Every Day*

"This book brings mindfulness literature to a refreshing and academic new depth. Scholarly, yet deeply personal, the writing is clear, readily accessible, and eloquent. Alper's brilliant presentation of the mindfulness pyramid model illustrates how therapeutic interdependence is alive and creative. This is an essential book for any therapist interested in mindfulness."

> —**Paula Carmona, MSN, RN, PMHCNS-BC,** coauthor of *Peaceful Mind*

"*Mindfulness Meditation in Psychotherapy* offers a beautifully integrated model for incorporating mindfulness in psychotherapy. Steven Alper weaves together years of contemplative practice and clinical wisdom with current research on mindfulness, emphasizing it as a way of being and a method for investigating subjectivity. This comprehensive and artful book will benefit therapist and client. I highly recommend it."

> —**Shauna Shapiro,** coauthor of *The Art and Science of Mindfulness* and *Mindful Discipline*

"Steven Alper has poured his deep understanding of practice and of psychotherapy into this wise and accessible book. His candor about his own struggles ground the book in humility and wisdom, and he speaks directly to his reader in a voice that is reassuring, confident, and deeply humane. Psychotherapists with established meditation practices, as well as those who want to begin, will both find much of value here."

> —**Barbara Davenport, LCS,** graduate of the Chicago Institute for Psychoanalysis Program in Child Psychotherapy, and author of *The Worst Loss* and *Grit and Hope: 5 Latino Students & the Program That Helped Them Get to College* (UC Press, 2016)

"Reading Steven Alper's book, I was impressed by its thoroughness and comprehensibility. He takes the complicated task of weaving mindfulness meditation into the therapeutic process and makes it philosophical and practical. The model he creates is dynamic, clear, and relational, and reflects his embodiment of mindfulness. I appreciated the range of meditations included in the book and the depth of understanding and clarity he brings to their usage. The breadth of the book makes it indispensable as a resource for all serious-minded therapists who want to maintain the integrity of meditation and deepen not only their own practice, but healing itself."

> —**Elana Rosenbaum, LICSW,** certified mindfulness-based stress reduction (MBSR) teacher, psychotherapist, speaker, and author of *Being Well (Even When You're Sick)* and *Here for Now*

"Steve Alper has given the world a remarkable synthesis that will be profoundly beneficial for therapists both personally and professionally if engaged in wholeheartedly as a way of being. How could their clients not benefit as well?"

> —**Jon Kabat-Zinn,** founder of mindfulness-based stress reduction (MBSR), and author of *Full Catastrophe Living* and *Coming to Our Senses*

"Drawing on decades of personal mindfulness practice, dedicated exploration of wisdom traditions, and thoughtful psychotherapeutic work, Steven Alper offers us a detailed, comprehensive, well-researched, and up-to-date exploration of how mindfulness practices can enrich and inform virtually any form of psychotherapy."

> —**Ronald D. Siegel, PsyD,** author of *The Mindfulness Solution,* coeditor of *Mindfulness and Psychotherapy,* and part-time assistant professor of psychology at Harvard Medical School

"Every once in a while a book comes along that exactly fits a need for our profession. Alper's *Mindfulness Meditation in Psychotherapy* is one of those books. With the burst of energy and popularity of mindfulness meditation, this book guides therapists to integrating these skills into our own self-awareness and into a toolbox for our clients. Packed with sophisticated depth applications, as well as handy little tips, this book belongs on every clinician's shelf."

> —**David B. Wexler, PhD,** author of *When Good Men Behave Badly* and *Is He Depressed or What?*

"This is the sine qua non book for any psychotherapist who integrates mindfulness into their psychotherapy practice, or wishes to and desires a road map. To the best of my knowledge, there is no one out there in the field that has put the pieces together in quite this unique fashion. Steven Alper has synthesized three major theoretical paradigms extant in contemporary psychotherapy: Buddhist psychology and practice, the mindfulness movement, and relational psychotherapy. However imposing that may sound, all of it is highly readable and immediately applicable to an ongoing psychotherapy practice."

> —**Richard F. Avery, LCSW**, assistant professor in the department of psychiatry at the University of California, San Diego School of Medicine; and certified teacher of Compassion Cultivation Training (CCT) through the Center for Compassion and Altruism Research and Education (CCARE) at Stanford University

"Steven Alper has written the best set of guidelines I have read for integrating mindfulness meditation into psychotherapy, in a format that will benefit the beginning and the experienced meditator. He writes with great integrity to the spaciousness and nonverbal wisdom of meditation practice, at the same time that he offers essential practical advice and integration of evidence-based approaches. As an experienced meditator, I have already benefited from using his illuminating 'pyramid' model in my work with clients and in teaching students how the therapist's embodied meditation practice stabilizes the client's capacity for emotional experience."

> —**Roberta Isberg, MD**, assistant professor of psychiatry at Harvard Medical School, teacher of psychotherapy—including dialectical behavior therapy (DBT) and parent-child interaction therapy—in the Child Fellows program at Boston Children's Hospital, and graduate and current member of the Boston Psychoanalytic Society and Institute

"Brilliant and highly accessible, this book is not only about how to bring mindfulness into your practice of psychotherapy, it's about how to be a great therapist. In other words, mindfulness as described in this book is not a specialized form of therapy; it constitutes a basis for the foundational ingredients that make for excellent psychotherapy, such as authenticity, present-moment attention, curiosity, compassion, and unconditional positive regard. I hope this book is integrated into basic training for psychotherapists."

> —**Cassandra Vieten, PhD**, president and CEO of the Institute of Noetic Sciences, author of *Mindful Motherhood*, and coauthor of *Spiritual and Religious Competencies in Clinical Practice*

Mindfulness Meditation

in Psychotherapy

An Integrated Model for Clinicians

Steven A. Alper, MSW, LCSW

CONTEXT PRESS

An Imprint of New Harbinger Publications, Inc.

Distributed in Canada by Raincoast Books

Copyright © 2016 by Steven A. Alper
    Context Press
    An Imprint of New Harbinger Publications, Inc.
    5674 Shattuck Avenue
    Oakland, CA 94609
    www.newharbinger.com

Cover design by Sara Christian
Acquired by Jess O'Brien
Edited by James Lainsbury

Library of Congress Cataloging-in-Publication Data

Names: Alper, Steven A., author.
Title: Mindfulness meditation in psychotherapy : an integrated model for
  counselors and clinicians / Steven A. Alper, MSW, LCSW.
Description: Oakland, CA : New Harbinger Publications, Inc., [2016] |
  Includes bibliographical references and index.
Identifiers: LCCN 2015039306| ISBN 9781626252752 (paperback) | ISBN
  9781626252769 (pdf e-book) | ISBN 9781626252776 (epub)
Subjects: LCSH: Mindfulness-based cognitive therapy. | Psychotherapist and
  patient. | BISAC: PSYCHOLOGY / Psychotherapy / General. | BODY, MIND &
  SPIRIT / Meditation. | SOCIAL SCIENCE / Social Work. | MEDICAL /
  Psychiatry / General.
Classification: LCC RC489.M55 A47 2016 | DDC 616.89/1425--dc23 LC record available at
http://lccn.loc.gov/2015039306

Printed in the United States of America

18   17   16

10   9   8   7   6   5   4   3   2   1   First printing

Contents

Acknowledgments

This book reflects both my professional development and my development as a dharma practitioner, as well as the larger stream where the two seemingly separate streams merged in me. I first want to thank New Harbinger Publications—particularly my editors Jess O'Brien; production staff Michele Waters, Vicraj Gill, and Jesse Burson; Nicola Skidmore and freelance copyeditor James Lainsbury, without whose guidance and encouragement this book would not have been possible. I also want to thank Barbara Davenport and the Sunday night writers' group for encouragement and critical feedback on early versions of the manuscript, and Dale Featherling for his early editorial assistance.

Gratitude to Swami Muktananda, from the Kashmir Shaivism tradition, through whom I caught my first glimpses of the vastness of mind beyond ego-centeredness. Gratitude to my day treatment mentor and dharma brother Bill Bradshaw, who skillfully directed me to the dharma through Shambhala training, and through whose generosity I had the good fortune to receive teachings from H. H. the Dalai Lama, Chögyam Trungpa Rinpoche, Kalu Rinpoche, Tai Situ Rinpoche, and Jamgong Kongtrul Rinpoche, among other Tibetan teachers. Gratitude to the senior students of the Plum Village sangha, and to Prittam Singh in particular, who hosted me and my young family at the Plum Village summer opening of 1997, where we received teachings from Thich Nhat Hanh and the Plum Village Sangha.

Gratitude to my first dharma sisters and brother, Alby Quinlan, Nancy Newhouse, and Rick Avery, who formed the nucleus of what became the San Diego Thursday Night Sitting Group, and my spiritual home for the past nearly thirty-five years. Thanks also to Nancy Newhouse for arranging for my invitation, in 1994, to establish an MBSR program at UCSD Department of Psychiatry, and to Rick Avery for both his friendship and valued clinical mentorship in group and couples therapy, as well as self-psychology and intersubjectivity theory. Thanks to Sanford Shapiro and the San Diego Self-Psychology Study Group, whose peer mentorship, supervision groups, and professional training workshops greatly enriched and deepened my understanding of intersubjectivity theory and relational psychotherapy.

I also want to thank my dear friend Richard Gelbard, by way of whose steady encouragement I attended my first ten-day vipassana retreat through Insight Meditation West, in 1984, and to my first vipassana teachers from that retreat, Christopher Titmus and James Baraz, who broke open my heart. Thanks also to Jack

Kornfield, Christina Feldman, Stephen Batchelor, Sylvia Boorstein, Sharda Rogell, Joseph Goldstein, and to the many other Spirit Rock, Insight Meditation Society, and Gaia House teachers whose wise, compassionate, and generous teachings have touched me so deeply over the years.

Deepest gratitude to Jon Kabat-Zinn and Saki Santorelli, who pioneered a field where none before existed. And to Jon in particular, for his friendship, encouragement, and generous support of the programs at UCSD and Scripps Clinic in the early days through presenting grand rounds and public lectures at both institutions. Meeting Jon and Saki has transformed my life (as it has so many others) and launched me on this path, which has become my work, my practice, and my passion ever since. Deep bows and gratitude as well to my wise, warm, and wonderful MBSR trainers, Elana Rosenbaum and Ferris Urbanowski, and my extraordinary colleagues from that first West Coast MBSR teacher training at the Mary and Joseph Retreat Center. Thanks also to Betty Christiansen and Mary and Mark Kalina, for extending the opportunity to establish the MBSR program at Scripps Clinic and for their strong support of the program, particularly in its early days; and to Mimi Guarneri and Rauni Prittenen King for bringing the Scripps MBSR course into the Scripps Center for Integrative Medicine.

Thanks also to Drs. Zindel Segal, John Teasdale, and Mark Williams, who invited me to attend their first North American MBCT professional training in Orangeville, Ontario, Canada. Special thanks to Zindel Segal for offering me the opportunity to co-lead some of the early North American MBCT professional trainings at the Omega Institute and the UCSD Center for Mindfulness.

Finally, this book is dedicated to my beloved sons, Zack and Sam, my most fierce, loyal, and loving teachers. May it prove worthy of your patience and forbearance during the writing.

—Steven Alper
July 25, 2015

Introduction

This book is a practical guide to incorporating mindfulness in psychotherapy. I intentionally use the word "incorporate," rather than the more commonly used "integrate," because it connotes *embodiment*, and mindfulness is not simply a technique or theory to be added to or combined with other techniques and theories. Rather, we literally *learn* mindfulness with and in our bodies. More precisely, we learn mindfulness with the mind-body process, or embodied mind (Varela, Thompson, & Rosch, 1993). In psychotherapy we teach and communicate about mindfulness through who and how we are in the therapeutic relationship as much or more than through specific words and techniques. Thus, the effectiveness of mindfulness in psychotherapy depends on the degree to which we, as therapists, authentically *embody* mindfulness in our relationships with our clients.

I wrote this book to meet the need for a practical, generalist guide for therapists across a wide range of theoretical orientations, who work in a variety of clinical practice settings, and who might be interested in incorporating mindfulness in their clinical work.

My approach was to build an integrated, holistic model for understanding mindfulness in psychotherapy called the mindfulness pyramid model (see chapter 4). The model is organized around four dimensions of mindfulness that are particularly relevant for psychotherapy (represented by the four faces of the pyramid) and three vertically integrated levels that correspond to the therapeutic process (the therapist's practice, the therapeutic process and relationship as practice, and the client's practice) within which mindfulness can be cultivated.

How Is This Book Different?

This book is different from other books about mindfulness and psychotherapy in four major ways.

1. The basic premise of this book is that mindfulness, as it pertains to psychotherapy, is neither just a technique nor a theoretical perspective per se but a way of being with and relating to experience. Mindfulness is an embodied

orientation to life itself that undergirds and informs both theory and technique. As such, mindfulness is fundamentally transdiagnostic and transtheoretical, and it can positively inform your clinical practice whether or not you teach formal meditation practices to clients.

Because I approach mindfulness as transdiagnostic and transtheoretical, I hope that this book will be relevant and useful to therapists across a broad spectrum of theoretical commitments and clinical-practice orientations. Although it is primarily addressed to psychotherapists practicing in outpatient settings, faculty and clinical researchers in departments of psychology, psychiatry, social work, counseling, marriage and family therapy, and psychiatric nursing will also find the book of interest, as will clinical supervisors, interns, trainees, and graduate students in the various psychotherapeutic disciplines.

2. This book differs in emphasizing that the therapist's personal mindfulness practice—and its expression in the therapeutic encounter as *healing presence*—is the foundation for the efficacy of all mindfulness-based therapies regardless of the other therapeutic techniques used or theoretical understandings held. *Healing presence*, as the embodied expression of the therapist's mindfulness practice in the therapeutic relationship, is not just the vehicle for delivering the therapy. It *is* the therapy, as much (or more) than anything else the therapist or client says or does.

The therapist's healing presence informs and shapes the client's experience of the therapeutic relationship as well as the client's self-experience in the context of therapy. If teaching formal mindfulness meditation is part of treatment, the therapist's healing presence also informs the client's experience of doing formal mindfulness meditation. So this book is a practical guide for therapists to develop or deepen their own mindfulness meditation practice, and to understand how their personal mindfulness practice informs treatment and enhances therapeutic efficacy.

3. This book presents a comprehensive, integrated model for incorporating mindfulness in psychotherapy. The model is called the *mindfulness pyramid model*, and it is organized around the functions of mindfulness in psychotherapy rather than diagnostic categories, symptoms, or traditional theories of personality, psychopathology, and psychotherapy.

The mindfulness pyramid model suggests ways of understanding mindfulness as a common factor (Duncan, Miller, Wampold, & Hubble, 2010) that promotes treatment efficacy in all types of psychotherapy.

4. This book is different in its strong emphasis on mindfulness as a way of being and experiencing and as a method for investigating subjective experiencing, including inquiring into how subjective experiencing is constructed. In this way mindfulness represents a radical break from other approaches to psychotherapy. Rather than being simply another theory or technique, or a trait or

state in the conventional sense, mindfulness represents a completely different epistemology, or mode of knowing.

Mindfulness as mode of knowing is experiential, sensory, intuitive, and unmediated by thought or language. In the Zen tradition, mindfulness is sometimes called bare attention, or nondoing. Segal, Williams, and Teasdale, developers of mindfulness-based cognitive therapy, refer to mindfulness as "being mode of mind" as opposed to the more conventional and common "doing mode of mind" (2002, pp. 70–75).

The Importance of the Therapist's Personal Practice

Unlike most other therapies that are designed to address specific pathologies, mindfulness meditation addresses the universal, existential underpinnings of human experience, including our uniquely evolved predisposition toward suffering (see, for example, Goldstein, 2002, 2013; Hayes, Strosahl, & Wilson, 2003; Batchelor, 2005) and our unique capacities for awareness, intentionality, self-healing, awakening, and freedom (Trungpa, 1984; Pandita, 1992; Kabat-Zinn, 1990, 2005, 2013; Maezumi, 2001; Goldstein, 2013; Batchelor, 2005; Chödrön, 2005).

Because mindfulness in psychotherapy ultimately addresses generic human suffering rather than specific psychopathology, and because the architecture of human suffering is universal regardless of its content, at the deepest level our clients' suffering and healing is indistinguishable from our own (Santorelli, 1999). Thus, in the most practical sense, our capacity to be mindful of our own suffering—to be present with and bear witness to our suffering without turning away or being overwhelmed—is ultimately the source of healing presence in our work with clients (Glassman, 1998; Santorelli, 1999; Germer & Siegel, 2013).

In my experience as a clinician, supervisor, teacher, and meditation practitioner, personal and professional mindfulness practices inform and support each other, so in this book the personal and professional guides are, in a very real sense, inseparable. Whether or not you teach formal mindfulness meditation practices to your clients, your own meditation practice can profoundly benefit your clinical work. How much depends on your commitment to a discipline of practice and the depth of your own experiential understanding (Kabat-Zinn, 2013; Santorelli, 1999; Segal et al., 2002).

Preview of the Mindfulness Pyramid Model

The mindfulness pyramid model is a conceptual framework, model, and guide to the ways in which mindfulness works in psychotherapy. It is designed for use as a teaching and training tool and as an aid to understanding what's happening in therapy from the perspective of mindfulness practice. It is my hope that the mindfulness pyramid model will also stimulate new ways of thinking about mindfulness in psychotherapy and promote creative, skillful, and situation- and context-specific therapeutic responses. What follows is a preview.

Briefly, the mindfulness pyramid model consists of the four dimensions, or facets, of mindfulness most relevant to psychotherapy, visualized as the four faces of a pyramid (see figures 1, 2, and 3 in chapter 4).

1.   Formal mindfulness meditation practices

2.   Skills, inner capacities, attitudes, and perspectives

3.   Method of inquiry and investigation and mode of knowing

4.   Way of being and relating to experience

The four facets of mindfulness represented by the four faces of the pyramid can be incorporated at three levels, visualized as three horizontal segments (see figure 4 in chapter 4).

1.   The foundation and bottom level of the pyramid represents the therapist's mindfulness practice.

2.   The middle level of the pyramid represents the therapeutic process and relationship (also a mindfulness practice for the therapist).

3.   The top level of the pyramid represents the client's mindfulness practice.

Because the single pyramid represents the therapist's perspective, I expanded the model to account for the client's perspective by adding an inverted pyramid standing on its tip directly above and intersecting the first pyramid (see figure 8 in chapter 4). The intersection of the two pyramids creates a diamond in the expanded model, representing the intrinsically intersubjective nature of the therapeutic process and relationship (see figure 9 in chapter 4).

The mindfulness pyramid model can serve as a resource and guide for creatively and effectively incorporating mindfulness in therapy with a broad range of clients, and across a broad range of diagnostic categories and therapeutic modalities, limited only by the depth of the therapist's mindfulness practice and experiential understanding.

Overview

Chapters 1 through 3 introduce the terrain of mindfulness. Chapter 1 debunks the general myths about mindfulness and meditation, looks at the definitions of mindfulness and how and why they differ, and finally proposes a definition of mindfulness particularly useful for psychotherapy and clinical practice. Chapter 2 looks at the many ways mindfulness contributes to psychotherapy beyond enhancing treatment outcomes. Chapter 3 explores how mindfulness heals. Chapter 4 introduces the mindfulness pyramid model, which then serves as the organizing framework for the remainder of the book.

Chapters 5 through 9 elaborate on level 1 of the mindfulness pyramid model, the therapist's mindfulness practice. Chapters 10 and 11 explore level 2 of the mindfulness pyramid model, the therapeutic relationship and process as intersubjective mindfulness practices for the therapist. Chapter 12 explores level 3 of the model—the client's mindfulness practice. Finally, the conclusion summarizes the major themes of the book and offers thoughts about the potential evolution of mindfulness in psychotherapy and in society.

The Heart of the Practice Is Practice

The dilemma and challenge of writing a practical mindfulness guide for clinicians is embodied in the word "practical." As it applies to mindfulness, *practical* is "practice"—direct, experiential knowing. Writing about mindfulness practice, especially in the conventional style of professional writing, does not convey the direct, experiential knowing, the immediacy, or the intimacy that is the heart of understanding the practice.

So in this book I chose to interweave didactic text, clinical vignettes, and personal reflection with guided reflections and experiential exercises for you, the reader, designed to elicit an embodied understanding of mindfulness. Throughout I will also invite you to reflect on your own clinical and life experiences in light of your mindfulness practice. Such reflection can further deepen your understanding, whether you are a novice or a more experienced practitioner.

This book contains instructions for a variety of formal mindfulness meditations to help you establish and strengthen a discipline of practice, or to deepen an already established meditation practice. It also offers instructions for a variety of *mini-meditations* (brief, structured meditations of approximately two to three minutes) and *informal* practices (bringing mindfulness to bear on activities of daily life) designed to help you understand and experience mindfulness as an orientation to experiencing and a way of being and relating in daily life, and not only a formal meditation practice method. You can find downloadable guided-meditation audio recordings, as well as recordings of the guided reflections, experiential exercises, and mini-meditations, at the website for this book: http://www.newharbinger.com/32752. (You can follow the prompts on the site to access the files, or see the very back of the book for more instructions.)

The meditation instructions and guided meditations, structured reflections and experiential exercises, personal stories, and clinical vignettes, are all presented to help evoke an understanding of mindfulness as direct experiential knowing. Verbal definitions and descriptions of mindfulness are, by themselves, wholly inadequate for conveying an understanding of mindfulness as lived experience. In the words of an old Zen proverb, "The finger pointing at the moon is not the moon."

Effectively incorporating mindfulness in psychotherapy requires authenticity. In that spirit, the practices I present in this book are practices that I do, or have done, intensively.

I cite prior writing and research to acknowledge and honor important contributors and contributions to the field. I have learned much from these contributors, have been inspired by them, and feel forever indebted and deeply grateful to them all, particularly my personal mentors and teachers. I encourage you to read their books and articles (see the bibliography).

Nonetheless, intellectual understanding can't take the place of your own mindfulness meditation practice. Developing an in-depth, experiential understanding of mindfulness through regular, formal meditation practice, and then embodying your practice in daily life as wise, compassionate understanding and action, is the day-to-day, lifelong challenge of any therapist who wants to incorporate mindfulness in clinical practice.

The Basis for This Book

This book is based on my nearly thirty-five years of personal mindfulness meditation practice in the Shambhala, American Vipassana, Zen, and Tibetan Buddhist traditions. In addition, I have trained nearly 2,000 mental health professionals in formal mindfulness-based interventions and incorporating mindfulness in psychotherapy. For over thirty years I have practiced mindfulness-informed psychotherapy, working with individuals, couples, families, and groups (mostly adults) within a variety of theoretical perspectives, including object relations, self psychology, interpersonal therapy, intersubjectivity theory, cognitive behavioral therapy, and systems-strategic, structural, humanistic-existential, and narrative-constructionist approaches.

Useful Things to Keep in Mind as We Begin

Like swimming, skiing, or playing a musical instrument, mindfulness is a form of mind-body knowledge, or embodied knowing. It cannot be learned purely intellectually, because the body—or more precisely the embodied mind—has to learn mindfulness through direct experience and intentional practice. You have to "feel" it in the body as lived experience, and then deepen your experience and develop your skills over time through repetition and practice.

Mindfulness as embodied knowing involves ways of being and relating to experience that may be unfamiliar and novel. What follows are a few suggestions about attitudes and ways of being that will be helpful as we proceed.

Nondoing

Unlike learning an athletic or performance skill, which is competitive (even if only with oneself) and oriented toward striving for improvement and accomplishment, practicing mindfulness involves simply being open to the direct experience of aliveness in each moment, which paradoxically requires completely letting go of trying to achieve, accomplish, or "do" anything. Instead, mindfulness involves shifting out of the conventional *doing* mode of mind, the mode of relentless, goal-oriented doing and striving, and dropping into the mode of *nondoing*, of being receptive to the experience of each moment as it arises, one moment after the next.

Nondoing isn't the same as doing nothing. Paradoxically, professional athletes (Mumford, 2015), corporate executives (Carroll, 2008), physicians (Santorelli, 1999), attorneys (Keeva, 2011), teachers (Jennings, 2015), and therapists (Bien, 2006; Germer & Siegel, 2013; Pollack, Pedulla, & Siegel, 2014), as well as practitioners of many other professions, find that regular mindfulness practice enhances performance, in addition to their well-being. Nondoing means not focusing on the goal of an action. It means letting go of concerns, worries, or other thoughts about future or past events, and instead experiencing fully and completely the moment you are in, with all the senses awake.

For many of us this flies in the face of both individual and cultural conditioning. In psychotherapy, nondoing means learning to accept and being present with each moment, even moments that are emotionally painful or distressing, without conditioned judging or attempts to fix or get rid of the present moment. In practical terms this often means not judging deeply conditioned, automatic judging and bracing against unpleasant experience when it arises.

Since the present moment has always already happened, attempts to change it are futile, and struggling against the experience of the present moment inevitably causes suffering. If we can receive and accept the present moment exactly as it presents itself, we are much more likely to perceive it clearly and to respond skillfully in the next moment.

Just Say Yes

Shifting out of *doing* mode, the mode of judging and striving to fix, change, or accomplish, and into *being* mode—the mode of present-moment awareness without judgment, of simply allowing and letting be—is a skill and inner capacity cultivated through strong commitment and disciplined practice as well as something akin to (dare I say it?) *love*. Mindfulness practice challenges you to embrace, savor, and love your life unconditionally *in this moment, right now, the only moment you ever have to live*. Mindfulness practice is the discipline of saying yes to your life without conditions. Mindfulness is the practice of showing up for every moment with an open heart, simply because it's the only life, and the only moment, you can ever have.

For therapists as well as our clients, unconditionally embracing and loving the human condition in the messy, moment to moment reality of lived experience is not easy. It requires concentration, clarity of awareness, and the capacities for distress tolerance, emotion self-regulation, and composure. Mindfulness meditation practice systematically cultivates and strengthens these as well as many other skills and capacities.

Be Authentic

As previously stated, your own discipline of mindfulness meditation practice is essential for effectively incorporating mindfulness in your clinical work. In particular, teaching and guiding formal mindfulness meditation as a therapeutic intervention is likely to be ineffective, as well as uncomfortable, frustrating, or confusing for you and your clients, if the teaching and guiding don't come directly from your own experience.

With regard to mindfulness, you teach most powerfully what you embody, not what you say. Guiding mindfulness practice for others requires first discovering that raw edge of direct experience—exquisitely sensitive, tender, wondrous, and ultimately ineffable—within yourself. Without that discovery, the teaching falls flat. See Segal, Williams, and Teasdale (2002, pp. 54–61) for a fascinating and touching personal account of how three world-renowned cognitive behavioral psychologists and clinical researchers, who are committed to empirical, evidence-based clinical research and practice, came to this same conclusion.

Stay Inside Yourself

In no way do I mean to discourage readers who are new to mindfulness from beginning to meditate or from incorporating mindfulness in clinical work. I simply want to convey the vital importance of staying inside yourself, of embodying your own practice experience in your work rather than reading a script or teaching from a book (this one included), or repeating something you heard during a training.

I don't mean to say that books and trainings aren't useful. Of course they are. But with mindfulness they can only be starting points, because intellectual understanding alone is insufficient. Incorporating mindfulness in psychotherapy requires an experientially embodied understanding beyond mere conceptual knowing. Literally, you must understand mindfulness from the inside out; and this is the kind of understanding that can only be developed through your own regular discipline of mindfulness meditation practice.

You can think of this book as a guide to the "inside-out understanding" of mindfulness meditation and how to deploy that understanding therapeutically for the benefit of your clients. If you are new to mindfulness meditation, this book can help you establish, develop, and sustain a daily discipline of practice. If you are an experienced mindfulness practitioner, I hope I have written this book in a way that will help you cultivate and deepen your practice and experiential understanding of mindfulness meditation. I also hope the book will help you look with fresh eyes at how you might incorporate mindfulness practice in your clinical work and how you can do psychotherapy as a mindfulness practice for the benefit of your clients.

Effectively incorporating mindfulness in psychotherapy requires embodiment. Teach only what you know from the inside out—from your own practice and embodied knowing—and refrain from attempting to incorporate or teach what you don't know. You'll do just fine if you stay inside yourself. If you know just a little, embody and teach only that much. You can trust that it will be enough. Any more would be insufficient.

Keeping a Meditation Practice Log and a Mindfulness Journal

It's helpful to maintain a daily log of your formal mindfulness meditation practice as you read the book, mostly for self-reinforcement. I also recommend journaling about your experiences with the guided reflections and experiential exercises as well as your reflections on your personal and professional mindfulness practice experiences. Appendix B includes samples of a mindfulness practice log and journal. You will find formal meditation practice instructions in chapter 6 and other structured reflections and experiential exercises throughout the book. Audio downloads for the formal meditations and experiential exercises and downloadable copies of the practice log and journal can all be found at the website for this book: http://www.newhar binger.com/32752.

The Promise of Mindfulness Practice

Ultimately, I hope to convey in this book the deepest promise of mindfulness meditation: to be able to experientially "see into" and understand how we create needless suffering for ourselves and others through our reactions—instinctual and deeply conditioned, but no longer adaptive—to life's unavoidable distress and pain as well as its pleasures and joys. I also hope to show how mindfulness practice can help us and our clients develop the capacities needed to respond more skillfully to life's pleasure and pain, thus alleviating and avoiding needless suffering while increasing peace, happiness, joy, and ease.

To paraphrase the well-known American Buddhist teacher Joseph Goldstein (1993, p. 9), practicing mindfulness is practicing freedom. The essence of mindfulness practice is waking up to the freedom that is always available and accessible now, in this very moment—not practicing to be free in some distant, undetermined future.

Chapter 1

What Mindfulness Meditation Isn't and Is

Many people have fundamental misconceptions about meditation, in general, and mindfulness, in particular, mostly derived from pop culture, mass media, and personal experiences. In teaching mindfulness I find it useful to define meditation and mindfulness in very simple terms. Then I like to debunk any myths about mindfulness, first by clarifying what it isn't and then elaborating on what it is. That's the approach I'll take in this chapter.

Defining Meditation

Meditation has been defined simply as "the intentional regulation of attention from moment to moment" (Kutz, Borysenko, & Benson, 1985, p. 2). If you've ever intentionally maintained focus on anything in particular for even a minute or two, you've meditated. Most of the many different meditation practices from the world's great religious traditions fit into one of two major categories: concentration practices and awareness practices (Goleman, 1988, pp. 7–38). *Concentration practices* involve focusing one's attention on a particular object, such as a prayer, a visual image, a candle flame, a sound, a word, or a phrase, and allowing one's attention to be completely absorbed by the focal object. Everything else is excluded from awareness. Concentration practices are useful not only for strengthening focus but also for calming and stabilizing the mind, decreasing anxiety, increasing energy, and generating states of bliss and other nonordinary states of consciousness.

Awareness practices involve focusing attention in the present moment of experience and allowing each moment, as it arises, to be the focal object. Thus, rather than excluding everything but the focal object from attention, awareness practices involve focusing on the moment as a whole or, more accurately, expanding awareness to include the entire range of experience in each moment while excluding nothing. Mindfulness meditation involves being aware of each moment as it arises without engaging in reactive judgment or striving to change the moment.

Concentration is also important in mindfulness meditation, but it is cultivated by allowing a particular component of the present moment (for example, breath sensation, a different body sensation, or a sound) to be the primary focus in the foreground, or center, of the field of awareness while allowing all other elements of awareness to come and go in the background, or around the periphery, of the field. Thus, mindfulness practice involves receiving, accepting, and embracing each moment exactly as it presents itself to awareness without excluding anything; it involves deploying awareness in various ways within the moment.

Before saying anything more about what mindfulness is, let's first debunk some of the most common myths and misunderstandings about it by clarifying what mindfulness isn't.

What Mindfulness Isn't

- **Mindfulness is not a relaxation technique.**

- **Mindfulness is neither a relaxation state nor a trance state.**

- **Mindfulness is neither "trait" nor "state" in the conventional sense.**

- **Mindfulness is not clearing or emptying the mind of thoughts.**

- **Mindfulness is not a type of thinking, nor is it not thinking.**

- **Mindfulness is not a goal to strive for or attain.**

- **Mindfulness does not require sitting cross-legged in the lotus posture or any other particular pose or posture.**

Mindfulness Is Not a Relaxation Technique

Perhaps the most common misunderstanding about mindfulness meditation is that it is a relaxation technique. From the psychotherapeutic perspective this is understandable because mindfulness meditation can lead to the relaxation response. Also, some mindfulness meditation techniques superficially resemble well-known cognitive behavioral relaxation techniques, such as progressive relaxation, autonomic training, hypnosis, breathing exercises, and guided imagery.

Although the relaxation response often results from mindfulness meditation practice, it is a by-product, rather than the goal, of the practice. We will explore this aspect of mindfulness in much greater depth in chapter 3.

Mindfulness Is Neither a Relaxation State nor a Trance State

While mindfulness practice may superficially resemble relaxation exercises or hypnotic trance inductions, it would be incorrect to assume that they are identical, or even closely related. Conventional relaxation is often a natural precursor to sleep, and may induce sleep. Trance involves heightened presence and receptivity, but not necessarily clarity of awareness.

Mindfulness, on the other hand, is a heightened state of wakefulness, which can be characterized as a state of both relaxed concentration and heightened awareness. It is more like "falling awake" than falling asleep, and it is characterized by a relaxation that brings about heightened acuity and clarity of perception rather than increased drowsiness. Some hypnotic states are also characterized by heightened awareness, but they are usually more dreamlike, lacking the acuity, precision, interest, and energy that are prominent features of mindfulness.

Mindfulness Is Neither Trait nor State in Any Usual Sense

Mainstream personality theories, such as those associated with cognitive behavioral therapy, most of the psychodynamic and interpersonal therapies, and humanistic and body-oriented therapies, consider traits and states to be relatively enduring (traits) or fleeting (states) psychological attributes of people and personalities. Traits and states in these theories are assumed to reside within and belong to a specific person or self. Research conventions in psychology dictate that psychological attributes be defined as traits, states, or behaviors belonging to individuals or individual personalities.

Mindfulness researchers in psychology have debated whether mindfulness is a trait or a state and have settled on defining two distinct types of mindfulness: *trait* or *dispositional mindfulness* is a relatively abiding characteristic of personality, or psychological skill, and *state mindfulness* arises temporarily, then passes like any other mental state. Although this characterization is understandable in the context of academic research, in clinical practice I think it is less productive and potentially misleading.

To classify mindfulness as trait, disposition, or state presumes that mindfulness fits neatly into the conventional Western psychological paradigm of individual mind and personality, and it ignores what might well be mindfulness's most valuable contribution to understanding human psychology.

From a purely clinical standpoint, I think describing mindfulness as a quality of moments of experience, to paraphrase Jon Kabat-Zinn (1990, p. 5), is more accurate and pragmatic than the more conventional trait, state, or dispositional definitions. I would suggest that when mindfulness is truly present, identification with or attachment to a sense of separate self-experience is absent. Instead, there is "just being." In acceptance and commitment therapy, a third wave cognitive behavioral therapy developed by Steven Hayes and his colleagues Kirk Strosahl and Kelly Wilson (2003), this experience of self is referred to as the "contextual self." The field of transpersonal psychology was developed to address this expanded paradigm of self beyond the bounds of the body and egocentric personality (Boorstein, 1991). Mindfulness, as a quality of moments of experience, doesn't require a self to whom it belongs (Jotiko, 1993; Epstein, 1995, 2008).

Ultimately, mindfulness practice allows for experiencing and seeing through the sense of a solid, substantial, relatively unchanging "me, myself, and I" as merely a point of view, albeit from an evolutionary perspective a profoundly useful one (Goldstein, 1993). If the previous sentence sounds like gibberish, just pass it by and read on. Both you and your clients can still benefit from mindfulness practice. You might want to revisit this passage after reading through the book and experiencing the meditation practices and exercises.

Mindfulness Is Not Clearing or Emptying the Mind of Thoughts

Another common misunderstanding about mindfulness meditation is that it involves clearing or emptying the mind of thoughts. The media regrettably reinforces pop culture's conflation of mindfulness with "emptying the mind," as do teachers who instruct their students to "empty your mind of thoughts." Unfortunately, this instruction is little different than saying "think of anything but a pink elephant." It's hard to think of anything else in that moment.

Rather than emptying the mind of thoughts, mindfulness meditation involves shifting our relationship to thinking itself, and relating to thinking as an event without identifying with the content or meaning.

Mindfulness Is Not a Type of Thinking, Nor Is It Not Thinking

Because the word "mind" is conventionally associated with thinking, mindfulness is frequently misunderstood as focused, sustained contemplative thinking. It is important to understand that mindfulness is not thinking, but rather it is the awareness that underlies thought and allows us to notice thinking happening, without identifying with or getting caught up in the content of thought. Mindfulness allows us to be aware of thought in the same way that we can be aware of sight, sound, smell, taste, and touch as sensory events without letting them define us.

Conversely, because mindfulness is not thinking, it is often misunderstood to be the absence of thought or a way to empty the mind of thoughts. But mindfulness is not opposed to thought. Rather, mindfulness as an experience underlies all categories of thought, dualities such as thinking/not thinking or any other forms of thought or attempts to not think. Attempts to define mindfulness conceptually are often confusing, because mindfulness is fundamentally nonconceptual. Ultimately, mindfulness can be meaningfully understood only through direct experience beyond discursive thought.

Mindfulness Is Not a Goal to Strive For or Attain

Technically, mindfulness is a quality of the present moment of experience. Striving to attain a goal or a state of being implies focusing on the future, which is shooting oneself in the foot as far as experiencing mindfulness is concerned. Since the present moment is always already here, it isn't necessary to *do* anything to be mindful.

We are always already in the present moment. It's the only moment we can ever be in, although our minds can take us far away into anger, regret, fear, nostalgia, and fantasy so that we stop noticing what's happening in the present moment. Mindfulness is simply being present with all the senses awake, which is their natural state. This actually requires just being, or nondoing, rather than striving. When we let ourselves just be, mindfulness arises naturally.

Mindfulness Doesn't Require Sitting in the Lotus Posture, or Any Other Specific Practice or Posture

At my Thursday night meditation group, about fifteen people can be seen practicing mindfulness meditation together. Some sit cross-legged on meditation cushions on the floor. Spines are upright and erect. Heads effortlessly balance on necks and shoulders; eyes are gently closed. Hands are folded neatly in laps. This scene is the classic pop culture stereotype of meditation practice. Like some stereotypes it contains a grain of truth. And like all stereotypes, without a context it's at best a caricature, at worst a lie.

Mindfulness meditation defies stereotypes. In my meditation group, many of us sit on chairs or sofas rather than meditation cushions on the floor. A few of us may lie on our backs. We walk, stretch, and talk. Any moment, in any posture, can be a mindfulness practice if the practitioner relates to the moment with mindfulness.

Nonetheless, it's easy to mistake the superficial trappings of meditation practice for the essential heart of the practice. In mindfulness meditation, a relaxed, upright sitting posture with a solid base can help one embody an inner attitude of relaxed wakefulness and unshakable stillness, within which you can more readily observe the movements of the mind-body process. However, you can also sit upright and erect for long periods of time in what might appear to be an admirable sitting posture and yet remain lost in mental chatter or just be spaced out (I certainly have!). Mindfulness practice is less about a particular physical posture or activity and more about attitude, intention, and awareness.

Having hopefully debunked the more common misconceptions about mindfulness meditation by clarifying what it isn't, let's look more closely at what mindfulness is.

What Mindfulness Is

In the explosion of interest in mindfulness over the past thirty-five years, mindfulness has been defined in many ways (see Kabat-Zinn, 2005, pp. 3–7; Shapiro & Carlson, 2009, pp. 4–13; Goldstein, 1993, pp. 100–103; Linehan, 1993b, pp. 63–69; Luoma, Hayes, & Walser, 2007, pp. 91–99). Defining any experience is challenging at best, simply because what we say about the experience can't truly convey the felt sense of the experience. For instance, consider defining the experience of the color red or the experience of music or the experience of a rainstorm. Defining mindfulness with words is problematic in the same way.

Mindfulness Is Awareness of Experiencing as Well as That Which Is Experienced

Defining mindfulness is uniquely challenging because it is the experience of experiencing. For example, mindfulness of breathing involves feeling the physical sensations of breathing moment by moment while also being aware that feeling the sensations of breathing is happening. Mindfulness of seeing is noticing what is seen while also being aware of seeing as an event.

Are you aware of seeing as an event as you visually register this sentence? Are you also aware of reading as you visually register and construe meaning from the black marks on the page in front of you? Notice that the descriptions of what's happening communicate nothing about the subjective experience of how seeing and reading feel.

Nondoing

Mindfulness can also be viewed as a unique kind of activity. Paradoxically, mindfulness as an activity involves doing "nondoing." However, nondoing doesn't necessarily mean doing nothing, nor is it the absence of activity. For example, nondoing is frequently described as receiving and being aware of each moment just as it is, without trying to make the moment different than it is and without judgment or expectation. It may sound like a description of doing something that requires effort. It may even sound like quite a project, and I readily confess to having made it a major and maddening project for myself more times than I care to count. So have most other mindfulness teachers and practitioners that I know.

Although paying close attention without judging may sound like *doing something*, it actually involves intentional *nondoing*, which requires completely letting go of doing anything. Instead, if we simply let ourselves be, we begin to notice an innate and exquisitely sensitive capacity to experientially register each moment as it arises. This doesn't require doing; in fact, doing just gets in the way.

On the other hand, nondoing does not necessarily mean doing nothing. If you've ever experienced a sense of "flow" (Csikszentmihalyi, 1990) while working with clients, collaborating with colleagues, teaching, or playing a musical instrument or sport, or if you have been surprised by a particularly witty or skillful remark made by you or someone else that seemed to come out of nowhere, you have experienced nondoing in action, which is the doing that comes out of nondoing.

Such experiences have many things in common: the energy of friendly, eager interest and curiosity; exquisitely attuned engagement with the present moment; being able to get out of your own way; trusting yourself; and letting the context elicit an appropriate response. So mindfulness can also be defined as a mode of being that involves nondoing, but it's not necessarily doing nothing.

Why So Many Different Definitions of Mindfulness?

The experience of mindfulness is rich, subtle, and multifaceted. In contrast, all definitions of mindfulness are reductionist and partial, at best, and seem to reflect the motivations and aspirations of their authors.

For example, spiritual teachers often define mindfulness with an emphasis on alleviating suffering, developing wisdom and compassion, and realizing spiritual liberation or enlightenment (for example, Pandita, 1992; Rinpoche, 1997; Trungpa, 1984; Chah & Amaro, 2002; Chödrön, 2003, 2005; Nhat Hanh, 1988a, 1988b, 1990; Goldstein, 1993, 2002; Goldstein & Kornfield, 1987; Glassman, 1998; Glassman & Fields, 1996; Khema, 1991; Kornfield, 1993, 2000; Rosenberg & Guy, 1998; Rosenburg, 2000). Clinicians tend to define mindfulness in ways that make sense to their clients (Bien, 2006; Brantley, 2003; Dimeff & Koerner, 2007; Germer & Siegel, 2013). Clinical researchers define mindfulness in order to operationalize it as a variable, so that either mindfulness or its proposed effects can be measured in replicable studies (Baer, 2006; Linehan, 1993a; Hayes et al., 2003; Hayes, Follette, & Linehan, 2004; Segal et al., 2002; Williams, Teasdale, Segal, & Kabat-Zinn, 2007).

The Mindfulness Pyramid Model as a Functional Definition of Mindfulness for Psychotherapy

For the purposes of this book, I will define mindfulness in terms of the four dimensions, or facets, of mindfulness practice that I believe are most relevant for psychotherapy and clinical practice. These comprise the four faces of the mindfulness pyramid in the mindfulness pyramid model (see figure 1 in chapter 4), and together they form a functional definition of mindfulness in psychotherapy. The four facets of mindfulness most relevant to psychotherapy are mindfulness as

1. a type of formal meditation practice;

2. a specific set of skills, inner capacities, attitudes, and perspectives;

3. a method of inquiry into and investigation of subjective experiencing and how it is constructed, and the mode of knowing that arises from such inquiry and investigation; and

4. a way of being and relating to experience.

Mindfulness as a Type of Formal Meditation Practice

Mindfulness as formal meditation practice is characterized by precise, receptive awareness of each moment as it arises, one after the next, without conditioned, reactive judgment or striving. Mindful awareness incorporates attitudinal factors that include unconditional acceptance of the present moment; curiosity and interest in each moment as it arises; and the patience, trust, and willingness to receive each moment, however it presents itself, with an open, undefended heart and all the senses awake (Kabat-Zinn, 1990, 2005; Hayes et al., 2003). Such unconditional openness to life in every moment also requires and cultivates courage, compassion, commitment, equanimity, and resilience (Chödrön, 2003, 2005).

Mindfulness as a Specific Set of Skills, Inner Capacities, Attitudes, and Perspectives

Mindfulness skills, inner capacities, attitudes, and perspectives can be taught, cultivated, and strengthened in a variety of ways, including but not limited to formal and informal structured meditation practices. Jon Kabat-Zinn (1990) has described in detail what he calls "the foundational attitudes" of mindfulness practice in mindfulness-based stress reduction. Linehan (1993b) proposed her own version of mindfulness skills in dialectical behavior therapy; for their development, these skills rely less on formal meditation practice and more on group work and cognitive behavioral exercises. Hayes, Strosahl, and Wilson (2003) contributed the concept of "willingness": to actively embrace each moment regardless of its content. Willingness implies an even stronger commitment than the more passive term "acceptance."

Mindfulness as a Method of Inquiry into and Investigation of Subjective Experiencing, and a Mode of Knowing

Mindfulness meditation is a tool for systematically investigating and understanding how we construct experiencing through the way we relate to perceptions, physical sensations, thoughts, emotions, moods, and so on. Mindfulness allows us to see (mindfully experience) in real time how subjective experiencing is constructed as it happens, and it serves the purpose of generating insight into how we create needless suffering for ourselves; how such suffering can be avoided or deconstructed; and how joy, happiness, peace, and other positive mind states are constructed and deconstructed.

Mindfulness meditation, in this sense, is a secular version of the meditation practice in Buddhist psychology called *vipassana*, usually translated as "insight meditation" or "clear seeing." Vipassana is a disciplined, systematic, and powerful method of phenomenological inquiry (Olendzki, 2010). Major proponents of phenomenological inquiry in American philosophy and psychology include nineteenth-century philosopher and social activist Henry David Thoreau (Thoreau, 2006) and William James (James, 1983; Wild, 1970), the father of American psychology. Mindfulness practice as phenomenological inquiry and investigation and mode of knowing can produce liberating insights into how we construct happiness and suffering through the ways that we relate to experiencing. Such experientially grounded insights can lead to an unshakable joy and inner peace that is not contingent on circumstance—the "freedom" that Joseph Goldstein referred to in describing insight meditation, in the title of his book, as "the practice of freedom" (Goldstein, 1993).

Mindfulness as a Way of Being and Relating to Experience

More than a formal meditation practice, mindfulness practice is a way of being that can be embodied in each moment of our lives. Any moment we experience with appreciative, engaged, precise, and unconditionally accepting, nonjudging, and nonstriving awareness, whether we are brushing our teeth, showering, sweeping the kitchen floor, cooking, doing therapy, interacting with colleagues or friends, parenting, or being intimate with a partner, is no less a mindfulness meditation than sitting in formal meditation practice.

Summary

In this chapter we looked at different definitions of mindfulness and how they reflect the needs and aspirations of their authors. I then proposed a functional definition of mindfulness specifically for psychotherapy. The definition incorporates four facets of mindfulness practice and how they relate to the therapist, the therapeutic relationship and process, and the client. This definition of mindfulness is broader than most, but not without precedent (for example, see Kabat-Zinn, 1990, 1994, 2005, 2013; Santorelli, 1999). I strongly believe that this kind of expansive understanding is vitally important for incorporating mindfulness in psychotherapy.

In chapter 2 we will explore the many ways that mindfulness practice can enhance psychotherapy and benefit both therapists and clients.

Chapter 2

Why Mindfulness in Psychotherapy?

A large and rapidly growing body of published clinical research supports the efficacy of mindfulness-based interventions in treating a broad range of mental health problems and stress-related medical symptoms and illnesses (visit *Mindfulness Research Monthly* online, published by David Black at https://goamra.org/publications, for an up-to-date listing of all research and clinical articles published in refereed journals). In this chapter, rather than review studies you can read about elsewhere, we will examine how mindfulness enhances psychotherapy and also benefits therapists, clients, and the psychotherapy professions beyond improved treatment outcomes (as important as those are). What follows are the proposed benefits of using mindfulness in psychotherapy:

Emphasizes health and wholeness rather than pathology

Focuses on direct experience beyond thought and language

Reemphasizes the body as a central focus of therapy

Revalues phenomenological inquiry

Revalues discipline and practice

Makes therapy existentially resonant and authentic

Serves as an antidote to the problem of reification in psychological theory and terminology

Challenges belief in a fixed personality essence, or self-identity

Bridges the science and the art of psychotherapy

Helps prevent therapist burnout

Emphasizes Health and Wholeness Rather than Pathology

Mindfulness-informed psychotherapies focus on shifting your relationship to life's inevitable pain and distress rather than altering or eliminating them. Beyond a singular focus on alleviating symptoms, mindfulness practices also promote health and well-being. Mindfulness practices also develop and strengthen specific skills, inner capacities, attitudes, and perspectives that increase happiness, vitality, and joy as well as provide the possibility for profound and stable experiences of peace, ease, and freedom in body and mind.

Focuses on Direct Experience Beyond Thought and Language

Mindfulness-based psychotherapies value present moment awareness as a powerful source of learning and healing for both therapist and client. Mindfulness is neither thinking nor sense perception per se, but rather the awareness underlying both, with which we can observe thoughts and sense perceptions as events. For example, mindfulness of seeing is being aware of both what you are seeing and the fact that seeing is happening (noticing seeing as an experiential event).

Mindfulness meditations systematically train and refine awareness. A regular discipline of mindfulness meditation can strengthen the capacity to self-regulate attention and to register subjective experience with nuance and subtlety and without conditioned, emotional reactivity and perceptual and cognitive distortions.

Reemphasizes the Body as a Central Focus of Therapy

Mindfulness meditation restores the importance of the body in mainstream cognitive behavioral therapy and psychodynamic therapies. It also offers balance and clarity for humanistic therapies of the 1960s and 1970s that perhaps overemphasized the importance of cathartic emotional expression and gratification of emotional desires as part of the reaction against the cultural repression of the 1950s.

Although many therapies of the past seventy years have had a significant focus on the body, beginning with Wilhelm Reich's variant of psychoanalysis (and including neo-Reichian therapies, such as bioenergetics and Radix, and therapies based on sensory awareness, such as focusing and somatic experiencing), they have mostly remained outside of the mainstream academic institutions and professional licensing and certification processes.

In contrast, mindfulness-based therapies are rapidly emerging in mainstream academic psychotherapy research and training. The foundational mindfulness practices in these therapies focus on awareness of sensory experience, particularly breathing and body sensations. These practices are profoundly helpful with reinhabiting our bodies and facilitating mind-body integration, in contrast to Western and Westernized cultures, which have encouraged alienation from the body.

Revalues Phenomenological Inquiry

Phenomenological inquiry and research involves systematically investigating subjective experiencing with our own refined, disciplined subjective awareness. Although having a significant role at the beginning of modern psychology (Wild, 1970; Jones, 1963), by the 1950s phenomenological research had been largely dismissed by research psychologists in favor of empirical approaches, such as behaviorism, cognitive psychology, and, in the psychotherapy realm, cognitive behavioral therapy (Cushman, 1995).

Empirical scientific research is the most powerful knowledge-production system the world has ever known. Although phenomenological research is not nearly as effective or reliable for producing knowledge, it can cultivate and develop self-knowledge, wisdom, and ultimately compassion. Ironically and fortunately, the newer mindfulness and acceptance-based cognitive behavioral therapy (CBT) treatments (most prominently dialectical behavior therapy, acceptance and commitment therapy, and mindfulness-based cognitive therapy) have led full circle back to emphasizing phenomenological inquiry, wisdom, and compassion within therapy by incorporating mindfulness practice, in some form, as a central element of the treatment. Together these treatments are referred to as the *third wave* of cognitive behavioral therapy (see Hayes et al., 2004).

Revalues Discipline and Practice

Mindfulness has rapidly made strong inroads into mainstream cognitive behavioral (Linehan, 1993a; Segal et al., 2002; Hayes et al., 2003; Hayes et al., 2004) and psychodynamic relational therapies (Epstein, 1995, 1998, 2005, 2008; Siegel, 2007, 2010, 2012; Germer & Siegel, 2013). I believe this is because mindfulness is a discipline of practice—that helps the practitioner to develop an embodied understanding of how unconscious, conditioned reactions cause needless suffering, and also the psychological skills and inner capacities needed to reduce such suffering and to live with greater skill and ease.

Makes Therapy Existentially Resonant and Authentic

Therapeutic mindfulness practice develops cognitive, emotional, and somatic self-regulation and distress-reduction skills that are existentially authentic. They are not just techniques, but rather skillful responses to looking deeply into (Nhat Hanh, 1988a, 1988b) and experientially understanding and accepting the existential truths of life, such as impermanence, the inevitability of pain and loss, and our uniquely human propensity to create unnecessary (adventitious) suffering for ourselves. We can then apply our experientially anchored understanding and psychological strengths developed through mindfulness practice to living more skillfully, with less distress and greater ease.

Many mindfulness-based therapies require that the client engage in a daily discipline of formal mindfulness meditation practice. This actually increases the sense of authenticity, because just like life, mindfulness meditation practice is often not easy; in fact, sometimes it can be quite challenging and unpleasant. The formal mindfulness meditation component in each of these therapies helps both therapists and clients to develop the understanding, skills, and inner capacities required to engage life's inevitable difficulty and distress in a way that optimizes happiness and reduces unnecessary suffering.

Serves as an Antidote to the Problem of Reification

Many of our theories about psychopathology and psychotherapy employ terminology that inadvertently reifies processes in describing them, making them sound more like things than processes. These include our clients' implicit theories as well.

I see this often with clients who are distraught about having a particular emotion or thought. For example, recently a potential new client named Lou phoned, reporting that his wife told him he had to "work on his anger." He was chronically irritable and emotionally abusive, and he frequently yelled at his wife and son. Both he and his wife talked about "his anger" like it was substantial and enduring, as "something" Lou "carried around" like a bundle of explosives that could go off at any moment. "It" was scary and burdensome.

This way of thinking about emotions, common among therapists as well as the population at large, predisposes us to certain thoughts and strategies. For instance, how can I "get rid of" my anger? If I can't get rid of it for good, can I at least "get it out" temporarily by exercising, screaming, or pounding a pillow? (Exercise isn't a bad coping strategy, and I often encourage it, if it's not just avoidance. Screaming and hitting pillows, not so much.) Because Lou feels angry so frequently, he identifies with his anger in a way that defines him as a person: "I am an angry person."

Mindfulness practice offers an alternative mode of relating to experience, one based on understanding that we live in moment to moment increments—sensation moments, perception moments, emotion moments, thought moments, always the present moment, one after the next.

In the deepest sense, objects and things are actually "happenings" (more like verbs than nouns), even you and me. Every seven years we change out almost every cell in our bodies. At the subatomic level there is only energy, matter, and space. Mostly space. Not even our bodies are solid. Something as fleeting as an emotion certainly isn't. Anger is just the dominant flavor of some moments of Lou's experience, so it's really more accurate to talk about "anger moments" than "my anger."

When you experience a physical itch or tingle, most likely you don't let it define you. For example, you wouldn't say, "I am a tingle person" or "I am an itch person." Just as we typically disidentify with and objectify a tingle or an itch, we can objectify and disidentify with moments of anger. We can simply notice each anger moment mindfully, without judging it, creating a story about it, or being compelled to action by it.

This doesn't mean abdicating responsibility for how we behave—not at all! But it might mean experiencing anger moments (and other distressing moments) as more workable, because they don't seem as substantial and solid, and you don't believe in them as strongly.

Exercise 2.1: Think of Yourself as a Verb Rather than a Noun

1. For an hour or two, experience yourself as a verb, as a mind-body process unfolding and changing moment by moment. Think of yourself as being fluid rather than solid.

2. For example, if you have a headache, try thinking of it as throbbing or stabbing that is happening in a "head moment," an event moment in a chain of event moments.

3. Express body-mind states as impersonal events happening moment by moment rather than descriptions of self. For example, tell yourself *Hunger is happening* rather than *I am hungry*.

4. Notice if and how imagining yourself as a verb changes what you perceive, as well as your experience of perceiving.

Challenges Belief in a Fixed Personality Essence or Self-Identity

Mindfulness meditation can experientially challenge conventional beliefs about personality and identity as having a fixed, unchanging core or essence throughout our lives. In addition to making possible an experiential understanding of how subjective experiencing is constructed, this may be the most radical contribution that mindfulness makes to psychology and psychotherapy.

Narrative and constructivist personality theories and psychotherapies have philosophically challenged notions of a fixed "essential self" (Cushman, 1995; Gergen, 1991). Mindfulness meditation practice can experientially challenge the belief in a fixed, essential self through systematic, disciplined inquiry into and investigation of the mind-body process as it unfolds moment by moment.

Bridges the Science and the Art of Psychotherapy

Psychotherapy has often been described as a mix of science and art (Shapiro & Carlson, 2009). Cognitive behavioral therapies perhaps weigh in more heavily as science, and psychodynamic and other relational therapies—as well as structural, strategic, and systems-based therapies—as art, but all can be practiced with greater emphasis on the science or the art, depending on the temperament, discipline, training, and theoretical commitments of the clinician. Psychotherapies outside the academic mainstream often have little or no scientific validation and are based solely on a foundation of theory, therapist observation, clinical trial and error, and art (the clinical wisdom, skill, insight, intuition, and healing presence of the therapist).

Mindfulness is now a major focus of scientific research in psychotherapy. Ironically, although experimental variables have been defined to quantify and measure mindfulness, in actuality mindfulness is the central, radically experiential component of what is likely the most systematic, rigorous, and disciplined program of empirical, phenomenological research ever developed: Buddhist psychology (Olendzki, 2010).

Subjecting mindfulness meditation to scientific scrutiny involves the scientific, empirical investigation of a phenomenological, empirical mode of knowing. Perhaps in this way mindfulness practice can help bridge the divide between psychotherapy as empirical science and psychotherapy as empirical phenomenological mode of knowing, sometimes described as the "art of psychotherapy."

Helps Prevent Therapist Burnout

A regular discipline of mindfulness meditation practice is the best way I know of to prevent burnout in any job or profession, particularly psychotherapy. Therapists are especially vulnerable to burnout because of occupational risk factors, such as regularly dealing with pain, suffering, and trauma and institutional and systemic pressures and demands; there are also common therapist personality traits that make us particularly vulnerable to burnout (Miller, 1980).

Mindfulness practice cultivates mind-body skills, inner capacities, attitudes, and perspectives that are vital for therapist self-care. Most basic is the skill of "bearing witness" (Glassman, 1998), or shifting out of "doing mode of mind" into "being mode of mind" (Segal et al., 2002) when listening to our clients' accounts of pain and trauma. Bearing witness, or listening from being mode of mind, requires capacities for distress tolerance and emotion self-regulation that allow us to relate skillfully to our own reactions while listening compassionately to a client's account of pain and trauma, without feeling compelled to either fix the client's pain or to shut down or emotionally distance ourselves. Bearing witness involves the wisdom, discernment, and trust that come from understanding, from the inside out, the power of healing presence. It helps us to understand the difference between true compassion (which brings us closer) and sympathy (which distances).

Mindfulness practice is, in a very real sense, like being on vacation without going on vacation. Although regular breaks and vacations are, of course, important, ultimately vacations are just situations and experiences we construct that are novel, very engaging, or extremely simple, making it easier to be fully present in the moment. We think we are more present because we are enjoying ourselves, when actually the opposite is true. Being fully aware and engaged with just the present moment brings joy and an increased sense of aliveness. At the same time, it's restful and refreshing.

Summary

In this chapter we looked at a variety of benefits that mindfulness brings in response to the question, Why mindfulness in psychotherapy? In chapter 3 we will explore responses to a second question: How does mindfulness heal?

Chapter 3

How Mindfulness Heals

In this chapter we will explore therapeutic modes of action for mindfulness, beginning with how mindfulness is itself transformative and healing.

Mindfulness Itself Transforms and Heals

Many therapies acknowledge that awareness is a necessary precondition to what is considered the central therapeutic mode of action (for example, emotional insight, cognitive restructuring, narrative reconstruction, and so on).

Mindfulness reintroduces the radical idea that a particular form of awareness is intrinsically healing, namely present moment awareness that is nonjudging, without agenda, unconditionally accepting, empathically attuned, kind, authentically friendly, curious, and interested (Rogers, 1980; Duncan et al., 2010).

To begin, it's vital to understand that the present moment, the only moment we can ever directly live or experience, has always already happened. Once present it can't be changed. We can choose only whether and how to engage it.

Mindfulness meditation develops and strengthens mind-body skills, inner capacities, attitudes, and perspectives that allow us to be present and respond to each moment with optimum skill (see chapter 7). Mindfulness in the present moment allows us to respond more skillfully in the next moment; to more effectively deal with life's challenges; to notice opportunities for learning, happiness, and even joy in difficult circumstances; and to reduce adventitious suffering or even avoid it altogether. In the remainder of the chapter we will look at how each of the mental factors that comprise mindful awareness is itself intrinsically healing.

Radical Acceptance

Radical acceptance (Brach, 2003) is the practice of receiving and fully experiencing each moment, one after the next, without conditions; that is, embracing each moment regardless of its content, whether it's pleasant or unpleasant, whether you like it or dislike it. Radical acceptance doesn't require agreeing with, approving of, or condoning the moment. Rather, it is simply acknowledging that the present moment has already happened, and therefore the most skillful response is to receive it openheartedly and without conditions. Doing so gives us the best chance of perceiving it clearly and accurately, and responding skillfully in the next moment.

A similar concept found in acceptance and commitment therapy is *willingness* (Hayes et al., 2003; Hayes & Smith, 2005). However, the more active term "willingness" suggests literally welcoming the present moment, because it is as precious as any other moment of our lives that we will never get back. If the moment is unpleasant and disliked, all the more reason to receive it willingly. Trying to avoid or resist what is unpleasant or disliked just increases distress in the next moment.

The Wisdom of No Escape

How we relate to each moment of our lives is a practice with powerful transformative consequences. If we practice patience, wisdom, empathy, or nonreactivity in the present moment, those qualities are reinforced and increasingly available in succeeding moments. If we practice impatience, being ill-attuned, or getting caught up in conditioned emotional reactivity or judgment in the present moment, we reinforce and strengthen those reactions, and increase the likelihood that they will arise in the moments that follow.

Each moment conditions the next. Pema Chödrön, a well-known American meditation teacher and Buddhist nun in a Tibetan Buddhist lineage, coined the phrase "the wisdom of no escape" (1991) to describe this deceptively simple but profound truth. Formal mindfulness meditation practice allows us to turn our own bodies and minds into experiential laboratories so that we can directly investigate and more deeply understand this truth for ourselves.

Another way of understanding the wisdom of no escape is to realize that you are never free from practicing. You are always practicing something. The question is, what are you practicing right now?

Personally I seem to relearn the wisdom of no escape on a regular basis. The most recent powerful lesson was about writing. Having never written a book before, I found that the more I wrote, the easier the writing became, and the more I enjoyed it. If I procrastinated or avoided writing, it seemed much, much harder, and I enjoyed it less. Okay, I dreaded it!

I also learned that there was no escaping the book. I could choose to write or not write. Both activities occupied the same psychic space. But not writing ultimately felt bad and accomplished nothing. Writing almost always felt better, and sometimes it felt wonderful—creative, productive, and lots of fun. Also, as I developed a more disciplined writing practice, even the difficult moments were less distressing.

The wisdom of no escape teaches that there is no vacation from responding to the past and shaping the future. Nonjudging awareness transforms your relationship to the present moment, allowing you to shift your relationship to the past and your response to the present in order to take responsibility for the future. Certainly these are also the basic goals of all psychotherapy, regardless of theoretical orientation or methodology.

The wisdom of no escape, though it may sound bleak, is actually very good news. You don't have to uproot all of your reactive, negative tendencies. Rather, mindfulness practice allows you to observe emotional reactivity without being compelled to action (or being frozen) by it. You can free yourself from the power of conditioned emotional reactions without having to either express or suppress them. Just be mindful of emotional reactivity as it happens. You don't have to do anything about your emotions, except to be mindful of them.

The wisdom of no escape encourages a focus in the present moment, which is also the only moment in which joy can be experienced. As Charlotte Joko Beck, a well-known Zen teacher and the author of several books, says, "Joy is who we are when we're not preoccupied with something else" (1993, p. 232).

Embracing Impermanence

When I was packing for a move to a new house I came across the slide rule I used in the eighth grade. For younger readers, slide rules were the nonelectronic precursors of handheld digital calculators. I showed the slide rule to my then seven-year-old son Zack, who was already adept at using a computer. I told him it was what I had used to work out math problems before calculators and personal computers. He examined it with the fascination of an archaeologist unearthing an ancient relic. It was a poignant moment. The gulf between his childhood world and mine was palpable. Not just the technology itself, but the profound upheaval wrought by the rapidly accelerating pace of technological innovation and change.

As I reflected on the radically different context in which I had come of age, it affirmed for me once again the reality of continuous and unrelenting change as life's only constant. Not only is the world around us constantly changing, but so are we.

Drop into stillness for a few minutes right now and experience just being. Notice the changing physical sensations, thoughts, emotions, perceptions, and mental states. Optimal mental health requires cognitive flexibility (Luoma et al., 2007, pp. 72, 193–194), the capacity to accommodate and respond skillfully to continuous change.

Mindfulness meditation cultivates cognitive flexibility as well as a deep experiential understanding that life is just what it is. Having expectations about how life "should be," or feeling angry about life not being the way you want, reveals an unfortunate misunderstanding about how life works, which can lead to much adventitious suffering. Cultivating freedom from preconceptions and rigid, unrealistic expectations is central to the practice of embracing impermanence.

Uncoupling from Stress Reactivity

The cycle of stress reactivity is the positive feedback loop of event, perception, appraisal, and reaction, which is then perceived and appraised as another threat, causing another reaction that is perceived and appraised as threat, and so on. This loop triggers the fight-flight-freeze reaction, or sympathetic nervous system reactivity.

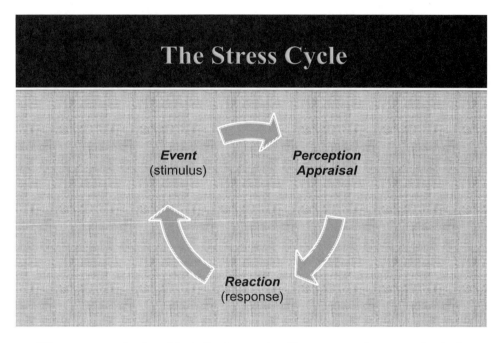

The Stress Cycle

Event (stimulus)

Perception Appraisal

Reaction (response)

The stress cycle is self-reinforcing and self-sustaining because the linkages between threat perception, appraisal, and reaction are instinctual, or they are so strongly conditioned as to be effectively automatic and beyond conscious control. Mindfulness training can enhance your ability to pay close attention to each moment without getting caught up in stress reactivity, letting you break the automatic linkages between threat perception, appraisal, and reaction and allowing you the freedom to respond rather than react.

I intentionally want to emphasize the distinction between "reaction" and "response" to underscore the fundamental truth that even when you are not free to choose what happens, you are always free to choose how you respond to what happens based on your innate capacity for mindfulness. The mode of action of mindfulness in therapy is thus linked to what is most fundamentally human: our capacity for self-awareness and our freedom to choose.

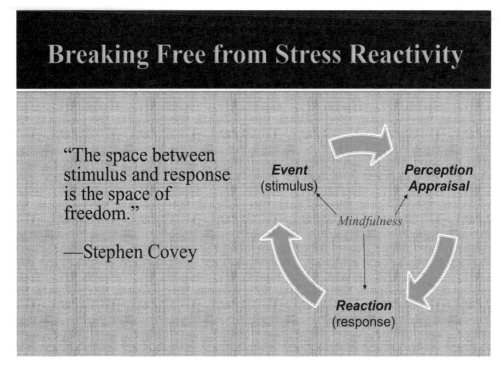

Breaking Free from Stress Reactivity

"The space between stimulus and response is the space of freedom."

—Stephen Covey

Event (stimulus)

Perception Appraisal

Mindfulness

Reaction (response)

There's a popular saying derived from the work of Viktor Frankl: "Between stimulus and response there is a space. In that space lies our freedom and power to choose our response" (Covey, 1999, p. 21). The "space" here is mindfulness, which allows for response instead of reaction, in the way that I have used these two words. By switching from reaction to response, I mean switching out of autopilot mode into the mode of awareness and choice. The table below further illustrates the differences between "reaction" and "response."

Reaction	Response
Automatic	Intentional
Instinctual	Creative/spontaneous
Conditioned	Unconditioned
Predictable	Unpredictable
Repetitive	Unique
Habitual	Situation specific
Unconscious/rote	Conscious/aware
Aggressive	Assertive
Predetermined	Freely chosen

Mindfulness uncouples the automatic cause-effect linkages between event, perception, appraisal, and reaction by interrupting the instinctual or conditioned associations between the links. Bringing mindfulness to bear on any link in the cycle of stress reactivity allows for the freedom to respond rather than to react.

Restores and Promotes Healthy Self-Regulation

Because mindfulness potentially frees us from the positive feedback loop of stress reactivity, it also supports our natural organismic tendencies toward self-regulation and balance. Gary Schwartz, a well-known psychoneuroimmunologist at the University of Arizona, developed a five-stage model to illustrate how the mind-body connection leads to illness through disconnection, sustained dysregulation, and lack of awareness, or to health through sustained self-awareness and self-regulation. Schwartz's model is summarized in *Full Catastrophe Living* (Kabat-Zinn, 2013, p. 279).

The first stage of the vector leading to illness is *disattention*, which means that you choose to ignore a stimulus (often an annoying or irritating stimulus) for any reason. It may be minor, out of your control, or low priority compared to other things. If disattention persists, then the second stage, *disconnection*, ensues.

In disconnection you have become habituated to the stimulus, so you are no longer capable of perceiving it even though it still affects you. For example, imagine that you are filling out managed care reports or doing billing. Suddenly you become aware of feeling hungry (it is almost noon), but you're on a roll and don't want to stop to eat. Within ten or fifteen minutes you no longer feel hungry. You have habituated to and disconnected from the hunger stimulus, although physiologically nothing has changed. You keep working. You finish just before 3:00 p.m. with a sense of relief and accomplishment. Then you notice that you feel a bit tired and irritable and have a headache. You have entered stage three, *dysregulation*.

If you respond to the dysregulation by paying attention (mindfulness) and then getting something to eat (nourishing yourself), you self-regulate and restore health and wholeness. In stress-related illnesses the symptoms we habituate to and disconnect from are often more serious, leading to more serious states of dysregulation and ultimately to disease.

Disorder and disease are most likely to develop wherever we are genetically or environmentally most vulnerable. People with family histories of anxiety disorder, depression, or substance abuse may be more vulnerable to these disorders when stressed. When relationship partners attempt to deny unhappiness or adapt in unhealthy ways, such as with distancing or passive aggressive behavior, the mind-body connection still ensures that there is a negative impact on health, which could consist of emotional or physical symptoms, or both. Perhaps you have worked with verbally and emotionally abusive couples in which one spouse's sarcastic or disdainful comments or controlling behavior is superficially accepted or ignored by the other but acted out in the bedroom or through undermining the other's parenting, compulsive spending, or affairs.

In consulting with executives in an executive health clinic, I have worked with many who become alienated from their partners and children as a result of very demanding travel schedules. Even without significant family histories, they often seem to be at greater risk for developing a variety of psychiatric disorders (alcohol abuse, compulsive overeating, anxiety and mood disorders), as well as experiencing marital dysfunction, due to the combination of the stresses and challenges of business travel and being away from loved ones.

Schwartz's model of the mind-body connection in illness is also useful in understanding how the mind-body connection contributes to health, including mental health. The first stage is *attention*, specifically mindful attention to each moment of experience, which implies being open and receptive to feeling sensations in the body. For those of us, including our clients, who have ignored our bodies and the capacity to experience physical sensation, this may require a significant shift in awareness.

When we pay attention to lived experience in our bodies—sensations, sounds, smells, thoughts, emotions, moods—we automatically reconnect with ourselves, reinhabiting our bodies and lives through directly experiencing each moment as felt sense in the body as it arises. Then *self-regulation* often occurs naturally, because we are by nature self-regulating organisms. At the very least, awareness leads to understanding of the behavior required to self-regulate and restore a sense of wholeness, balance, systemic order, and ease (Kabat-Zinn, 2005).

The Present Moment as Refuge

In addition to uncoupling the automatic linkages between perception, appraisal, and reaction, mindfulness allows us to literally step outside of linear time as defined by past, present, and future and into the eternal time of the present moment. The experience of the *eternal now*, of one present moment after the next, beyond thoughts and ideas about past and future, has profound implications. In particular, anchoring oneself in the eternal now alters the subjective experience of both emotional and physical pain and suffering, and it allows us to develop the capacity to be peaceful and at ease regardless of circumstances.

Unconditional Acceptance, Accurate Empathy, and Genuineness: The Nonspecific or Common Factors of Therapist Efficacy

It would be fair to say that the therapist's personal mindfulness practice is the necessary foundation for incorporating mindfulness in psychotherapy work because it cultivates the therapist's heart. In his well-known children's book *The Little Prince*, author and aviator Antoine de Saint Exupéry's main character imparts this famous bit of wisdom to the lost boy: "It is only with the heart that one can see rightly. What is essential is invisible to the eye" (Saint Exupéry, 2000, p. 63).

In my experience, this statement summarizes an underlying truth about psychotherapy. Seeing "with the heart" is the essence of the therapeutic relationship. The relational variables, those most difficult to see with the eyes, are determinative of therapeutic outcome.

Over sixty years ago, Carl Rogers (1957) theorized that there were three necessary and sufficient conditions to bring about positive change in psychotherapy: unconditional positive regard, accurate empathy, and genuineness. A number of clinical researchers have since validated Rogers's work, in what has come to be known as *common factors research*. The common factors of therapist efficacy identified by subsequent researchers mostly cluster around the three therapeutic attributes originally identified by Rogers. All three can be systematically developed and strengthened through mindfulness meditation practice (Duncan et al., 2010). We will explore Rogers's three factors below.

Radical Acceptance and Unconditional Positive Regard

Unconditional positive regard is radical acceptance of one's client, involving unconditional friendliness, genuine interest, curiosity, and caring concern. Unconditional positive regard also involves unconditional presence, meaning you bring the full focus of awareness to the client in each moment. If you have ever been in the presence of someone who gifts you with 100 percent of their friendly, caring attention, someone who really wants to know you compassionately and has no interest in evaluating or judging you, then you know how powerful and transformative this experience can be.

Empathic Attunement

Empathy is the attitude of receptive, decentered, precisely attuned presence as a mode of knowing. Ideally, empathy is an attitudinal factor that we bring to each moment of mindfulness meditation, as well as to each moment of listening and attending to our clients in psychotherapy. Heinz Kohut (2014), the founder of psychoanalytic self-psychology, described *empathy* in psychoanalysis as "a tool for introspection", which bears directly on the method of inquiry and investigation and mode of knowing factor of the mindfulness pyramid model. Empathic attunement is both the driver and the outcome of mindful inquiry in meditation practice.

Authenticity and Genuineness

Genuineness is the willingness to know and be known exactly as we are in each moment, without defensiveness or evasion. By doing so we can know each moment as it is, and in the present moment with our clients we allow ourselves to be known as well. In therapy this means bringing authentic presence to each moment of the therapeutic encounter, embodying the willingness to be vulnerable and known in each moment as we invite our clients to do the same.

Mindfulness meditation cultivates and strengthens authenticity and genuineness as systematically as weight training develops strength and muscle mass and running develops aerobic fitness. These traits both undergird mindfulness practice and are strengthened by it. Mindfulness practice facilitates a more accurate attunement to the client in context, to what's happening in the therapeutic process, and to what the client needs in each moment to move forward in therapy.

Healing Presence

The attributes of therapist effectiveness together comprise the essence of *healing presence*, that combination of attitudes, skills, and inner capacities that potentiate healing in the therapeutic relationship regardless of the therapist's theoretical orientation or techniques. Mindfulness practice is thus a potent resource for teaching and cultivating healing presence in psychotherapy training programs.

Wellspring of Resilience, Self-Acceptance, and Self-Compassion, and Other Psychological Strengths for Clients

The same meditation practices that cultivate and enhance healing presence, therapeutic effectiveness, stress reduction, and burnout prevention for therapists and other health care practitioners can also strengthen our clients' inner resources for self-healing.

Clients who actively do mindfulness meditation as part of, or in addition to, therapy cultivate and strengthen innate resources and capacities for nonjudging awareness, relaxed concentration, radical acceptance, distress tolerance, emotion self-regulation, and self-healing. These attributes enable clients to relate more skillfully to the intrinsic difficulty, distress, and pain of life and to decrease adventitious suffering created by conditioned, habitual stress reactions and experiential avoidance.

Summary

This chapter offered an overview of the healing modes of action of mindfulness in psychotherapy. Chapter 4 elaborates on and further explores the mindfulness pyramid model.

Chapter 4

The Mindfulness Pyramid: An Integrated Model of Mindfulness in Psychotherapy

The mindfulness pyramid visually models the facets and elements of mindfulness meditation that are most relevant to psychotherapy, as well as how they relate to each other and the therapeutic process practice as a whole. I describe this model as "transtheoretical" because it's based on the assumption that mindfulness, whether or not it's labeled as such, undergirds and informs all effective psychotherapy regardless of theory or technique. The four facets below are depicted as the four faces of the mindfulness pyramid model in figures 1 through 3.

A. Formal mindfulness meditation practices

B. Skills, inner capacities, attitudes, and perspectives

C. Method of inquiry and investigation and mode of knowing

D. Way of being and relating to experience

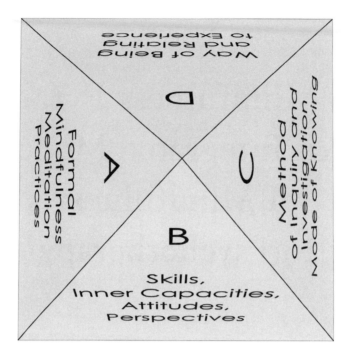

Figure 1. The mindfulness pyramid: The four facets of mindfulness in clinical practice, depicted as the four faces of the mindfulness pyramid

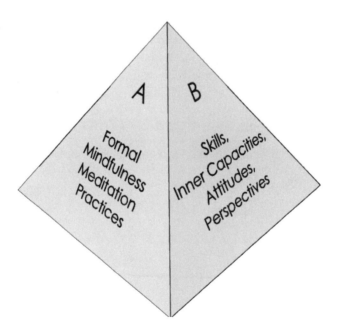

Figure 2. The mindfulness pyramid, faces *A* and *B*

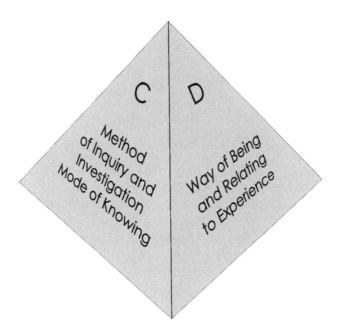

Figure 3. The mindfulness pyramid, faces C and D

The four facets of mindfulness can be incorporated at three levels of the therapeutic process, listed below. Visualize the three levels as three horizontal "slices" of the pyramid moving from bottom to top (see figure 4).

1. The foundation and bottom level of the pyramid represents the therapist's mindfulness practice.

2. The middle level of the pyramid represents the therapeutic process and relationship as mindfulness practice.

3. The top level of the pyramid represents the client's mindfulness practice.

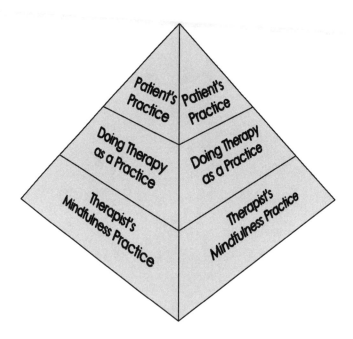

Figure 4. The three levels at which mindfulness is integrated in psychotherapy

The three levels are vertically integrated and of equal thickness, but they increase progressively in volume from the uppermost level (client's practice) to the foundation level (therapist's mindfulness practice). The greater volume of the foundation and middle levels is no accident. I believe it graphically represents the relatively greater therapeutic impact of these levels as well as the dependence of the middle and uppermost levels on those below.

Thus level 1 (therapist's mindfulness practice) is the most important level, the foundation upon which the incorporation of all other mindfulness in psychotherapy rests. The foundation allows you to embody mindfulness in level 2 (doing therapy as a practice) and in level 3, in which you "teach" formal and informal practices to clients. I enclose the word "teach" in quotation marks because teaching mindfulness comes as much from being as from doing. Efficacy at level 3 depends on levels 1 and 2, and level 2 depends on level 1. Even what appears to be doing, such as teaching and guiding formal mindfulness meditation practices, needs to come from the therapist's "being." If the therapist doesn't authentically embody his or her own mindfulness practice in the therapeutic process and relationship (level 2), and in teaching and guiding formal meditation practices (level 3), the client's practice (level 3) will likely be weak or compromised.

The four facets of mindfulness in psychotherapy are incorporated at all three levels of the pyramid, which represent three parallel streams—therapist, therapeutic process and relationship, and client—of embodied mindfulness (see figures 5 and 6). Experientially, the three levels are less distinct than the sharp dividing lines might suggest. However, I thought it most important to clearly convey the hierarchical relationship between the three levels.

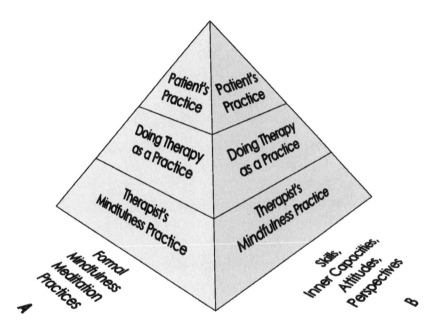

Figure 5. Depicting facets *A* and *B* integrated at all three levels of the mindfulness pyramid

Both in the mindfulness pyramid model and throughout the book I emphasize the therapist's mindfulness practice (level 1) as being the key to effectively incorporating mindfulness in psychotherapy. Chapters 5 through 9 focus on developing and deepening all four facets of the therapist's mindfulness practice and exploring how the therapist's embodied understanding of each of the four facets of practice informs the therapeutic relationship and process, as well as the explicit teaching of formal and informal mindfulness practices to clients.

As the therapist's practice and understanding deepen, doing therapy as a mindfulness practice (level 2) and teaching formal mindfulness meditation practices to clients (level 3) increasingly become organic expressions and extensions of the therapist's mindfulness practice (level 1), what in Buddhist psychology is referred to as "skillful means" (Surya Das, 2007, pp. 165–184).

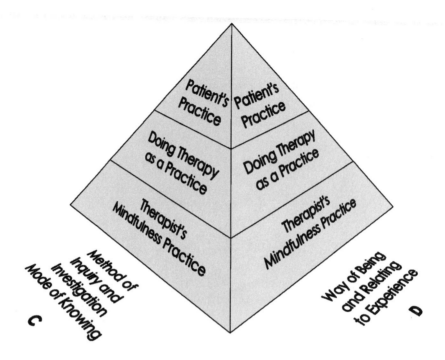

Figure 6. Depicting facets C and D integrated at all three levels of the mindfulness pyramid

Pyramid Redux

In summary, the mindfulness pyramid model depicts the four facets of mindfulness practice in psychotherapy as the four faces of a pyramid (figures 1, 2, and 3). The model also depicts three levels of the therapeutic process within which the four facets of mindfulness can be incorporated (figures 5 and 6). Level 1, the therapist's mindfulness practice, is conceptualized as the foundation for all mindfulness-based psychotherapeutic interventions.

Level 2, doing therapy as a mindfulness practice, represents the embodiment of the therapist's mindfulness practice in the unfolding present of the therapeutic relationship and process. At level 2 the therapist consciously assumes the role of the mindfulness of the relational field without necessarily discussing mindfulness with the client. Chapters 9 and 10 explore in greater depth the therapeutic process and relationship as a mindfulness practice at level 2, which also lays the foundation for effectively teaching formal and informal mindfulness practices to clients at level 3.

The Four Faces of the Mindfulness Pyramid Are Only Superficially Distinct

Structurally, the four faces of the mindfulness pyramid model are only superficially separate and distinct (see figure 7). As soon as you move inside the pyramid the distinctions vanish, and each of the four faces of the pyramid begins to merge with and contain the other three.

It's the same with the four facets of mindfulness practice. Each of the facets can be understood, deployed, and experienced as distinct. Yet each facet also contains and is supported by the other three at all three levels of practice. The hierarchical distinctions between the three levels also vanish as you move inside the pyramid, although they provide a useful visual aid for conceptualizing the vital importance of vertical integration for all mindfulness-informed and mindfulness-based psychotherapies based on the foundation of the therapist's meditation practice.

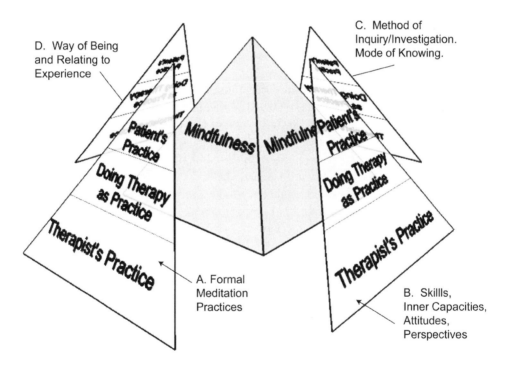

Figure 7. The four faces and three levels of the mindfulness pyramid: the therapist's perspective

41

Therapist's Mindfulness Practice—Manifesting Healing Presence

Typically, the client first encounters mindfulness in therapy as a quality of healing presence embodied by the therapist in the moment to moment unfolding of the therapeutic relationship. Healing presence is characterized by genuine interest, curiosity, caring, unconditional acceptance and friendliness, empathic attunement, warmth, authenticity, compassion, and fearlessness. The therapist's healing presence invites and encourages the client, both implicitly and explicitly, to be present to his or her own experience in a similar fashion. The therapist encourages (and supports) the client to receive and accept each moment of experience unconditionally and willingly, without resisting or attempting to change or get rid of moments that are unpleasant and without trying to cling to pleasant moments.

Being the Mindfulness of the Therapeutic Relational Field

The therapeutic relationship becomes an important mindfulness practice for the therapist, starting with the first moment of the therapeutic encounter. Our challenge as therapists is to function as the mindfulness of the therapeutic relational field— fully present and aware, nonjudging, nonstriving, accepting, interested, caring, friendly, patient, and encouraging one moment after the next; yet radically decentered, just allowing each moment to evoke the most appropriate response. Some moments call for listening. Other moments call for deeper inquiry, mirroring or validating, making observations, emotional support, humor, education, or confrontation, depending on the context and what's happening with the client in any given moment.

At times we may notice attention wandering (just as it does during formal meditation), and that we are no longer focused on the client within the therapeutic relationship and process (or, as I prefer to think about it for reasons I will elaborate on in chapter 10, the intersubjective relational field). Each time you notice that your attention has wandered away from the client in the present moment, simply acknowledge where it went, and then escort it back to the client. Your formal mindfulness meditation practice will strengthen your capacity for steadiness, composure, and clarity of focus in the therapeutic relationship in the face of emotional reactivity—both your client's and your own.

Teaching and Guiding Formal Mindfulness Meditation with Clients

The therapist's practice at level 3 involves explicitly teaching formal meditation practices as well as mindfulness skills, inner capacities, attitudes, and perspectives to clients. The viability and efficacy of the client's level 3 learning depends on how authentically the therapist embodies the meditation practices she is teaching and guiding.

When your client encounters your authentic embodiment of the practice, it clarifies and empowers her practice, and ultimately her embodied understanding of practice. Chapters 11 and 12 look more deeply into the client's formal mindfulness practice and into teaching and guiding formal meditation as a mindfulness practice for the therapist.

The Client's Perspective

So far the mindfulness pyramid model has represented only the therapist's perspective in the therapeutic encounter. However, the model would be incomplete without also representing the client's perspective.

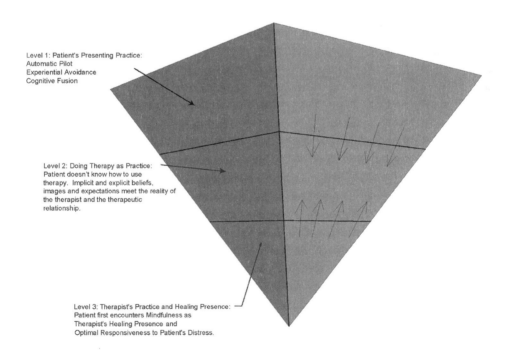

Level 1: Patient's Presenting Practice:
Automatic Pilot
Experiential Avoidance
Cognitive Fusion

Level 2: Doing Therapy as Practice:
Patient doesn't know how to use therapy. Implicit and explicit beliefs, images and expectations meet the reality of the therapist and the therapeutic relationship.

Level 3: Therapist's Practice and Healing Presence:
Patient first encounters Mindfulness as Therapist's Healing Presence and Optimal Responsiveness to Patient's Distress.

Figure 8. The mindfulness pyramid from the client's perspective: life isn't working, precarious balance, distress

Figure 8 represents a hypothetical client in a therapy session for the first time. Imagine that the top level of the inverted pyramid still represents the client's practice, the middle level represents the therapeutic relationship, and the bottom level represents the therapist's practice. A client usually seeks therapy because she is experiencing significant distress, and life isn't working. The client's efforts to remedy the emotional distress and to change her behavior in order to restore balance and ease have not succeeded.

Thus the top of the client pyramid (level 1) represents the client's practice coming into therapy, particularly the unsuccessful efforts to self-regulate emotions, change behavior, and decrease distress. Level 2 represents the client's hopes and expectations coming into therapy, including ideas about what therapy is and how it works derived from prior personal experience, the accounts of family or friends, or representations in media and popular culture; it also includes the ideas, hopes, and fantasies the client has about the therapist derived from prior phone contact, what the referral source said about the therapist (if the referral was made by an outside source), and anything else the client may have heard.

Level 2 also represents the client's initial encounter with the therapist's embodied practice as healing presence. This can include the first phone contact and any other interactions prior to the first session, up to and including the first session of the therapy, and any internalized representations of the therapist. Level 3 represents the therapist's practice as embodiment of her, hopefully experienced by the client in the preliminary contacts and the first session as healing presence.

Figure 9 represents the intersubjective process unfolding, for both therapist and client, and the felt sense of the therapeutic relationship. The unstable, inverted pyramid representing the client's experience in figure 8 is joined with the therapist's pyramid, depicted in figures 2 through 7, to represent the more stable structure of experience depicted in figure 9, which ideally depicts the intersubjective reality of the therapeutic relationship. With the therapist's help, the client "uses" the therapist as needed to develop a stronger, more stable self-experience.

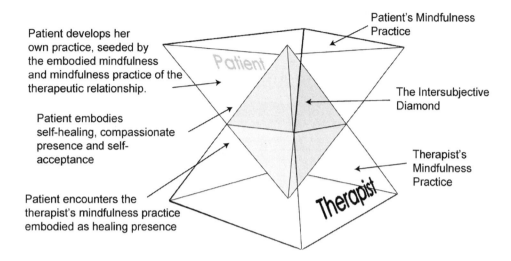

Figure 9. The mindfulness pyramid depicting the intersubjective reality of the therapeutic relationship. The intersubjective diamond depicts the relational space within which therapeutic change and transformation occur.

In my experience doing psychotherapy, intersubjectivity theorists (Stolorow & Atwood, 1992; Stolorow, Brandchaft, & Atwood, 1987; Stolorow, Atwood, & Brandchaft, 1994) come closest to understanding, at least with regard to relationships, what in Buddhist psychology is called *dependent origination*—the insight that nothing and no one has a separate, essential self, or self-experience, apart from everything and everyone else in the universe. This means that for both therapist and client, the experiences of self and other co-arise contingently in each moment of the therapeutic encounter.

Figure 9 represents the intersubjective encounter and relational co-arising that constitutes the client-therapist relationship. The therapeutic relationship and process is thus depicted as the intersection of the two pyramids. The upright pyramid on the bottom represents the therapist's experience, and the inverted pyramid on top represents the client's experience. The client's pyramid is embedded in and supported by the therapist's mindfulness practice, which the client hopefully experiences as the therapist's healing presence and, when appropriate, as explicit formal and/or informal mindfulness practice instruction.

The client can experience and internalize the therapist's mindfulness practice at all three levels of the inverted pyramid. The *intersubjective diamond* at the center of the intersecting pyramids represents the therapist-client encounter within the transformative crucible of the therapist's healing presence. (We'll explore the intersubjective diamond in more depth in chapter 11.)

The Four Faces of the Mindfulness Pyramid

Mindfulness, as previously stated, is much more than a formal meditation practice or therapy technique. At the deepest level, it's a way of life, or more accurately, a practice of being in relationship to each moment of life in a particular way. Mindfulness practice involves just being present with and experiencing each moment as it arises, one moment after the next, with care, tenderness, appreciation, gratitude, respect, and love.

Mindfulness is an innate capacity that we all possess to some degree. For most of us, however, consistently relating to life in this way doesn't come easily. It seems counterintuitive to open our hearts equally to moments of pleasure and moments of distress or pain. Rather, we instinctually try to avoid experiencing unpleasant moments and grasp for, and try to hold on to, pleasant ones.

Formal Mindfulness Meditation Practices

Formal mindfulness meditation practices are one way we can systematically strengthen the capacity to be mindful. In the same way that weight lifting builds muscle mass and increases strength and aerobic exercise develops cardiovascular fitness, formal mindfulness meditation practices strengthen the capacity to deploy mindfulness in daily life. Nonetheless, we don't do formal mindfulness practices in order to accomplish anything or get anywhere, whether it be strengthening mindful awareness or the attitudes and perspectives mindfulness develops. Doing so would be antithetical to the spirit of mindfulness, which involves nonstriving, letting go, and just being with each moment without trying to get anywhere or accomplish anything. Striving to accomplish something through mindfulness practice just leads to frustration and distress.

Mindfulness meditation as a form of nondoing, and ceasing from striving to accomplish anything, may seem fundamentally in conflict with psychotherapy's mission to alleviate suffering, which undoubtedly is a goal-oriented endeavor. But it is precisely within this paradox, or "dialectic" (Linehan, 1993a), that the healing power of mindfulness resides.

Skills, Inner Capacities, Attitudes, and Perspectives

Beyond formal meditation practices, mindfulness can be understood as a specific set of skills, inner capacities, attitudes, and perspectives (see figure 2) that can be taught and learned in therapy, both implicitly and explicitly, and then deployed in daily life to alleviate distress and to live more effectively and with greater ease. This approach to mindfulness is represented most significantly in two of the most important and influential third wave cognitive behavioral therapies: dialectical behavior therapy (Linehan, 1993a, 1993b) and acceptance and commitment therapy (Hayes et al., 2003; Luoma et al., 2007).

Although both mindfulness-based stress reduction and mindfulness-based cognitive therapy focus primarily on formal and informal meditation practices, each intervention also recommends specific attitudes and behaviors that support the development and strengthening of mindfulness. Buddhist psychology also has many lists of attitudes, behaviors, and psychological states that are recommended as healthy behavioral and mental habits in their own right, as well as to support and strengthen the development of mindfulness (Goldstein & Kornfield, 1987; Olendzki, 2010; Goldstein, 2013). In chapter 7 we will explore in greater depth the specific mind-body skills, inner capacities, attitudes, and perspectives that are relevant to incorporating mindfulness in psychotherapy.

Method of Inquiry and Investigation and Mode of Knowing

Mindfulness as a method of phenomenological inquiry and investigation is extraordinarily powerful and valuable for psychotherapy. It involves inquiring into and investigating each moment of experience as it arises; it is a form of self-exploration with the potential to develop profound insight and inner wisdom that is far more trustworthy than perception, emotion, or intellectual analysis alone.

Because mindful awareness operates below the level of conditioned, automatic thinking and emotional reactivity, it allows us to more objectively observe thoughts, emotions, sensations, perceptions, and mind states without identifying with them, which subsequently leads to being caught up in them. Through mindful inquiry and investigation and mindfulness as a mode of knowing, it's possible to see how the predisposition toward adventitious suffering is built into the very structure of language and cognition through a conditioning process called *cognitive fusion* (Hayes et al., 2004, p. 13). Mindfulness allows for cognitive defusion, deconstructing adventitious suffering, and the possibility of relating to experience in a way that leads to greater happiness, peace, and ease.

Mindful investigation of self-experience illuminates, at a micro level, the moment to moment movements of the mind-body process as it unfolds in real time. Through mindfulness we can see clearly how we create and intensify suffering through unconscious identification with instinctual or deeply conditioned reactive patterns of thought, emotion, and behavior triggered by stress. These stress reactions happen so rapidly that they are nearly imperceptible until we deploy mindfulness to become aware of them. We can also see clearly, through mindfulness, how we can decrease and even eliminate the suffering of automatic stress reactivity by simply disidentifying with it.

It's profoundly compelling to experientially discover in formal meditation, in real time, how we create adventitious suffering for ourselves, and how we can avoid doing so. Experiencing for ourselves how humans are wired for suffering through the dominance of language functions over nonverbal functions (Hayes et al., 2004, p. 13) but can also override automatic reactions through mindful awareness and skillful responses gives rise to compassion and a realistic sense of hope that a different, more skillful mode of being and relating is possible.

Way of Being and Relating to Experience

The mode of being and relating to experience is reinforced and strengthened within formal mindfulness meditation practice. We experience in our own mind-body process how embracing each moment with curiosity, openness, and acceptance, and to experiencing it without judgment or striving reduces emotional and physical suffering and cultivates states of happiness and inner peace that are remarkably stable because they aren't contingent on external circumstance. This is quite different from our conventional mode of experiencing, and for most of us it flies in the face of what we've learned about what causes suffering and what makes us happy.

Embracing mindfulness meditation as a discipline of practice creates the potential for a profound shift in our way of being and relating to life. Attachment to preferred outcomes and views is increasingly replaced by heartfelt curiosity, openness to experience, and appreciation and gratitude without preconceived expectations or judgments.

Final Reflections on the Mindfulness Pyramid

The use of the pyramid shape to develop a model for mindfulness in psychotherapy grew out of my experience teaching continuing education seminars for mental health professionals. I wanted seminar participants to understand (much as I would like you to understand) that the possibilities for incorporating mindfulness in psychotherapy are limited solely by our creativity and depth of understanding of mindfulness.

Over time, with sincere commitment to a discipline of formal meditation and to practicing mindfulness as a way of being and relating in daily life, your understanding of mindfulness will naturally deepen. You may also notice a natural "lightening up" and an enhanced capacity to respond creatively and with more flexibility to the needs of the moment, not just in clinical practice but throughout your life.

I groped for words to convey my understanding that all definitions of mindfulness, and the tools and techniques I was teaching, point to a singular truth about life that is beyond description and language and is only accessible experientially, in the present moment. I wanted to convey the beauty and depth of mindfulness practice, its paradoxical nature, and the felt sense that there is no separation between the object being known, the knowing itself, and the knower.

Hoping it would be true that a picture is worth a thousand words, I decided to develop a visual model. The model began as a simple triangle with three levels. Then it evolved into a pyramid, then two separate pyramids, and then interpenetrating pyramids as I tried to represent my experience of the various facets, levels, elements and dynamics involved in incorporating mindfulness in psychotherapy. As I continued to refine the pyramid model over time, I began to appreciate its symbolic resonances as well as its convenient shape.

Pyramids Old and New

The pyramids of Giza in Egypt were built at least two thousand years before the foundations of Western culture flowered in Athens and the other city-states of ancient Greece. When Alexander the Great conquered much of the known world, he brought Greek culture with him. Egypt, one of the great prizes of the Alexandrian Empire, stood both symbolically and literally at the crossroads of Eastern and Western civilizations and had a culture at least as rich as, and much older than, that of Greece. Both conquered Egypt and conquering Greece were transformed by the encounter.

The Egyptians adopted Greek gods, styles of dress, manners, language, and philosophy. The Greeks incorporated Egyptian advances in astronomy and mathematics into their teaching and adopted Egyptian gods and mystery schools, particularly that of Isis, who represented the sacred feminine. Mystery schools were mystical cults dedicated to a particular goddess, god, or rite that had esoteric knowledge (thus, "mystery schools") shared only with initiates.

Perhaps the current interest in mindfulness in Western medicine, clinical psychology, psychotherapy, and so many other fields is similar. The Western cultural paradigm of scientific, technological, and economic "progress" that dominates the world has encountered the wisdom traditions of the "conquered" cultures of Asia, particularly the different forms that Buddhism took as it moved across Asia from India to Japan, as well as yogic, Taoist, and Hindu traditions. These encounters subsequently triggered rediscoveries, within the conquering cultures, of the suppressed, contemplative traditions in Judaism, Christianity, and Islam, as well as the rejected and subsequently neglected wisdom traditions of conquered, indigenous peoples around the world.

The historian Arnold Toynbee is often credited with having said, "When historians look back on the twentieth century, the most important event will not be seen as the splitting of the atom, or the defeat of fascism in World War II, but rather the encounter of Buddhism and Western culture." Although the quote seems to be apocryphal (I was unable to track down a credible source in Toynbee's writings), there is nonetheless ample evidence to support what may or may not have been Toynbee's assertion (for example, Fields, 1981; Batchelor, 1994; Boyce, 2011; Ryan, 2013). The incorporation of mindfulness in medicine and psychotherapy, as well as business, education, law, jurisprudence, and many other professions, can be seen as one manifestation of this encounter.

More concretely, Egypt's Great Pyramid has four triangular faces that have almost identical dimensions despite their immense size. They rise at virtually identical slopes to a shared point at the top more than fifty stories high. Although each of the four faces appears quite distinct on the surface, if you imagine moving beneath the faces and inside the pyramid they quickly lose their separate, distinct identities within the underlying mass of stone.

Penetrate beneath the surface of the pyramid faces and the appearance of each face as distinct is revealed as an illusion. In fact, each face of the pyramid is composed of "non-face elements" (Nhat Hanh, 1988a), the same rock from which the entire pyramid, including the other three faces, is constructed. Similarly, the four facets of mindfulness in psychotherapy, represented by the four faces of the mindfulness pyramid, are interconnected and made of the same stuff. Each is only superficially distinct. In fact, each is just a different expression of the same underlying whole.

Summary

The core of this chapter was about incorporating mindfulness in psychotherapy using the mindfulness pyramid model. The rest of the book elaborates on the four facets of mindfulness most important for psychotherapy, as represented by the four faces of the pyramid, and the three parallel levels of process within which mindfulness can be cultivated, as represented by the three levels of the pyramid.

Chapter 5 further explores the therapist's mindfulness practice and why and how it is the necessary foundation for effectively incorporating mindfulness at levels 2 and 3 of the pyramid model. In addition, chapter 5 lays the groundwork for establishing and deepening your mindfulness practice in relation to the four facets of mindfulness practice most relevant to psychotherapy, which we will explore in subsequent chapters.

Chapter 5

The Therapist's Mindfulness Practice as Foundation

Chapters 5 through 9 explore the therapist's mindfulness practice as the foundation for incorporating mindfulness in psychotherapy. I am convinced that being committed to your own mindfulness practice because you value it personally is a prerequisite for effectively incorporating mindfulness in psychotherapy. Though this conviction is shared by many leaders in the field (see Kabat-Zinn, 1990; Santorelli, 1999; Segal et al., 2002; McCown, Riebel, & Micozzi, 2010), I come to it through my own mindfulness practice and clinical practice experiences, my experiences teaching mindfulness-based stress reduction (MBSR) courses and facilitating mindfulness-based cognitive therapy (MBCT) groups as well as training therapists in MBSR and MBCT, and leading workshops for therapists in incorporating mindfulness in psychotherapy.

In chapter 5 we will explore in greater depth why and how the therapist's personal practice serves as the necessary foundation for incorporating mindfulness in therapy. If you already have an established, ongoing mindfulness practice, this chapter will help you reflect on how mindfulness may already inform your clinical work as well as how you might intentionally incorporate it further. If you are new to mindfulness, hopefully this chapter will strengthen your motivation to establish your own mindfulness meditation practice.

Embodiment

Therapists need to maintain a personal, ongoing mindfulness practice because mindfulness is an *embodied knowing*. In doing therapy, the therapist experientially embodies openhearted, receptive, nonjudging, nonstriving, friendly, curious, inquisitive, and compassionate awareness as literally a *felt sense* in the moment by moment unfolding of the therapeutic relationship and the therapist's mind-body process. Words are inadequate to directly describe this experience. Metaphor and imagery can help.

See if you can recall an experience of *flow* in relationship, when you just clicked with your partner without apparent effort and the shared moment seemed particularly vivid and alive. Perhaps you can recall an experience of exquisite attunement to a client in therapy, leading to a particularly skillful verbal response (or perhaps to saying nothing, the two of you just inhabiting the fullness of the silence together).

Moments of flow can also be emotionally challenging, but all are similar experientially in feeling very vivid and alive and in the sense of time slowing down. There is a mode of whole-body knowing and responding that is based on the joining of past experience, training (sensorimotor, emotional, and cognitive), and/or mindfulness (present moment, relaxed concentration, and awareness of sensory, motor, and perceptual inputs). This mode includes all of the attitudinal elements of mindfulness listed in the preceding chapters, organized and focused with exquisite sensitivity to register and respond to the experience of the present moment.

Experiential Metaphors for Mindfulness

Experiential metaphors can be extremely helpful for developing an embodied understanding of mindfulness. These can be first-person experiences, client experiences, accounts of the experiences of others, or verbal metaphors or poems that engender an emotionally and somatically powerful experience as well as cognitive insight that deepens embodied understanding. Personally, my experience learning to ski provided an apt experiential metaphor for developing mindfulness as embodied knowledge and mode of being.

I learned to ski as a young adult a number of years before I started practicing mindfulness. I felt awkward and uncomfortable as a beginner. Just dealing with the equipment and the chairlifts was frustrating, let alone actually going down the mountain. I fell a lot, and the more I fell the more I tried not to fall.

I instinctually braced against the slipperiness of the hardpack snow and the feeling of gravity pulling me down the mountain by stiffening my legs and clenching the soles of my feet. This flattened the skis beneath me, which felt even more out of control. Flat skis (resting on the bottoms rather than the edges) tend to shoot out from under you, especially if you are tense. So the more I tried not to fall by tensing up, the more I fell.

It was a beautiful day, and all around me were smiling people who seemed happy and exhilarated. Knowing that there was something about skiing I was totally not getting only increased my frustration. My friend Richard, who was teaching me to ski, saw what I was doing and kept telling me to relax. But the more I tried to relax, the tighter I got.

Looking back, I realize that I was trying to avoid falling by tensing up, and I was also bracing against the natural tendency of the skis to turn downhill, which left me feeling like I was losing control and about to fall. At the same time I was trying to force my skis to go downhill. It was exhausting.

Beginning Again

The next day was sunny and beautiful. Richard and I hit the slopes early, before the crowds. A fresh covering of light, dry powder made the prospect of falling less daunting.

"Let your knees be soft and flexible," Richard instructed, "and bring your weight forward over your skis. As your knees bend, let them drive your shins forward hard against the front of your boots, allowing your torso to come forward over the tips of your skis so your weight and center of gravity are directly over the soles of your boots. Now follow me as you let your skis turn down the mountain and begin to run downhill.

"Unweight your left ski, which will become your uphill ski as you begin to turn left, and feel how the weight naturally transfers to the uphill edge of your right ski, which is now your downhill ski. Next, unweight your right, or downhill, ski, and as you begin to turn right, let your weight naturally shift to the uphill edge of your left ski, which is now your downhill ski. Keep leaning forward over your skis, and follow my turns down the mountain, letting your weight shift from ski to ski to initiate turns and letting gravity do the work of turning and setting your edges."

I followed Richard's wide, slow turns all the way down the mountain. Paradoxically, the more I relaxed into my skis and let go to the pull of gravity, the more control I had. I began to actually feel, through my skis, knees, legs, and hips, the pitch and contours of the slope, and the fluffy powder covering the hardpack.

That day I began to understand what everyone had seemed so exuberant about the day before. Skiing was about relaxed concentration and focus, being completely present in each moment, and being attuned (with an embodied knowing) to the pitch and contours of the slope, the snow conditions, and the limitations of my ability and energy in each moment. It was a completely embodied awareness, mind and body together and whole, not two—no separation.

I discovered that enjoying skiing required getting the self-conscious "I" out of the way. I learned that control in skiing required leaning out over the tips of my skis and letting go to the pull of gravity, settling into and trusting my edges, letting the mountain tell me what to do, and evoking an appropriate response by sensing the pitch and contours of the slope, and the consistency of the snow, through my skis. It was exhilarating.

Use the exercises below to identify and reflect on experiences or moments in your own life in which you felt like you had to tense up or hold on tight in order to stay in control and avoid losing your balance, but through experience learned that tensing and holding on actually intensified and accelerated the loss of control and feelings of distress, while letting go and surrendering paradoxically allowed for greater control and ease and more creative and skillful responses.

Exercise 5.1: Personal Experiential Metaphors for Learning Mindfulness

1. Recall an experience in which you got stuck trying to do something that couldn't be forced or controlled, but only allowed.

2. Recall a time when you instinctually tightened or braced against a feared or unwanted outcome while pursuing a desired outcome, and the tightening or bracing not only prevented you from achieving the desired outcome, but perhaps inadvertently contributed to actualizing the feared or unwanted outcome.

3. Write about your reflections in your journal. What was the situation? How did you perceive and experience it? How did you react or respond? What was the result?

Exercise 5.2: Personal Experiential Metaphors for Mindfully Letting Go

1. Recall an experience when you stopped trying to make something happen and instead just let it happen, or you stopped trying to control an outcome that was out of your control. Reflect on the event itself, as well as the physical sensations and emotions you experienced.

2. What helped you to let go?

3. Write about your reflections in your journal.

Exercise 5.3: Client Experiences as Metaphors for Learning Mindfulness

1. Call to mind a client whose presenting complaints or symptoms arose from similar patterns of tensing or bracing against the way things already are, from trying to achieve through effort something that one can only allow to happen, or from trying to control an outcome that was not within the client's control.

2. Now call to mind another client whose presenting complaints or symptoms also reflected trying to control outcomes not within the client's control or resisting, bracing against, or refusing to accept what had already happened or the moment as it already was. In strategic therapy, such binds are called "be spontaneous paradoxes." I can create one simply by telling you to "be spontaneous." *Spontaneity* on demand is, by definition, contradictory. We cannot *do* spontaneity. We can only *allow* it.

3. Recall one or two clients who successfully stopped struggling against what had already happened or the moment as it already was. What did you sense about your client's experience? What was your experience of the therapeutic relationship in that moment?

4. Journal about your experience with this exercise. Which clients did you recall? What was the nature of each client's distress? How did each client try to avoid or get rid of unwanted events or experiences? What were the results?

First Experiences with Formal Mindfulness Meditation Practice

Formal mindfulness meditation practice is transformative. If you commit to it, it changes you. Your own formal mindfulness practice experience informs your sense of what mindfulness practice might offer clients.

In the next section I reflect on two of my first experiences doing formal mindfulness meditation. I then invite you to reflect on your own first experiences and the impact they (and subsequent experiences) have had on your clinical work. If reading this book is your first encounter with mindfulness meditation, I will ask you to reflect on your motivations and aspirations for reading it and your hopes as you begin your own journey with mindfulness.

First Experiences with Meditation and Mindfulness

My own first experience of meditation was with an ancient Indian devotional tradition that emphasized concentration meditation practices, including mantra repetition, chanting, and guru yoga. I was drawn to it out of curiosity, and because it was presented in the context of a conference for health care professionals that offered continuing education units, which was unusual at that time (1980).

The meditation practices led to bliss and fascinating states of nonordinary, expanded consciousness. There was also a wonderful sense of community among the practitioners. Nonetheless, after a few years I became disillusioned, because the practice seemed to have limited practical application or benefit in the "real" world.

I mentioned this to my boss and mentor at the time (I worked in a psychiatric day treatment program), knowing that he was a longtime practitioner of Tibetan Buddhism. He recommended I look into a secularized version of basic Buddhist mindfulness practice called Shambhala training (Trungpa, 1984) that had been developed specifically for Western students.

Soon thereafter I attended my first silent meditation retreat. From Friday evening through Sunday afternoon I sat cross-legged on a cushion on the floor, with fifteen or twenty other meditators, in a small, rustic Zen center near San Diego. I was physically uncomfortable. Being unaccustomed to sitting cross-legged, my knees ached, and my lower legs kept falling asleep.

The meditation instructions were simply to "follow the breath" by feeling it flowing in and out, labeling each in-breath "in" and each out-breath "out." If we noticed that the focus had wandered off the breath, we were instructed to make the mental note *thinking*, and then to bring the focus back to the sensations of breathing. This was our sole assignment for the weekend.

Friday night and all day Saturday I obediently practiced, struggling with the physical discomfort of long periods of sitting cross-legged as well as agitation, restlessness, aversion, boredom, and doubt. *What is the point of all this?* I wondered. *Why subject myself to such discomfort?*

Sunday morning seemed easier somehow. Not that I was physically more comfortable. On the contrary, my knees, thighs, back, and shoulders ached, and I still felt restless and agitated. But I noticed that I wasn't fighting the meditation so much (probably out of sheer exhaustion), and oddly I felt relatively calm and at ease, despite the physical discomfort.

Sunday afternoon there was a palpable change in the weather, both inner and outer. Internally, I noticed a gradual shift to an experience of silence and stillness that felt exquisitely sensitive, receptive, and aware. Outside the meditation hall, a gathering storm had turned the sky gray and overcast. The air had grown thick with moisture, and a veil of stillness fell over the valley, muting the birdsong and the chatter of crickets and frogs, which I noticed only in their absence.

The rain began to fall almost imperceptibly, drop by drop, at random intervals, slowly increasing to a steady downpour accompanied by distant rumblings of thunder. There were no other sounds. You could almost hear the silence out of which the sounds of the rain and thunder arose. The texture, quality, and color of the light in the meditation hall were also changing rapidly. (This was an *eyes open* style of meditation practice.) The smell of wet grass and eucalyptus was intoxicating.

Suddenly there was a loud crash, and the steady rain burst into a torrent. The next thunder crash came with a sizzling crackle of lightning, illuminating and vaporizing the rain sheets. I sat completely still and silent, rapt and amazed. There was a glimmer of a completely unfamiliar mode of awareness somehow unencumbered by self-consciousness. It was as if I had disappeared, and in the moment there was just the storm, knowing itself as itself.

After a few minutes the rain began to slow, and soon it stopped completely. Only the sounds of water droplets falling from the leaves of the eucalyptus trees and the eaves of the Zen center broke the silence. Suddenly, the air erupted with the raucous singing of birds, announcing the end of the rain. Everything seemed to become more vivid and alive.

I now know that "everything" was just as it always was, except for me. For a few minutes my awareness seemed unusually acute and refined, and my sense perceptions seemed extraordinarily vivid and alive, without the usual filters of conditioned judging; habitual, discursive thinking; the identity processing of *this is me, this isn't me*; or the labeling and organizing of perceptions into preconceived cognitive categories. I can fill that in now, after the fact—rain, birds, trees, grass, meditation hall, body, mind—but in the actual experiencing there was just hearing, smelling, sensing, feeling, seeing, thinking, being.

After that first weekend retreat I maintained a fairly consistent daily practice. The occasional brief lapses were usually no more than a missed day or two. When I missed a day of practice I could feel it as a physical sensation of subtle agitation and density, as if my body were congested and more solid, and not in a pleasant way. I would also experience a subtle, barely palpable anxiety, which increased if I missed more than one day, and a more noticeable—at least to me—decrease in mental sharpness. I also continued to attend weekend retreats on a fairly regular basis. Though there were no other dramatic experiences like the first weekend, I noticed feeling increasingly grounded and emotionally stable, as well as what I can only describe as a subtly heightened sense of aliveness.

Two Years Later

About two years after that first retreat, I was attending a weekend retreat at a Shambhala meditation center in downtown Los Angeles. It was late Sunday morning, and the retreat was coming to an end. Sounds of people and traffic were coming in through the open windows, and I was beginning to think about returning to my life in San Diego and also noticing increasing pain in my knees.

Suddenly the awareness that had previously been cool, still, and spacious was agitated, thick, hot, and contracted. There was no longer much space, and what awareness was still there had contracted around and identified with the knee pain and the thoughts about returning to life in San Diego.

Anchoring awareness in the sensations of breathing restored a measure of calm and composure and let me notice my aversion to the pain in my knees as well as the accompanying thoughts. *I hate this pain in my knees! I don't think I can stand it much longer without moving! I don't care if it disrupts the silence and disturbs other people. I'm ready for this retreat to be over! But then I have to go home and pay bills, and deal with the landlord. Blah, blah, blah... I don't want, I want, I like, I don't like, I wish I didn't have to... I, me, I, me, I, me.* All the judging, worrying, and planning—the self-centered mental chatter—was overwhelming the rapid-fire Spanish coming in from the street, the sounds of traffic and the lowrider car horns blaring "La Cucaracha, La Cucaracha."

Suddenly there was interest in the arising and passing away of the sounds and the thoughts, of the voices within and without. Then I noticed *inside and outside* as just one more thought. There was even curiosity and interest about the knee pain—burning, unpleasant, aching, stabbing, intense, stretching, tensing, stiffening—and then a sudden melting away of the tension, and with it the surprising recognition of how much I had been pushing away and bracing against the unpleasant sensations and thoughts all along.

Suddenly and abruptly there was a new understanding that seemed to arise out of the knee pain—that the tensing and bracing against the painful knee sensations, and the thoughts and emotions about the sensations, were not simply reactions to the pain. They actually caused and constituted the pain, to a large extent. As I unconsciously tensed, the knee pain and worry automatically intensified, to which I reacted by tensing even more. I had been caught in a completely unconscious, reactive spiral that I inadvertently caused and then intensified by automatically tensing and bracing against unpleasant sensations in the knees. The tensing and bracing were driven by negative, judgmental thoughts and emotional aversion to the intense, unpleasant sensations, which caused more tensing and bracing, further intensifying the pain and evoking more judgment and aversion, and so forth and so on, round and round.

With that realization, which felt quite physical, like an embodied insight *in the knees*, a palpable sense of both physical and psychological letting go and relief seemed to happen by itself. The worrying and knee pain that remained were much less intense and disturbing, and there was plenty of space for them to be there.

Exercise 5.4a: For Readers Who Have an Ongoing, Established Practice

1. Recall your earliest experiences of mindfulness meditation practice.

2. What do you recall most vividly?

3. What did you take away from those earliest experiences of mindfulness meditation?

4. Were you intrigued, inspired, discouraged, motivated, excited, or turned off?

5. What other reactions did you have?

6. How did your early experiences of mindfulness meditation inform your sense of its therapeutic potential? How have subsequent experiences changed it?

7. Journal about your reflections and reactions to the exercise.

Exercise 5.4b: For Readers Who Are New to Mindfulness Meditation

1. Reflect on your motivations for reading this book.

2. Reflect on your hopes and aspirations for establishing your own mindfulness meditation practice and for incorporating mindfulness in your clinical work.

3. In light of your responses to questions 1 and 2, what are your reactions to the book so far?

4. Journal about your responses to the questions above.

Preparing for Formal Meditation Practice

Before committing to a discipline of formal mindfulness meditation practice, it can be useful to ask yourself some questions. First, what is your current practice? Right now, in this moment? We are always practicing something, even if it isn't mindfulness. Practicing mindfulness is actually relatively rare, even if you have an established formal meditation practice.

For instance, I just noticed that for at least the past half hour, while writing at the computer, I haven't been aware of my breathing, which is now intentionally deep, because in the moment prior I was holding my breath. I am also aware of no judgment about it, just a feeling of bemused irony since I am writing a book about mindfulness.

Formal meditation practice, at least initially, radically simplifies activity and focus so it is easier to be mindful. For example, just sitting and feeling breathing happening, moment by moment, is breath-awareness meditation. Or just lying on your back, motionless and registering sensations in the body one moment after the next, is body scan meditation. Or just walking, and paying close attention to the physical sensations of the movements moment by moment, is walking meditation.

Formal mindfulness meditation practices strengthen our capacity to be mindful in daily life, where it is most beneficial, because the alternative is usually conditioned, automatic behavior that often creates or exacerbates adventitious suffering. Mini mindfulness practices, or *mini-meditations*, are brief, structured practices that focus on bringing mindfulness to everyday experience. The mini-meditations function as a bridge between formal mindfulness meditation and informal practice, or mindfulness in daily life. Exercise 5.5 below is a mini-mindfulness meditation that will prepare you for the formal mindfulness meditations in chapter 6.

Exercise 5.5: What Is Your Practice Right Now?

1. This is an exercise in mindfulness of thinking. As best you can, don't *try* to think about either the questions that follow or your responses. Just hold each question in awareness, and let the question itself evoke a response from your own inner wisdom and embodied knowing, receiving any responses that arise without expectation or judgment.

2. Become aware of your posture right now. What physical sensations does the posture produce? Did you consciously choose this posture? If not, reflect on how you got into it.

3. Feel the sensations of breathing in the posture. Now make any changes to the posture you want to make to be more comfortable. Notice if the posture affects your breathing? If so, how? Notice if the posture affects the quality of attention you bring to this exercise. If so, how?

4. Finally, notice reading *happening*. Become aware of looking at, seeing, and recognizing the nonrandomly constructed and distributed black marks in this sentence. Become aware of construing order and meaning in them.

5. Write about your responses to the exercise in your journal.

Motivation, Aspiration, Intention, and Commitment

It's important to ask yourself why you want to practice mindfulness meditation before you begin to practice. As Jon Kabat-Zinn has frequently said, "Mindfulness meditation is not for the faint-hearted" (2005, p. 21). It's not a feel-good exercise. In fact, it often involves intentionally opening to and fully experiencing painful or distressing emotions, thoughts, and physical sensations.

In this light, mindfulness meditation can better be understood as a powerful technology of mind-body-spirit transformation, awakening, and conscious evolution that develops the capacity to live with our hearts, minds, and senses completely open to life as it is in each moment, without the distorting, self-protective filters of desire, aversion, hope, fear, denial, fantasy, delusion, evasion, or escape.

It takes courage to embrace life openheartedly in this way, as the French root for courage—*coeur*, which means "heart"—suggests (Kabat-Zinn, 2005). It takes courage to unconditionally open our hearts to life's beauty, fragility, and transience; to love and the inevitability of loss; to all of life's poignant ironies, including the universality of pain and suffering. If we incorporate mindfulness in psychotherapy, it means opening our hearts to our clients in the same way.

In addition to *requiring* courage, mindfulness also *develops* courage, as well as wisdom, compassion, distress tolerance, resilience, and the capacity to be present with both our own and others' suffering without shutting down or being overwhelmed.

There is a wonderful story about Tenzin Gyatso, fourteenth Dalai Lama of Tibet (and global icon of openheartedness and compassion in the face of Chinese oppression), that illustrates the courage, wisdom, compassion, and resilience that mindfulness practice helps develop. I offer it to you in preparation for exploring your own motivations and aspirations in establishing a mindfulness meditation practice, or deepening an already established practice.

A reporter at a press conference once asked the Dalai Lama if he hated the Chinese. His response was, "No, I don't hate the Chinese." The reporter pressed him. "How is that possible? They have killed a million of your people, and they are destroying your culture." The Dalai Lama responded, "Yes, that is true. The Chinese have taken everything from us. Shall I let them have my mind also?"

The following exercise is designed to help you explore your motivations and aspirations for practicing mindfulness meditation. Audio versions of this exercise and the ones that follow are available for download at http://www.newharbinger.com/32752.

Exercise 5.6: The Well

1. Sit up comfortably tall in a straight-backed chair. Embody a posture that expresses dignity, wakefulness, and presence.

2. Let awareness drop into the belly-breath sensations, focusing on sensations of expanding and rising on the in-breath and releasing and falling on the out-breath.

3. For a few moments just rest in the breath sensations, allowing the mind and body to settle and become still.

4. Now experience yourself as a well. Your physical posture is the structure itself, and the changing flow of the mind-body process itself, awake and aware, is the water in the well.

5. Now imagine the following questions are a pebble being tossed into the well. Why do you want to learn about mindfulness meditation? What are your motivations? What are your deepest hopes and aspirations?

6. As the pebble breaks the surface, you notice the most obvious responses to the first question. For example, *I want to see if mindfulness can help me be more effective with my clients.* Or, *What is mindfulness, and why all the fuss about it?* Notice your responses without criticism or expectation.

7. As the pebble drops deeper the water becomes calm and clear. You may notice responses that touch on deeper motivations, both personal and professional. For example, *Maybe mindfulness practice can help me with my own battles with anxiety, depression, cynicism, or burnout. Maybe it can help restore the sense of vitality and joy I seem to have lost.* Note your own responses without judgment or expectation.

8. Finally the pebble comes to rest at the bottom of the well. The water is utterly still and clear. You can make out the outlines of your deepest hopes and aspirations, perhaps barely conscious, or unarticulated, until now. What do you notice?

9. Take a few minutes to journal about your responses to the questions represented by the pebble falling through the different levels of the well, as well as general responses to the exercise. What responses arose? Did any of your responses surprise you?

Exercise 5.7: Intention and Commitment

1. Sit up comfortably tall once again, and let your awareness drop down into the physical sensations of sitting. As the mind-body process quiets down, allow the awareness to collect and gather on the sensations of breathing in the belly.

2. For several minutes let the awareness focus and concentrate on the belly-breath sensations, moment by moment.

3. After a few minutes, or whenever you feel ready, expand the field of aware-ness to include the entire body sitting and breathing. Experience the body as a changing flow of sensations, with the belly-breath sensations at the center.

4. For a few minutes rest in the awareness of the body as a field of changing sensa-tions, with the belly-breath sensations at the center. Let the mind and body settle and be still.

5. When you feel ready, pose the following question to yourself. *Am I willing to commit to thirty minutes of formal mindfulness meditation as a daily discipline of practice?* Notice whatever response arises, without judgment. If the response is yes, reflect on the plans and arrangements you need to make to support follow-ing through on your commitment. Record both your commitment and your plan to follow through in your journal, as well as any other reflections or observations about the exercise that you found interesting.

6. If the response is no (or "don't know"), then ask yourself, *How many minutes of daily, formal mindfulness meditation am I willing to commit to?* If a number other than zero arises, ask yourself what plans and arrangements you need to make to ensure you follow through on your commitment. Record both your commitment and your plan in your journal, along with any other observations.

7. If the answer is zero or none, then ask yourself, *What is my intention with regard to doing formal meditation practice in conjunction with reading this book?* Again, observe any response that arises without expectation or judgment. Record it in your journal, along with any other reflections or observations you found interesting.

For readers who already have an established discipline of formal mindfulness meditation practice, the following exercise will help you to reflect on your current practice in relation to your clinical work and to reading this book.

Exercise 5.8: Reflecting on Your Current Mindfulness Meditation Practice

1. Sit in a comfortable, upright posture, and allow awareness to drop down into the belly, becoming mindful of breathing sensations in the belly moment by moment, and shifting out of doing mode into being mode. Receive each question that follows without figuring out or searching for the answer. Simply hold the question in awareness, and let the question itself evoke the response that is true for you right now from your own inner knowing.

2. What motivated me to begin my meditation practice? How have I sustained it?

3. What is my practice now? Does it involve formal meditation on a regular basis? Which formal practices does it include? Does it also include informal meditation or daily life practices? What do they consist of?

4. What has the experience of mindfulness meditation practice been like for me? What impact has mindfulness practice had on my life?

5. How has my mindfulness practice informed my clinical work? Has my clinical work affected my meditation practice in any way?

6. What do I hope to gain from reading this book? For my clinical work? For myself?

7. Write about your responses to the questions above in your journal.

Summary

In this chapter we explored how and why the therapist's mindfulness meditation practice is the essential foundation for incorporating mindfulness in psychotherapy. We also explored the importance of personal experiential metaphors for learning mindfulness and for understanding how mindfulness works in therapy. In chapter 6 we begin our systematic, in-depth exploration of the mindfulness pyramid model with level 1, facet A—the therapist's formal meditation practice. We'll explore and experience formal mindfulness meditation practices that are particularly useful for psychotherapy and can effectively serve as the foundation of the therapist's formal mindfulness practice.

Chapter 6

Therapist's Practice: Formal Meditations

This chapter presents the formal mindfulness meditations that are integral for establishing the therapist's formal meditation practice discipline. It also offers opportunities for guided reflection and journaling and discussions of the potential benefits of each practice.

The downloadable guided meditation recordings for each practice, found at the website for this book (http://www.newharbinger.com/32752), are meant to be used for real-time meditation guidance. The written meditation instructions in this chapter are not intended for that purpose, being far too wordy and detailed. Rather I offer them to point out and illuminate some of the less obvious experiential dimensions of practice that you might want to investigate on your own as your practice deepens.

If you are an experienced meditator and already have a well-established mindfulness practice discipline, you might use the written meditation instructions as a tool for deepening your understanding. I intentionally used words and phrases that I've found particularly helpful in supporting and deepening concentration and mindfulness when I guide meditations. If you are drawn to a particular use of language, feel free to use it. Just be sure it resonates with your experience and that you can embody it from the inside out.

More important than any specific words you choose to guide client practice is your genuine *embodiment* of the practice you are leading. With genuine embodiment your words are a palpably authentic expression of your experience of the practice. When and if you choose to guide meditation practices for your clients, let your words emerge from your own moment by moment experience of doing the practice along with your clients. If you find words, phrases, or language patterns that you particularly like or resonate with the guided meditation instructions in this book, feel free to use them, so long as you first experientially embody them through your own meditation practice and make them your own.

Scripted, guided meditation feels like someone is doing meditation to you rather than with you. If you are reading or reciting a script, you can't also be meditating. Rather you are directing your client's experience while distancing and disconnecting from the experience and your client.

Guiding formal meditation entails doing the practice with your client in real time. This means narrating your own embodied experience of the practice as it unfolds, informed by attuned responsiveness to your client's moment to moment experience and to the therapeutic relationship. Ultimately the best guidance is more than just meditation instruction; it's also an invitation to closeness and connection with the guide through shared mindfulness—being present together in the moment. I discuss use of language in guiding meditation practice more thoroughly in chapter 11.

In summary, the guided meditation instructions in this chapter and the corresponding audio downloads are intended primarily as aids in establishing and deepening your own formal mindfulness meditation practice discipline, though they may also give you ideas about using language to guide formal practice.

Establishing a Formal Meditation Practice Discipline

Establishing a mindfulness meditation practice discipline is no different than establishing any other habit. The keys are repetition, consistency, and developing a routine. For the sake of routine and consistency, it's best to meditate at the same time every day. If you can wake up a little earlier each day to make time to practice, even better. If you meditate first thing each morning, it's much easier to be consistent and to establish a routine. It's also easier to stay awake during the practice after a good night's sleep.

But any regular time is better than none, as long as you commit yourself to practice at that time consistently and make it a routine. If your schedule is so irregular that it's impossible to meditate at the same time every day, then at least formally schedule dedicated meditation time into each day.

At least initially, consistency and the regularity of daily practice are more important than how long you meditate during any single practice period. It's much better to meditate ten minutes at the same time every day than to meditate an hour one day and then not again for five days, even though the total time spent practicing is the same in each case. Most important is establishing a regular, consistent discipline of practice. Once you've done that you can begin to extend the duration of your practice sessions.

It's also helpful to keep track of your formal meditation practice in a dedicated mindfulness meditation practice log, mostly because looking back at the entries is self-reinforcing. A print log is provided in appendix B (and available for download at http://www.newharbinger.com/32752). There are also a number of smartphone applications that include meditation practice logs, timers, recorded meditation bells, and a variety of guided mindfulness meditations as well as other forms of meditation. Some applications include user communities and discussion groups organized around shared practices and common interests.

Set Aside a Space Just for Meditation

If possible, set aside a space in your home to be used only for formal meditation practice. If you have an extra room that you can dedicate to mindfulness practice, it is not only a boon to your practice but it provides an added dimension of peace and calm to your home. Thich Nhat Hanh, a world-renowned Vietnamese Zen monk and meditation teacher, has written about the benefits of creating a "breathing room" (1991, pp. 45–46), both literally and figuratively.

If you don't have an extra room (most of us don't), even a small area or corner of a room set aside just for mindful sitting and breathing is sufficient. If you live alone, the breathing area adds a special dimension to your home, a sacred space within which you can take refuge from the demands of life and simply let yourself be. The breathing area can also serve as a retreat for family members or roommates caught up in stress reactivity and needing or wanting a breathing break.

The breathing area or room itself can become a tremendous support for your practice. If you consistently use it for a daily routine of mindfulness practice, eventually just entering the space will trigger a shift from doing mode to being mode; the setting itself will begin to evoke the foundational attitudes of mindfulness.

Experiential Introduction to Mindfulness: Mindful Eating

Mindful eating is very useful as an introduction to mindfulness. It quickly dispels stereotypes about mindfulness by using as a mindfulness practice what is a routine activity (at least have a guaranteed supply of food and to eat regularly) for those of us lucky enough to. Because we often eat without awareness, eating is the perfect activity to introduce mindfulness as a way of paying close attention to each moment with curiosity and interest, without expectation or judgment, and without striving to get somewhere or accomplish anything.

Exercise 6.1: Mindful Eating Practice

1. For this exercise you will need an apple, a knife, a cutting board, and a napkin or paper towel.

2. Cut the apple into six or eight wedges. For the purpose of this exercise, forget as best you can that this is an apple, and imagine that you have no idea what it is and have never seen anything like it before.

3. Now imagine you are an alien from another galaxy, part of the science crew of a spaceship exploring distant, unknown planets. Your ship has arrived in Earth's orbit, and you are the leader of a small team that has traveled down to the surface to make preliminary observations.

4. In front of you are some wedge-shaped objects, the likes of which you've never seen before. Carefully pick up one of the objects with your thumb and first two fingers, and begin to examine it visually. Rather than actively looking at the object, just let your gaze come to rest on the object and notice seeing happening. There's no need to do anything. Seeing happens by itself, and the object begins to reveal itself to you in the seeing. Notice curiosity and interest arising, because you've never seen this object before, or anything like it. Now notice how the interest and curiosity seem to energize the seeing, so your observations effortlessly become more detailed and refined. Again, there is no need to do anything. Just see the object.

5. If you'd like, rotate and turn the object to see different surfaces and perspectives; see color, shape, texture, moisture, reflectivity, and other features. Each time you turn the object, let your gaze settle on the new surface or perspective and allow yourself to start again, seeing the object with fresh eyes.

6. After another minute or two of seeing, bring the object up to your ear and notice hearing. Notice both what you hear and hearing as an event in awareness. Remember that you can't identify any sounds because you are an alien. But you can notice hearing happening and qualities of sound, such as pitch, volume, tone, duration, and texture, as well as silence.

7. After a minute or two of hearing, bring the object just beneath your nostrils and notice smelling—both the fragrance of the object, if any, and smelling as an event.

8. Now rub the object on your lips and notice touch sensation—qualities of touch, such as pressure, temperature, moistness, dryness, texture, pleasantness, unpleasantness, and also touch sensation as an event.

9. Finally open your mouth and bite off a small piece of the object. You have to take my word that it's safe, because as an alien you don't know. Notice sensations of biting, tasting, salivating, and chewing; notice how the jaw, mouth, lips, teeth, tongue, and palate know how to perform their complex choreography without your direction or interference; notice how the impulse to swallow arises as the taste fades, and how swallowing also just happens without your needing to do anything. Feel the sensations of swallowing as long as you can. After the last sensations fade, rest awhile in the after-sensations of swallowing.

10. In the stillness after swallowing, you may begin to notice the sensations of the movements of breathing. If you'd like, let your eyes close and take two or three minutes to experience the breathing sensations moment by moment, without judgment or striving, and with the same interest and curiosity with which you explored the wedge-shaped object.

11. Now imagine that you have returned to the mother ship, and you must report back to your tough, no-nonsense chief science officer about your observations. She isn't interested in your opinions, judgments, likes, or dislikes. She is only interested in your observations, in descriptive, nonevaluative language.

12. So reflect on your observations investigating the object and record them in your journal. Remember to go through all six senses, the sixth sense being awareness itself; in this instance, awareness is how you noticed that experiencing through the other five senses was happening (for example, noticing seeing as an event in awareness).

13. You may notice that it isn't easy to limit yourself to objective, nonjudging observations. If you notice the language of preference (liking or disliking) or judgment (good or bad, better or worse, or right or wrong) sneaking into your observations, simply reframe the preference or judgment as an event you observed. For example, rather than writing "I liked the sweet taste" or "it tasted too sour," you could write "tasted sweet" or "tasted sour" and then, as a separate observation, "noticed liking happening" or "noticed dislike happening."

14. When you've finished recording your observations in your journal, let go of the alien science expedition scenario and reflect more generally about the exercise and your reactions to it, writing these reflections in your journal also. What was it like to let go of "apple" as a preconditioned cognitive category and to perceive the object with beginner's mind? How successful were you doing it? What did you notice about investigating the object with all your senses? What surprised you, if anything? Finally, what, if anything, did you learn about eating?

Final Reflections on the Mindful Eating Practice

We often eat on autopilot, paying little or no attention to what or how much we are eating, let alone the sensory experience of eating. If we eat alone, we may be so focused on other activities, such as reading, watching television, or playing with a smartphone or tablet, that eating goes practically unnoticed, and we barely taste our food.

When we eat mindfully, the experience comes alive. There is a vivid, embodied awareness of seeing, smelling, tasting, and touch sensation, and we are fully present to the synchronized choreography of hand, arm, jaw, mouth, lips, teeth, tongue, salivary glands, esophagus, and stomach set to the rhythms of instinct and desire. When we eat on autopilot, we completely miss out on the extraordinary experience and sensual pleasure of eating.

Mindful eating can benefit all of us. It is particularly useful in treating eating disorders, in which food is rarely savored and eating is often not associated with pleasure or gratitude.

Breath-Awareness Meditation

For many reasons the breath is a wonderful focal object for mindfulness meditation:

- It's always there (as long as we're alive), so it's relatively constant.

- Most people can readily feel the sensations of breathing.

- Although the presence of the breath is relatively constant, the sensations of breathing change continuously with changes in volume, rhythm, rate, and so on, which makes the breath more interesting as a focal object and thus easier to maintain focus on.

- Literally right under our noses, the breath offers ready access to the present moment as a refuge or safe harbor whenever needed.

- Breathing is one of only a few physiological processes that is both voluntary and involuntary. We can control and regulate the breath with conscious intention. But when we aren't paying attention to breathing, the body breathes just fine.

- Breathing is so basic to staying alive, however, that when we do pay attention to it there's often a tendency to try to control it. For many people it can be difficult simply to feel breathing happening without immediately trying to regulate or control it, even though 99.9 percent of the time, at least for most of us, the breath works just fine without intervention or guidance.

- The breath can be a powerful metaphor for the desire to control what doesn't need to be, or can't be, controlled. It can also serve as a metaphor for difficulties with simply allowing and letting be, particularly with regard to anything we perceive as vital to survival or well-being.

Posture in the Breath-Awareness Meditation

In breath-awareness meditation, posture is key. A relaxed, upright, erect posture allows the breath to flow freely. It also literally embodies the quality of awareness that supports, and is cultivated by, the meditation practice, a quality that can be described as "relaxed wakefulness" or "relaxed and alert."

Rigidity, slouching, instability, and other less-than-ideal postural attributes tend to reinforce qualities of awareness that are hindrances to mindfulness, such as dull, sleepy, inattentive, irritated, agitated, and distracted. Whereas conventionally we may interpret relaxation as a signal to go to sleep, in the breath-awareness practice the mind-body process is trained to experience relaxation as a signal to "fall awake." Wakefulness in this context means letting go of expectations and judgments and softening and opening to each moment without reservations but rather with interest, clarity of perception, and exquisitely attuned responsiveness.

Though relaxed wakefulness isn't the goal of the breath-awareness practice per se, it is a vital component of mindfulness, which is why embodying relaxed wakefulness in the posture is important in cultivating mindfulness of breathing.

Exercise 6.2: Breath-Awareness Meditation

1. Sit up comfortably tall, preferably on a hard-backed chair or, if it's comfortable for you, a meditation cushion on the floor.

2. If sitting in a chair, sit toward the front of the chair with your feet flat on the floor. Your hands can rest one on top of the other in your lap or on your knees or thighs, whatever position is most comfortable. Let the spinal column be erect and upright without being rigid or stiff.

3. As best you can, allow the natural structure of the spinal column to support the torso without using the backrest of the chair. Or, if you'd like, experiment with lodging the sacroiliac joint and the back of the pelvic girdle into the lowest portion of the backrest, where it meets the seat of the chair, to create a stronger foundation for the erect spine.

4. If you are sitting on a cushion on the floor, it's best to find a comfortable, cross-legged position in which your knees rest on and can be supported by the floor. If this is impossible, you may want to experiment with additional support under your knees in the form of pillows or folded blankets, or try sitting in a chair.

5. Now let the awareness drop down into the physical sensations of pressure and touch created by the sitting posture. Not thinking about the sensations of pressure and touch, but rather allowing awareness to saturate and register the felt sensations of pressure and touch in the soles of the feet, buttocks, and backs of the thighs as they arise, moment by moment. If sitting on a cushion, feeling the pressure and touch sensations arising moment by moment where your backside makes contact with the cushion, where your knees make contact with their underlying support, and where your hands rest in your lap or on your knees or thighs.

6. As best you can, receiving each moment of pressure and touch sensation with friendly curiosity and care, realizing there is no right or wrong, no better or worse; there is nowhere to get to, nothing to strive for or attain. Just feeling the sensations of pressure and touch, moment by moment, however they are.

7. Now feel the spinal column rising up out of the sacroiliac joint, each vertebra stacked neatly atop the one below to where the spine inserts into the skull. Not thinking about or visualizing the spine, but rather experiencing the spine, moment by moment, as physical sensation. Perhaps registering sensations of hardness, uprightness, or of how the body is configured in space and the torso and head supported by the erect spine in the sitting posture.

8. However you experience the physical sensations of the spine, letting awareness saturate those sensations moment by moment. Now letting the muscles of the neck, shoulders, chest, back, and belly soften around the upright spine, and as best you can allowing the structure of the upright spine by itself to support the head, neck, and torso with minimal muscle participation.

9. Continue to feel the sensations of pressure and touch without judging or striving as they change from moment to moment. Give yourself plenty of time to settle into the wakeful stillness of the sitting posture.

10. Now within the stillness of the sitting posture, begin to notice the sensations of breathing in the belly. If at first you can't feel the belly-breath sensations, allow yourself to intentionally and deeply inhale into the belly and lower back, then into the midchest and midback, upper chest, upper back, and shoulders before letting out a long, slow exhalation, experiencing sensations of release and letting go on the out-breath. If the sensations of breathing in the belly are still hard to find, repeat the deep belly breathing with the long, slow exhalation.

11. Now let go of any efforts to control or regulate the breath, and experience breathing as a sensation in the belly, however the breath presents itself to awareness.

12. Let the awareness be a moment by moment, nonjudging awareness. There is no better or worse way to breathe, no right or wrong, just each breath moment exactly as it presents itself—long or short, deep or shallow, smooth or coarse, flowing or constricted; it doesn't matter. Receiving each breath moment, however it is, with curiosity and appreciation.

13. Just *being* with the experience of breathing without *doing* anything. Registering each moment of belly-breath sensation, one after the next, without trying to get anywhere or accomplish anything.

14. You may notice that from time to time the awareness wanders off the breath sensations in the belly, perhaps caught up in thinking or sounds or other sensations in the body. This is nothing to worry about; it's just what minds do. They wander. When you notice that your focus has wandered off the breath, simply acknowledge where it went and then very gently bring it back to the sensations of breathing in the belly, wherever the breath is in the cycle of in-breath and out-breath.

15. Regardless of how many times your mind wanders, one hundred times or one thousand times, each time simply acknowledge where it went, without criticism or judgment, and gently bring the focus back to the breath sensations in the belly. The *noticing that the mind has wandered and then coming back to the breath* is as important and useful a part of the practice as *being focused on the breath*. We work against the mind's resistance to remaining focused in order to develop concentration and clarity in the same way we use resistance training to build muscle mass and cardiovascular training to develop aerobic fitness.

16. If you'd like, for the last few minutes of the breath-awareness practice, imagine yourself riding the waves of the breathing. Riding up the swells of the in-breath and riding down the troughs of the out-breath. Moment by moment, and breath by breath.

17. Letting go to the buoyancy and support of the breath. As best you can, letting yourself be cradled and rocked by the breath while allowing the sensations of breathing to anchor awareness in the present moment.

18. Experiencing the breath as a refuge or a safe harbor beyond hope and fear, which are always about the future; and anger, guilt, remorse, and regret, which are always about the past. For the last few minutes of the practice, just resting in the present moment sensations of breathing, one moment after the next.

19. As we come to the end of the breath-awareness practice, reflecting on the gift of mindfulness you have given yourself, the gift of being truly present for your life.

20. When you're ready, forming a conscious intention to open your eyes. Then letting that intention open your eyes, and noticing seeing happening—not just what you are seeing, but also seeing as an event in awareness.

21. Take a few minutes to reflect on and journal about what you noticed and experienced during the breath-awareness meditation. As best you can, write about your experience objectively and nonjudgmentally, like you did with the apple in Exercise 1.1.

22. If you paid close attention during the breath-awareness practice, perhaps you noticed that the sensations of breathing are themselves continuously changing, and therefore each breath moment is distinct and unique. Perhaps you also noticed that awareness tended to wander off the breath, distracted by thinking, other body sensations, sounds, or mind states such as boredom or restlessness. Perhaps this happened quite frequently. Maybe you fell asleep or felt like crawling out of your skin. Any and all of these experiences, as well as others you may have had, are absolutely fine.

23. Remember that mindfulness involves simply being present for and accepting of each moment of experience without expectation or judgment, regardless of its content. There is no other goal, not even relaxation. If you noticed that your mind wandered, perhaps constantly, that's great. It's simply one of the things that minds do—frequently in fact. Minds wander reactively here and there, seemingly out of control and chattering incessantly without invitation, as if they had minds of their own. But that's okay. It's just the nature of the conditioned, reactive mind.

24. When you notice that the mind has wandered off, that's mindfulness of wandering. When you notice incessant mental chatter, that's just mindfulness of thinking. If you notice sleepiness, restlessness, agitation, or boredom, that's also fine. It's wonderful, in fact. These are all moments of mindfulness, of noticing what's actually happening. They are moments of waking up out of the sleepiness, restlessness, agitation, or boredom and "seeing" it rather than "being" it. Moods and mind states change continuously, much like the weather. If you notice what's happening, that's wonderful, because you're less likely to get caught up in and swept away by the mood or mind state.

25. Be sure to log your breath-awareness practice in your meditation log (see appendix B) or with a smartphone application, if you prefer. (Make copies first if you are using the log sheet; since each sheet has space to log a week's worth of daily practice, or seven meditation sessions, you will need fifty-two sheets per year.)

Final Reflections on the Breath-Awareness Meditation

The breath is the ultimate focal object for mindfulness meditation. Breathing in is the first thing we do (if all goes well) when we come into this world, and breathing out is the last thing we do as we leave. In between the breath is basically continuous, an ever-present, faithful companion to which we give little thought or attention, let alone appreciation, unless it malfunctions.

The Hebrew word for both "breath" and "spirit" is *ruach*. In the creation story in the book of Genesis, God is depicted as ruach (spirit or breath), and ultimately God breathes his breath (spirit) into Adam to bring him to life. This is the origin story of the sanctity of human life for Abrahamic religions. We literally all breathe (or are breathed by) the same breath as Adam—in Hebrew *Ruach Elohim*, the breath or spirit of God. By the grace of that breath we live, and absent that breath we die.

Lack of awareness of breathing is a form of life denial, and perhaps ultimately it is a way to deny death. Yet how often have you not noticed your breathing for hours? At the deepest level, awareness of breathing is awareness of being alive as well as awareness of mortality.

The breath is also exquisitely sensitive to emotional reactivity and stress. Careful attention to breathing reveals a great deal about the breather. When you freeze in fear, you hold your breath; this is an ingenious evolutionary adaptation to avoid betraying your location to a predator or attacker with the sound of your breathing. When anxious we tend to constrict our breathing; when angry we tend to force deeper breaths, oxygenating our muscles to be ready to attack.

In sleep, the breath may become slower, shallower, and more regular. When we are very relaxed, the breath often slows and deepens. In very deep states of meditation, the breath may become quite subtle, to the point that it may seem to disappear completely.

All of this happens without conscious awareness or intention. If you aren't already, be aware of the physical sensations of breathing as you read this paragraph. Have you noticed that almost as soon as you intentionally notice the breath by feeling it, you almost involuntarily begin to regulate and manipulate it? Perhaps you make it deeper, or longer, or more even. Although the breath has breathed itself perfectly well for years, suddenly you find yourself needing to control the breath.

As discussed in chapter 4, breathing is one of the only physiological functions that is both voluntary and involuntary, and it is also continuous. How we relate to breathing is an embodied metaphor for how we relate to living. It is also literally true that breath is life. The thin stream of air that you draw in through your nostrils and into your lungs is all that stands between life and death for any of us. How convenient and reassuring to forget about it.

Moment by moment awareness of breathing can be calming and centering; it is a powerful practice for quieting the mind and body. On a deeper level, this awareness also connects us to the fragility, preciousness, and poignancy of each breath and every moment of our lives

Is it any wonder that when you bring close attention to the breath you instinctually try to control it? This response is a manifestation of our deepest instinct for survival. Without breathing we die. Controlling the breath then becomes an embodied metaphor for your efforts to exercise control over things (for example, your own emotions, others' emotions and behavior, and situations and outcomes over which you have no control, including the moment you are in, which has always already happened and can't be changed).

When you are mindful of how you are relating to breathing in each moment (for example, allowing, letting go, letting be, accepting, curious, nonjudging, nonstriving, controlling, regulating, bracing against, forcing, tightening, holding), your mind-body process becomes a powerful teacher. Each moment becomes a transformative teaching about how lack of awareness and automatic reactivity increase suffering and distress and how mindfulness and the possibility of a more skillful response tend to decrease suffering and distress.

Body Scan Meditation

In the body scan meditation we expand the moment by moment awareness of breathing sensations to include systematic investigation of present-moment experience in the body as a whole. As with breathing, focusing awareness on body sensations, one moment after the next, gets you out of your head and anchors awareness in the physical, lived reality of body sensations in the present moment. This is more solid footing from which to relate to habitual discursive thoughts and reactive emotions, which are almost always focused on the future or the past. I recommend that you use audio download track 6, "Body Scan Meditation," to guide you through the body scan practice before reading the instructions below.

Please remember that the instructions for the body scan in Exercise 6.3 are much wordier than the ones in the audio track on the website or how you would guide a body scan for clients. They are not presented as a script; rather, they are presented in an effort to evoke a felt sense of the impact of certain wordings and phrases on the listener.

Exercise 6.3: Body Scan Meditation

1. Arrange a time and place where you won't be interrupted. It's best if you can lie on your back on the floor on a thick carpet, blanket, or mat. If it's comfortable, let your legs be uncrossed and fully outstretched in front of you with the feet falling away from each other, and let your arms lie by your sides with palms turned up toward the ceiling. To take pressure off your low back, you may need to bend your knees so your heels move toward your buttocks and the soles of the feet are flat on the floor.

2. Make any other adjustments that allow you to surrender as completely as you can to the pull of gravity and the support of the floor. If lying on the floor is difficult, you can do the body scan sitting upright or in a recliner.

3. Let your awareness drop down into the physical sensations of pressure and touch where the back of the body makes contact with the carpet, blanket, or mat. Feeling the entire back body making contact with the floor. Feet, legs, buttocks, and hips. Low back, midback, and upper back. Spine and shoulder blades. Hands, arms, shoulders, and back of the head.

4. As best you can, letting go completely to the pull of gravity and the support of the floor. No need to hold yourself up.

5. Now imagine with each in-breath, inhaling energy, vitality, freshness, and nourishment, and with each outbreath exhaling fatigue, tension, toxins, and holding.

6. With each cycle of the breath, continuing to inhale energy, vitality, freshness, and nourishment, and to exhale fatigue, tension, toxins, and holding. Completely letting go.

7. Whenever you feel ready, intentionally breathing deeply into the lower abdomen, and feeling a more pronounced rising of the belly, low back pressing firmly into the floor beneath. On the out breath feel the awareness traveling down from the lower abdomen through the left hip and buttock, down through the left thigh, knee, calf, shin, ankle, foot, and into the toes of the left foot. Aware of sensations in the left big toe, the left little toe, and the three toes in between, moment by moment, one toe moment after the next.

8. Letting awareness of the sensations in the left toe region be a nonjudging, nonstriving awareness. As best you can, letting go of judging, striving, worrying, or questioning, and letting it all just come and go in the background of awareness. Focusing awareness in the foreground on sensations in the left toe region, arising, changing, and dissolving moment by moment.

9. Registering sensations of tingling, pulsing, itching, vibrating, warmth, coldness, moistness, dryness, softness, hardness, no sensation, numbness—whatever is happening, one moment after the next. No need for thinking. Just experiencing the left toe region directly as sensations arising, changing, and dissolving moment by moment.

10. Embracing each moment of sensation without expectation or preference. Receiving each moment, one after the next, with friendliness, hospitality, curiosity, and interest. Appreciating the "being" of the left toes without asking them to "do" anything. Resting in the life of the toes as a changing flow of sensations.

11. Now, expanding the field of awareness to include the sole and heel of the left foot, the top of the left foot, the left ankle, and the Achilles tendon, and finally expanding awareness to include the entire left foot region, from the toes, sole, and heel to the top of the foot, ankle, and Achilles tendon; experiencing the left foot region as a whole as a field of sensations; arising, changing, and dissolving, one moment after the next.

12. Pulsing, vibrating, cool, warm, rough, smooth, hard, soft, itching, tingling, no right or wrong, no good or bad, no better or worse, just experiencing each left foot moment as sensation, one moment after the next, with a receptive, non-judging, and nonstriving awareness. Nowhere to get to, nothing to strive for or attain, not even relaxation. Letting the left foot be however it is, moment by moment, and letting yourself be however you are, moment by moment.

13. Bringing awareness to the sensations of aliveness in the left foot region. Experiencing the life of the left foot as a continuous flow of sensation and no sensation arising, changing, and dissolving moment by moment. What's happening in this left foot moment? And this left foot moment? And now what's happening? Experiencing the *being* of the left foot as sensation, without asking the left foot to *do* anything.

14. Now, moving the focus of awareness to the left calf and shin region, from the top of the ankle to just below the knee. Feeling the life of the left lower leg as sensations, arising, changing, and dissolving, moment by moment. Registering sensation in the left calf region without preference or judgment, and without needing to *do* anything.

15. If you notice that the focus has wandered off the left calf sensations, it's not a problem. Just acknowledge where the focus went, and gently escort it back to this moment of sensation in the left calf region.

16. Feeling the changing flow of sensations or lack of sensation in the lower left leg moment by moment, without judging or striving. Now letting the focus of awareness move to the left knee, experiencing the left knee region as sensation—knee cap, back of the knee, inner and outer aspects of the knee joint—and registering the inner architecture of the knee joint as sensation.

17. Now expanding the focus to include the left thigh, the left hip joint and hip, and the pelvic girdle. Finally letting awareness extend down through the right thigh and right calf into the right foot, and illuminating the life of the right toes and foot as a changing flow of sensation.

18. Systematically moving awareness through the right toes, foot, ankle, and up thorugh the calf and shin, knee, thigh, hip socket, and hip. Finally expanding the field of awareness to include the entire left foot and leg region as sensation; arising, changing, and dissolving one moment after the next.

19. Now allowing awareness to saturate the pelvic region as a whole.

20. Awareness illuminating sensations in the buttocks, the anal region, the genital region, the pubic bone, the pelvic floor, and the abdominal floor. No right or wrong, no good or bad. Just noticing and being with sensations, moment by moment.

21. Perhaps noticing texture, temperature, and intensity of sensations in each moment, and whether the sensations are pleasant, unpleasant, or neutral.

22. Now moving the awareness into the lower abdomen and belly, and experiencing the lower abdomen and belly as a flow of sensations. Rather than *thinking* about the belly as a thing or a concept, directly *experiencing* the belly as sensation, one belly moment after the next.

23. Now expanding the field of awareness around the belly and abdomen to include the low back, midback, upper back, shoulder blades, diaphragm, rib cage, chest, sternum, breasts, armpits, and shoulders; directly experiencing the entire torso as sensation, moment by moment. Noticing and appreciating the life of the torso as sensation, arising, changing, and dissolving one moment after the next.

24. Now bisecting awareness into two equal beams, and directing a beam of awareness down each arm, into the wrists, hands, and the fingers of each hand. Experiencing the being of the fingers, wrists, and forearms as sensation, without asking them to do anything.

25. Now experiencing the elbows, upper arms, and shoulders as a flow of sensation, arising, changing, and dissolving from one moment to the next.

26. Whenever you're ready, expanding awareness into the neck, shoulders, and throat region and experiencing the shoulders, neck and throat as a changing flow of sensations.

27. We frequently hold tension in the upper torso, arms, shoulders, neck, and throat. Common colloquial expressions reflect this. We might call someone "a pain in the neck," speak of "shouldering a burden," "choking back grief," or "swallowing rage or pride." Such expressions reflect the intuitive wisdom of the body.

28. Take your time to bring a particularly kind and compassionate awareness to the shoulders, neck, and throat. Listen carefully to what they are communicating, and experience the life of the shoulders, neck, and throat with tenderness and care, and without judgment or striving.

29. Now moving the awareness into the head region. Experience the life of the face, lower jaw, upper jaw, transmandibular joint, lips, teeth, gums, and tongue as sensation. Just noticing.

30. Now expanding the awareness to include the cheeks, nostrils, nasal passages, nose, cheekbones, eye sockets, eyelids, eyeballs, and eyebrows. Experiencing the being of the upper face, nose, and eyes without asking anything of them.

31. What's happening in the forehead region? Around the temples? Experiencing the ears as sensation, and noticing hearing as an event in awareness.

32. Feeling sensation in the skull, scalp, hair, and the back of the head where it touches the floor. Experiencing the region between the ears and between the forehead and the back of the skull as sensation.

33. Now in your own time, whenever you're ready, letting the field of awareness expand to include the body as a whole, lying down and breathing from the top

of the skull, scalp, and hair to the heels, soles of the feet, and toes. Experiencing the body as a whole, as a symphony of sensation and no sensation. Resting in the body as sensation, however it presents, one moment after the next. Appreciating the *being* of the body as sensation without asking it to *do* anything.

34. For the last few minutes of the body scan, resting in the sensations of the entire body breathing. Letting the breathing be however it is—short or long, erratic or rhythmic, smooth or coarse, shallow or deep. As best you can, feeling breathing happening by itself. Feeling the breath breathing you.

35. Finally, experiencing the mind-body process as a whole, the one you call "yourself," embedded in a succession of larger and larger wholes: your family, your community, your local ecosphere, the global biosphere. Your breathing embedded in the larger breathing of the planet: inhaling the oxygen exhaled by the forests and oceans, and exhaling the carbon dioxide inhaled by the forests and green plants. As best you can, feeling yourself being breathed by this larger breath. For the last few minutes of the body scan, resting in stillness and appreciating the experience of participating in and being breathed by this larger breath.

36. Take a few minutes to reflect on your experience of the body scan; write about your observations and experience in your mindfulness practice journal. What sensations did you notice, and in which areas of the body? Where did you experience the most intense sensation? Where did you experience less sensation, more subtle sensation, or no sensation? Were you aware of pleasant, unpleasant, and neutral tones of sensation?

37. What was it like for you to experience each area of the body directly as sensation rather than visualizing or thinking about the parts of the body conceptually, or as images? How was it different from your usual way of relating to your body?

38. Were there areas of the body where it was more difficult to stay focused and aware? Which areas? Reflect on what happened in those instances as best you can without judgment, and write about your experience without judging it.

39. Remember to log your body scan practice using the meditation practice log form in appendix B, a smartphone application, or some other form of record keeping of your choosing. Formally recording your practice is a wonderful way to reinforce consistency and discipline and to sustain momentum in establishing a practice.

Final Reflections on the Body Scan Meditation

"Mindfulness" and "mind" are often understood, in conventional usage, as being purely "mental." Very few people associate mindfulness with the body. Yet mindfulness meditation is fundamentally a somatic, or body-oriented, practice; it is a somatically anchored awareness. Based on the experience of mindfulness meditation, it makes no sense to conceptualize mind and body as separate. Recent advances in cognitive and affective neuroscience, interpersonal neurobiology, and the neuroscience of attachment have validated the accuracy of this nondualistic view of mind and body. Research confirms that brain structure, function, and development can be altered by cognitive and affective inputs (Hölzel el al., 2010; Hölzel et al., 2011; Rosenkranz et al., 2013).

The history of Buddhist meditation practice provides 2,500 years of phenomenological, empirical validation of a nondualistic view of mind and body (Thera, 1998; Bodhi, 2005; Olendzki, 2010). When you do the body scan, you can investigate and perhaps verify this for yourself. For example, as your practice deepens, you might begin to notice how conditioned, reactive judging and muscle contraction, stiffening, and bracing happen simultaneously. The judging and aversion and the tightening and contracting of the musculature are the same movement of the mind, inclusive of thoughts, emotional reactions, physical reactions, and sensations in the body. We can also experience letting go as an integrated mind-body experience—an experience of simultaneous emotional and physical release.

Mindful Movement Meditation

Mindful movement is exactly what it says: movement as a mindfulness practice. Most often it takes the form of hatha yoga, chi gung, or tai chi chuan, but it can also be dance or free movement. What makes it mindful movement is the awareness of each moment of movement sensation as it arises, one moment after the next, without a focus on the goal of movement or a valuing or weighting of one moment of movement as being more important than any other. It's also a wonderful practice for focusing on mindfulness of intention.

Exercise 6.4: Mindful Movement Meditation

1. The primary instruction for mindful movement is that you are always the ultimate arbiter of how you should move in any given moment. If any instruction feels unwise for your body for any reason, ignore that instruction and simply rest, or modify the movement so it is safe and reasonable for you.

2. Lie on your back on the floor on a mat or thick rug with your legs fully outstretched in front of you and your arms on the floor by the sides of your body.

3. Begin with yogic breathing, a three-part deep inhalation through your nostrils: first the breath fills your abdomen, belly, and lower torso; second it expands into the midtorso, midback, and chest; and third inhale fully into the upper chest and shoulders.

4. Allow the exhalation to be prolonged, letting it make a sound as it flows out of the your body slowly and completely. Enjoy any sensations of letting go and release accompanying the out-breath. Repeat for two more cycles of breath.

5. On the next in-breath, let your arms and hands float up toward the ceiling and fully extend, and then allow your arms to float down fully extended behind your head (as much as possible without straining) so that your hands and fingers point away from your feet.

6. One of the benefits of mindful movement practice is the opportunity it affords to explore limits, physical limitation in particular. With any particular movement allow the body to move up to the physical limit of the posture without straining or pushing through. Instead, inhale deeply into the limit and notice what happens.

7. If there is more space, then move into it and explore how the limit has changed. If the limit stays the same, then continue to dwell right at the edge, breathing into the limit of the movement or backing off a bit if your body tells you to back off.

8. On the next out-breath, let your arms float back up over your head fully extended and pointing toward the ceiling, and then slowly, slowly lower them back down to your sides, letting go completely so they are supported by the floor.

9. Repeat the movement: float your arms up slowly, slowly until they are fully extended toward the ceiling, and then fully extend them behind your head on the in-breath until they rest on the floor behind you; then back up, over, and slowly back down to the sides on the out-breath. Let your awareness be fully present in each moment of movement sensation without anticipating the future or getting stuck in the past.

10. Rest in stillness for two cycles of in-breath and out-breath. On the next in-breath bring the soles of your feet in toward your buttocks so they are resting flat on the floor and your knees are bent and pointed toward the ceiling.

11. On the out-breath flatten your low back on the floor as your pelvis tilts forward, pubic bone pointing toward your head. The sacrum should come off the floor slightly, but not the low back.

12. Now breathe deeply into your belly, letting it inflate up toward the ceiling and allowing your low back to arch slightly off the floor as your pelvis tilts away from you on the fulcrum of your tailbone.

13. Breathing out, allow your awareness to saturate each moment of the movement as your low back flattens onto the floor, your pelvis tilts again toward your head, and your tailbone comes up off the floor slightly, pubic bone pointing toward the head.

14. Breathing in again, feeling the pelvis tilting away from your face as the belly inflates and rises and the low back arches slightly off the floor. Be sure your awareness is present in the movement sensations.

15. Continue the pelvic tilting, or rocking, for a minute or two, varying the speed and intensity if you like, allowing the movement to come out of the breath and to be an expression of the breath.

16. When you want to end the pelvic rocking, come to stillness, extend your legs out in front of you, and again surrender completely to the pull of gravity and the support of the floor.

17. Breathe a few cycles of in-breath and out-breath while lying fully extended on your back. In yoga this posture is called *shavasana*, or "corpse pose," because it calls for complete surrender and complete wakefulness simultaneously.

18. On an in-breath bend your knees so they point up toward the ceiling; then on the out-breath wrap your arms around your knees, clasping your elbows or wrists with your hands, and pull your knees into your chest. As an alternative, just grasp your knees with your hands and pull them down toward your chest. Rock back and forth and side to side on your sacrum and low back, allowing the weight of your legs over your belly or chest to give your low back a pleasant massage.

19. Check to see where your awareness is. Is it present in each moment of sensation? Is it present at all? Were you caught up in planning, judging, remembering, or fantasizing? If you notice that your awareness wandered, congratulate yourself; noticing that your awareness wandered means you are paying attention in the present moment again. Then refocus your attention to the sensations of movement or, if you are still, the sensations of breathing.

20. Return to the corpse pose. After resting for a few breath cycles, bring just your left knee to your chest, keeping your right leg flat on the floor as best you can. If it's comfortable, hold the left knee to your chest for a few breath cycles; then return your left leg to the floor and bring your right knee to your chest, letting your left leg remain flat on the floor as best you can. If it's comfortable, hold the posture for a few breaths; then bring full care and attention to each moment of sensation as you return the right leg to the floor.

21. Rest in corpse pose for a few minutes, allowing awareness to move up through the body from the soles of the feet to the crown of the skull, including scalp and hair, and waking up to sensation in every part of the body.

22. Write about your experience of the mindful movement practice in your journal. What did you notice? Was there straining or striving in the movement? Were you competing with yourself to see how far you could stretch? If so, how did you respond?

Final Reflections on Mindful Movement Meditation

If you have done any yoga at all, you may have felt frustrated by this very elementary and brief introduction to mindful yoga practice. There are many extensive and elaborate mindfulness yoga instructions available (for example, Kabat-Zinn, 1990, 2013; Boccio, 2004; Cushman, 2014); I highly recommend such books if you are interested in exploring mindful movement. However, the purpose of Exercise 6.4 was simply moment to moment awareness of movement sensation without judging or striving or conferring greater or lesser importance on any particular moments, especially moments marking the beginning or end of movement or intense sensations within a movement.

There can be a tendency to pay more attention to the beginning, ending, and apex moments of movement, particularly to moments of maximum intensity and extension, than to moments in between, which may seem less interesting. What did you notice in this regard?

Sitting Meditation

In some ways sitting meditation is the stereotype of meditation practice. When asked about meditation, most people have an image of a Buddha-like figure sitting cross-legged, upright with a straight back, hands in lap, eyes closed, with a subtle smile. Sitting meditation is so much identified with meditation that meditators often use the words "sitting" and "meditating" synonymously.

There are reasons for the apparent popularity of the sitting posture. The upright spine promotes energy and wakefulness, while the crossed legs and bottom on a firm cushion on the floor provide a solid, stable foundation for stillness. Within the stillness of the sitting posture, the continuously changing body sensations, perceptions, mind states, thoughts, emotions, and moods within the changing landscape of awareness are more palpable and clear. The sitting posture itself can become a still, transparent container within which the movements of the mind-body process become increasingly clear, and eventually they might also begin to settle and become still.

The instructions for the sitting meditation practice below are long and elaborate. They move systematically through focus on breath sensations; other body sensations, and the body as a whole as a field of sensations; noticing hearing and awareness of discreet sounds, as well as the soundscape as a whole; awareness of thinking, emotion, moods, and mind states; and finally opening to *choiceless awareness*, in which the present moment as a whole, however it presents itself, one moment after the next, is the focal object.

There are vast terrains to explore in formal sitting meditation practice, and much to learn. I encourage you to read the instructions below all the way through and then section by section based on the focal object of your particular practice. Please visit the website for this book (http://www.newharbinger.com/32752) for a variety of audio sitting meditations, including the one below, that focus in-depth on particular focal objects.

Exercise 6.5: Sitting Meditation

1. Set aside a period of time when you won't be disturbed. Choose to sit on either a chair or a meditation cushion (zafu) on the floor, whichever allows for the most stability, ease, stillness, and wakefulness.

2. As best you can, sit with an upright, erect, and flexible spine, if it's comfortable for you, and allow your eyes to close, embodying from the inside out a sense of dignity, uprightness, wakefulness, and presence in the physical posture.

3. If you'd like, imagine a hook on top of the back of your head just above the spine. Visualize another hook in the ceiling straight above. Now imagine a fishing line between the two hooks; imagine this line lengthening and elevating the spine with a gentle, upward pressure. As best you can, feeling the upward pressure opening up space between the vertebrae, lengthening and elevating the spine from the seventh cervical vertebra, which inserts into the skull, all the way down to the first lumbar vertebra arising out of the sacroiliac joint.

4. Now settling into the sitting posture around the elevated, upright spine. Head is balanced on the neck and shoulders with the chin parallel to the floor. Shoulders and arms are hanging loosely off the spine. Hands are resting on the knees or thighs or one on top of the other in your lap, whatever is most comfortable.

5. If you are sitting in a chair, let the feet be flat on the floor with legs uncrossed. It's best not to lean back against the backrest. Instead, if there is a space between the backrest and the seat of the chair, wedge your sacroiliac joint and upper glutes into the space for more stability. Feel how the natural lumbar curvature in the spine is accentuated as it supports the erect torso.

6. If you are sitting on a zafu or cushion on the floor, be sure your knees are supported. Imagine a gentle upward pull on the fishing line connecting the top of the skull to the ceiling. Let your spine lift and lengthen. Notice how the abdomen and the rib cage open as the spine becomes more erect, making more space for the breath. Allow the belly and chest to remain soft and receptive.

7. Let the awareness settle fully into the sitting posture, feeling the posture as sensation in the body, particularly the touch points where the body makes contact with the floor, cushion, or chair. Giving full care and attention to the sensations of touch and pressure in each moment, one moment after the next, with an accepting, nonjudging, and nonstriving awareness. Receiving each moment exactly as it presents itself, as best you can, without wishing it to be any different than it is.

8. Within the stillness of the sitting posture, begin to notice the sensations of the movements of breathing in the belly. Feeling the belly rising and expanding on the in-breath and releasing and falling on the out-breath. Allowing the awareness to gather and collect in the breath sensations in the belly, moment by moment. As best you can, let go of any impulse to control or regulate the breathing. Simply register each belly-breath moment as sensation without judgment or striving, one moment after the next.

9. Let the awareness of the belly-breath sensations be continuous, from the first moment of the out-breath, through each subsequent moment of the out-breath, to the last moment of the out-breath. If there is a pause between the last moment of the out-breath and the first moment of the next in-breath, then experience the

pause, as best you can, without impatience or judgment. Then feel the sensations of the in-breath for the full duration of the in-breath.

10. Observe the breath as best you can with interest, curiosity, appreciation, and gratitude. Each breath moment is unique, precious, and life sustaining. So often we take breathing for granted. For the next few minutes let yourself be fully present and awake to the breath, exquisitely sensitive to each breath moment, one moment after the next.

11. When you notice that the attention has wandered off the breath, simply acknowledge where it went, and gently bring it back to the breath in the present moment. No matter how many times the focus wanders off the breath, each time simply acknowledge where it went, thereby reconnecting with the present moment, and gently bring the attention back to the breath sensations. Wandering mind is not a problem. Wandering is just what the conditioned, reactive mind does. Mindfulness practice involves waking up to the reality and inevitability of wandering mind and learning to relate to it skillfully.

12. Each moment of waking up to the focus of attention having wandered off the breath, noticing where it went, and deliberately escorting awareness back to the breath, rather than being a problem, is cause for celebration. It is as useful and important a part of the practice as being focused on the breath.

13. Now, in your own time, expanding the field of awareness around the sensations of breathing to include the entire body as a field of sensation, from the top of the head to the soles of the feet and the toes. Experiencing the body as a flow of sensations arising, moving, changing, and dissolving, one moment after the next. Warm and cool, moist and dry, tingling, itching, twisting, piercing, soft, hard, tense, relaxed, vibrating, pulsing, throbbing, stabbing, numb, dull, and many other sensations, as well as no sensation. No right or wrong, no better or worse, nothing to accomplish or strive for. Just experiencing sensation as it arises each moment without resisting or judging; experiencing with friendliness, curiosity, and interest.

14. Sometimes a particular sensation can become quite intense. Subtle or strong, brief or sustained, focused or pervasive. If that happens, let the area of intense sensation become the focus of practice. If the intensity is painful or distressing, as best you can, be aware of the unpleasant sensations as objectively and concretely as possible. Is it burning, pressure, tension, stretching, pulling, twisting, throbbing, stabbing, tearing, or some other sensation? Where is the sensation located? Is the intensity and unpleasant quality continuous or variable?

15. Sometimes it can be helpful to soften around the area of intensity. Imagine breathing into the area, bathing the intense sensation in the breath. Not to alleviate or get rid of the sensation, but rather to soften and expand the space around it in a spirit of welcoming and hospitality. This practice gently counters the tendency to stiffen or brace against unpleasant sensation, inadvertently increasing

and sustaining it; instead mindfulness practice cultivates radical acceptance, nonjudging, the capacity for softening, allowing and letting be.

16. Let yourself be interested in and curious about the sensation. Notice that sensations often change continually from moment to moment—in intensity, texture, location, temperature, type, and quality. If your focus wanders away from the sensation, simply notice where the focus went and gently bring it back. Bringing full care and attention to each moment of sensation, one moment after the next, as best you can.

17. If the intensity feels overwhelming and your attention becomes diffuse or fragmented, then let your awareness refocus on the sensations of breathing in the belly, concentrating and focusing on the moment by moment flow of sensations of each in-breath and each out-breath and letting all other sensations in the body come and go freely in the background, without preference or judgment.

18. When concentration is restored, you can return to the previous area of intensity, if it is still there, or allow the focus to move to another area of strong sensation, or expand the focus once again to include the body as a whole. Or, if you prefer, continue to rest in the sensations of breathing in the belly.

19. At this point the meditation practice becomes a bit more complex. It includes a wide variety of potential focal objects and ranges. Potential focal objects include any sensations in the body and noticing the registering of sensations as an event in awareness. Potential focal ranges include a discrete, tiny sensation moment all the way to an expanded focus on the whole body as a rich and continuously changing symphony of sensation.

20. Sometimes it can be helpful to employ a technique called *mental noting* to help keep the awareness focused on its chosen object. This is particularly the case as we continue to expand the domain of the sitting meditation to include sounds, thoughts, mind states (including emotions), and choiceless awareness—just sitting without a specific focus. Mental noting involves silently saying a word that describes the focal object as a way to remember it and stay focused on it from moment to moment. It's best to use words that are very simple, concrete, and descriptive rather than evaluative. For example, when focusing on belly-breath sensations, noting *rising* on the in-breath, and *falling* on the out-breath. When focusing on other body sensations, attempting to be as precise and succinct as possible. Words like cool, warm, touch, pressure, aching, throbbing, stiff, itching, and tingling are useful. Use words that best reflect your experience of what's happening in each moment. Be mindful that the mental note does not overpower the experience it is describing. As a guiding principle, let the actual experience of the focal object occupy about 95 percent of the field of awareness, and the mental note 5 percent; it should be like a silent whisper in the background of awareness, aiming awareness at the focal object.

21. When the current focal sensation weakens or passes or another sensation becomes stronger, at your discretion allow the focus to move to the stronger

sensation, if that's where it wants to go, or you can return to the belly-breath sensations, other sensations that capture your attention, or to the body as a whole.

22. If you notice a sensation that is particularly strong or unpleasant, it is useful to practice turning toward it with curiosity and interest, embracing and opening to it as best you can. Create more space for the unpleasant sensation by breathing into the area around it. Allow the unpleasant sensation to be however it is, without trying to alleviate the intensity or to get rid of it.

23. For the next few minutes, continue to practice in this way with body sensations. If the mind wanders, simply acknowledge where it went and bring it back to the focal body sensation in that moment, or let the awareness gather and collect on the breath if the concentration is waning.

24. Now if you would like, expand the field of awareness to include hearing, not only what you are hearing but also hearing as an event in awareness. Notice that you don't have to *do* hearing. Hearing just happens; it's the natural sensitivity and consciousness of the ears that our brains register and interpret as sound.

25. As best you can, notice the tone, pitch, volume, duration, texture, and intensity of each hearing moment without identifying or labeling the sound or its source. Notice that some sounds are sustained and others momentary, some loud and some soft, some intense and full, others thin. Notice the variety of tones, pitches, and textures. Appreciate the exquisite sensitivity of the hearing faculty, registering and discerning fine gradations of volume, pitch, texture, tone, and intensity without your having to do anything.

26. If you haven't already done so, beginning now, also notice the spaces between sounds, perhaps even glimpsing the vast, spacious, all-encompassing silence out of which all sounds arise and back into which all sounds subside and dissolve. A famous concert pianist said that what distinguishes the best pianists is not how well they play the notes, but how well they play the silences between the notes. See if you can hear the silences between the notes as well as the notes of the soundscape. Perhaps you will hear the even deeper silence that is the context of sound, the spacious silence undergirding both sounds and the spaces in between.

27. For the next few minutes, continue to practice mindfulness of hearing with a nonjudging, nonstriving, moment by moment awareness of both discrete sounds and the spaces between them and perhaps even the boundless silence out of which all sound arises.

28. When you are ready, let go of the focus on hearing and re-anchor awareness in the present-moment sensations of sitting and breathing. Rest in mindfulness of sitting and breathing for a few minutes, until the awareness feels concentrated, settled, and stable.

29. Now, once again expand the field of awareness, this time to include thinking. Noticing thinking happening and thoughts as events in awareness without

buying into the meaning of the thought or being seduced by the content or story line of the thought.

30. Because thoughts can be difficult to notice as events (we tend to fall into them in the same way we might become engrossed in a compelling movie, musical performance, or sporting event), it can be especially helpful to use the mental noting technique to be aware of thinking as an event. A very simple note (like *thinking, thinking*) is often best. It helps to realize that internal self-talk is a form of thought. So self-statements, such as *Where are my thoughts?* or *I don't seem to have any thoughts,* or *I must not be doing this right* can all be labeled with the simple mental note *thinking, thinking.*

31. If you find yourself getting lost or confused, bring awareness back to the belly-breath sensations and the physical sensations of sitting, moment by moment, in order to gather, collect, and stabilize awareness and concentration. Then once again expand the awareness to include mindfulness of thinking, noticing thinking as an event in awareness without getting caught up in the story line of the thoughts. Continue to practice mindfulness of thinking for the next few minutes.

32. When you are ready, expand the field of awareness once again to include the entire body sitting and breathing but without a preferred focal object. Just receiving each moment of experience as it arises, one moment after the next, with interest, curiosity, and an open heart and without judging or striving.

33. This is the practice of choiceless awareness, and the focal object is the present moment of experience in all its richness. In choiceless awareness, rather than focusing on a particular aspect of the present moment, such as sensation, sound, or thought, the practice involves just being present with each moment as it arises, without preference regarding the content of the moment. In practical terms, this means that sometimes body sensations are in the foreground, sometimes sounds, sometimes thoughts, sometimes breathing sensations, sometimes emotions, and sometimes mind states, which are combinations of thoughts and body sensations. In choiceless awareness you remain receptive to each moment with an open heart. With so much happening in each moment, it is easy to get lost or confused in the practice. Mental noting can be a very useful aid. Simply by naming what's happening in the foreground of awareness from moment to moment, or by focusing on and noting the space of awareness itself, within which all other phenomena arise and pass, you can stay focused in the present.

34. After resting for a few minutes in the practice of choiceless awareness, gather up awareness in the belly-breath sensations, just resting in the buoyancy and support of the breathing for the last few minutes of the sitting meditation.

35. Take a few minutes to reflect on your experience of the sitting meditation. What did you notice? Reflect on what it was like to notice hearing, thinking, mind states, and emotions as events happening, just observing without getting caught up in or identifying with the content.

36. It can be particularly difficult to observe thoughts as events without getting caught up in the story line and content. What did you notice in your practice of mindfulness of thinking? What mind states, emotions, and types of thoughts did you observe?

37. Finally, how did you experience choiceless awareness? It can be difficult at first. It helps to identify with the space of awareness, or the context within which all other phenomena are arising, changing, and fading away—like a vast, spacious sky, within which clouds or various sizes, shapes, and colors come and go; identifying with the sky as the space of awareness itself.

Final Reflections on Sitting Meditation

Sitting meditation affords the best platform for clearly perceiving and experiencing the mind-body process as it unfolds moment by moment. In particular, it's the best platform for observing and coming to understand experientially how we construct and deconstruct suffering through our reactions or responses to pleasant, unpleasant, or neutral tone in the moment. The sitting posture is unparalleled in its ability to promote relaxed wakefulness by allowing one to be effortlessly upright.

Because the sitting posture promotes such a solid, stable foundation, whether one is in a chair or on a meditation cushion on the floor, it makes possible profound stillness, within which one can experience movements of sensations, sounds, thinking, emotions, perceptions, moods, and mental states, including concentration and mindfulness, with much greater clarity. Because the sitting posture creates the potential for strong, powerful stillness and choiceless awareness of the full range of experience in each moment, it is unparalleled as a meditation practice. For this reason, whatever you choose as your primary formal practice, I still strongly recommend incorporating some sitting meditation practice as well.

Walking Meditation

After breathing, eating, discovering our bodies, learning about the different ways we can move our limbs, pulling ourselves up to sitting, learning to crawl, and exploring as much of our surroundings as we can through crawling, we eventually learn to stand up and walk. Standing up and walking is the culmination of about a year of intense effort and exploration, which becomes increasingly frustrating as we discover the limitations of crawling. It's slow, you can't reach very high up, and everyone else is much, much taller than you. So, motivated by some combination of frustration, desire, and the innate drive for mastery, we manage to pull ourselves up to a standing posture while holding on to anything for support. We learn to take our first steps (usually sideways) while continuing to hold on to a piece of furniture or a loved one's legs or hands for support.

One day, who knows how or why, we decide it's time to let go, to attempt to stand on our own without holding on. Those first few wobbly moments, especially if witnessed and delighted in by a loving parent or caretaker, are for most of us moments of sheer triumph and exhilaration, even if they are quickly followed by a fall! Standing unsupported is often followed shortly thereafter by the first wobbly attempts at walking unsupported. We have to feel our way into it, the balancing upright on just our legs, the forward motion that feels a little like falling, the synchronized, alternating weighting and unweighting of right and then left feet and legs.

Certainly the wisdom of evolution does most of the work, but we still have to feel into it and embody it through practice, practice, practice. At first we walk simply to experience walking: to embody it, to get it, to master walking for its own sake. We walk for the sheer joy of experiencing this remarkable form of locomotion of which we humans are capable.

Very soon, however, walking becomes instrumental—a means to an end, a way to get from place to place. Walking becomes an automatic skill. Not only do we not need to think about walking, we can actually sleep through it! As adults, we rarely fully experience walking because we are so focused on where we are going and what we will do when we get there.

Walking meditation is an antidote to "sleepwalking through walking" (and perhaps through life!). It involves reinhabiting walking, reawakening to the sensory experience of walking as it unfolds in each moment. We already know how to walk. Walking meditation lets us reconnect with the sensory experience of walking, apart from where it gets us.

Exercise 6.6: Walking Meditation

1. Stand upright and erect if you're able, feet about hip-width apart and knees soft. Let your eyes focus softly on a spot on the ground about six feet directly in front of you. If you're not able to stand upright, make any adjustments necessary to adapt the walking meditation practice to your abilities.

2. Take some time to settle into the standing posture. Appreciating the experience of standing upright and tall, if you're able; feeling the erect spine elevating up to where it inserts into the skull, supporting the head, neck, shoulders, arms, and hands; no need for direction from you. Head positioned back over the spine for support, and chin either parallel to the floor or tilted down a bit, whichever is most comfortable.

3. Sacroiliac joint, pelvic girdle, knees, and ankles working together effortlessly to provide stability and balance, transferring the weight of the head and torso through the feet to the support of the floor and the earth beneath.

4. All of this happening on its own without your conscious direction, though at the beginning of your life it took you six months to a year to figure it out—actually to feel and sense it out, because there wasn't yet language with which to think about it.

5. Standing balanced, stable, solid, rooted, alert, and at ease. Embodied. Present. Awake. Just experiencing the sensations of standing without needing to do anything. Appreciating, as best you can, just standing on the earth. It's an almost unfathomable evolutionary achievement, which took more than two billion years, or perhaps fourteen billion, depending on how you think about it.

6. Now unweight your right leg and feel all of the weight shift down through your left leg and onto your left foot. As the weight shifts onto your left leg and foot, let yourself lift the right foot off the ground, move it forward a short distance (your foot knows what's right for you), and place it on the ground again, shifting the weight onto your right foot and leg while unweighting your left leg and foot. Now lifting the left foot, moving it forward, placing it on the ground, and letting the weight shift back onto the left foot and leg as the right leg unweights and the right foot lifts.

7. Can you feel the left foot lifting itself, moving itself, and placing itself, all with no instructions required? Feel how elegantly the weight shifts from right to left and left to right while moving forward. It's already perfectly choreographed. No need for direction. Just being fully present in the body, and feeling walking happening as movements and sensations in the feet and legs—lifting, moving, and placing.

8. Let the legs and feet do what they already know how to do from years of practice and experience of walking as sensations of weighting, unweighting, lifting, moving, and placing, first one foot and leg, then the other.

9. When you've walked eight or ten steps forward, let yourself stop for a few moments, appreciating the sensations of stopping and standing. Then turn 180 degrees and walk back the other way to where you started. Be present for each moment of the walking as sensations of weighting and unweighting, lifting, moving, and placing first one foot and then the other. Just noticing and feeling walking happening, moment by moment.

10. Continue practicing this way for about ten minutes, coming to stillness again when you've come back to the spot where you started. Just standing for a minute, inhabiting the experience of standing as a flow of changing sensations in the same way you inhabited walking. Moment by moment feeling sensations of standing, erect, upright, and balanced on your feet and legs, weight transferring down through the pelvis, legs, and feet into the floor. Perhaps noticing that balance itself is a dynamic process, even while standing still.

11. Remain standing in silence for a few more minutes, reflecting on your experience of walking meditation practice; then write about the experience of walking meditation in your journal, particularly what it was like to practice mindfulness of a habitual movement usually done on automatic pilot. Finally, be sure to log your practice in your meditation practice log or smartphone application.

Final Reflections on Walking Meditation

In mindfulness in daily life practice, you may have noticed, or may discover, that the transitions between activities are when we tend to lose focus. Moving meditations, like mindful walking, are particularly helpful in cultivating and strengthening the ability to sustain mindfulness when moving from one activity to the next.

Can you remember instances of rushing from one room to another to get or do something, only to realize you'd completely forgotten what you wanted to get or do? Or getting so involved in a conversation, enjoying a favorite song while driving, that you missed your turn or freeway exit? Or eating cookies or spoonful of ice cream for a snack, and suddenly looking at the empty box or carton, having missed most of the actual eating? Sustaining mindfulness in the midst of activity is a unique challenge, and walking meditation in particular helps with developing the skills and inner capacities to do so.

Loving-Kindness and Compassion

In Buddhist psychology, cultivating the four immeasurable virtues is considered an essential foundation for mindfulness practice. Loving-kindness is the first of the four virtues, which include compassion, sympathetic joy (being truly happy for the happiness of others, without jealousy or envy), and equanimity. Until recently in contemporary Western psychology, meditations developing loving-kindness, compassion, and equanimity in particular, were subsumed under the umbrella of mindfulness practice. Now several researchers and scholars have developed therapies focusing specifically on cultivating compassion for self and others (Germer, 2009; Gilbert, 2009; Neff, 2011; Jinpa, 2015). Many of these partially conflate loving-kindness and compassion practices or emphasize self-compassion, which I think is fine for the purpose of psychotherapy. In Buddhist psychology, compassion practices are generally considered to be more advanced. In the new therapeutic compassion trainings that I've experienced, compassion practices tend to be modified so they are more like loving-kindness practices.

Loving-kindness meditation focuses on developing radical acceptance, or openheartedness, a vital component of mindfulness that requires us to be equally partial to each moment, whatever its contents. Radical acceptance allows for maximum clarity of perception in each moment because perception isn't distorted by conditioned judgment, aversion, or grasping. Seeing the present moment clearly allows for an optimally skillful response in the next moment, developing a positive feedback loop of clear seeing and skillful response, with each moment conditioning the next.

If, instead, we greet the moment with conditioned judgment, aversion, or grasping, or act from delusion (not perceiving what's happening clearly, because of ignorance or prejudice), we are more likely to respond unskillfully in the next moment, which increases the likelihood of creating adventitious suffering. So despite its lofty name, loving-kindness, or radical acceptance, is actually extremely practical—one could even say necessary—for optimal mental health and well-being.

Loving-kindness meditation is particularly helpful for people who can't tolerate mindfulness meditation because they are too agitated or restless or are unable to tolerate the obsessive self-judgment, rumination, or worry that can become louder and more prominent in the context of formal mindfulness meditation practice. Because it explicitly cultivates and strengthens radical self-acceptance, loving-kindness is particularly useful in treating harsh self-judgment, obsessive self-criticism, and other forms of depressogenic thinking, as well as shame and feelings of unworthiness.

In Buddhist psychology, loving-kindness is said to be the natural antidote ("far enemy") of anxiety and fear because they are opposite movements of mind. The original Pali word for "mind" in Buddhist psychology can be best translated as "heart mind." Loving-kindness, or radical acceptance, is the movement of the heart mind in the direction of unconditionally opening to and receiving the experience of each moment without resistance or aversion. In contrast, the heart contracts and closes in the experience of fear and anxiety, creating more anxiety, which causes the heart to contract more in an unvirtuous positive feedback loop. Loving-kindness practice is also said to promote sound, uninterrupted sleep.

Exercise 6.7: Loving-Kindness Meditation

1. Sit up comfortably tall in a well-supported posture. Let the eyes close if it's comfortable, and allow awareness to drop down into the "heart space" just behind the lower part of the sternum in the center of the chest. This is not the anatomical heart space, but rather the emotional heart space, that area in the center of the chest where we feel sadness, grief, loss, and longing as well as love, caring, compassion, empathy, and tenderness. It's the same area that clutches and tightens when we're anxious and afraid, and melts, radiating warmth, when we love.

2. Focus on the sensations of breathing as the breath passes in and out through the heart space. Feeling the heart space expanding and opening with the in-breath, and releasing and softening with the out-breath.

3. As you continue to experience the sensations of breathing in this way, begin to visualize and feel a warm, radiant, white light glowing in the center of the heart space. With each in-breath the light glows brighter and warmer, and with each out-breath it radiates out in all directions: front and back, up and down, and to either side, spreading the warm white light of loving-kindness to every cell in your body and out into the room.

4. As you continue to breathe, imagine inhaling energy and freshness and exhaling toxins and holding from the heart space as the warm white light intensifies and radiates out to every cell in your body. As you continue breathing, imagining every cell in the body soaking in the soothing energy, warmth, and radiant white glow of loving-kindness.

5. Continue breathing in this way, and as best you can, begin to feel the entire body soften, release, and open. The warm white light glowing ever more brightly in the center of the heart space, radiating the healing warmth and soothing energies of loving-kindness in all directions, to every cell in the body.

6. Now visualize in the mind's eye an image of yourself, either as you are now or as a child or infant. Just receiving any image of yourself that arises in the mind's eye. Now, see an image of yourself in the mind's eye dropping down into the center of the heart space, immersed and saturated in the warm, radiant glow of loving-kindness.

7. With each in-breath, direct the energies of loving-kindness toward the image of yourself in the heart space. Sincerely wishing yourself health and well-being, happiness, vitality, joy, love, wisdom, compassion, patience, faith, prosperity, and abundance.

8. Now, repeat the phrases below, either out loud or silently to yourself, directing the intentions and aspirations contained in the phrases toward the image of yourself in the heart space. Let yourself genuinely and deeply feel the aspirations and intentions in the phrases.

   The phrases may sound like supplicatory prayer, but they are intended as expressions of aspirations for ease and well-being. Whether you feel your heart opening or hardening in any given moment doesn't matter. Each repetition of a phrase is like a repetition in weight training, strengthening the capacity for radical self- acceptance. Repeat the four phrases three times, directing the aspirations and intentions expressed by the phrases toward the image of yourself in the heart space.

   May I be happy and peaceful.

   May I be safe from all internal and external harm.

   May I be free from emotional and physical suffering.

   May I live with joy and ease of being.

9. Now letting go of the image of yourself from the heart space and receiving the image of a loved one or respected mentor or teacher in the heart space. Directing the energies and aspirations in the phrases to the image of the loved one or respected mentor or teacher in the heart space as you say them out loud or silently to yourself three times.

   May you be happy and peaceful.

   May you be safe from all internal and external harm.

   May you be free from suffering.

   May you live with joy and ease of being.

10. The practice continues in the same way, directing the phrases successively toward the image of a neutral person; an enemy, adversary, or someone you dislike;

and finally toward all beings. Radiating loving-kindness onto all beings equally, just as the sun shines equally on the wicked and the good. This practice is just like progressively increasing resistance in weight training.

11. Remember that the loving-kindness meditation, as well as the compassion and equanimity practices we will be doing, are meant to be workouts in a literal sense, strengthening the muscles of loving-kindness, compassion, and equanimity by gently working against the opposite tendencies in the heart mind, if they are present, and developing capacity through repetition regardless.

12. For the last few minutes of the practice, just feeling the breath moving in and out through the heart space and letting the awareness soak in the energies of radical acceptance.

13. When you're ready, take a few minutes to reflect on the experience of the loving-kindness meditation, then write about your experience in your journal as well as about any interesting observations or questions that arose. Remember to log your practice in your practice log or smartphone application.

Final Reflections on Loving-Kindness Meditation

The loving-kindness practice is obviously quite different from the other practices we've done so far. It is a concentration practice, as defined in chapter 1, in which the focus of attention is a particular object, in this case the repetition of phrases, in conjunction with a visualization.

The object is to become completely absorbed in, and to strengthen, the experience and expression of the intentions and aspirations in the phrases while focusing on the energies of loving-kindness, experienced as physical sensations, emotions, and visual imagery in the heart space. Part of the practice is to note any resistance manifesting as the physical sensations of contracting, tightening, or bracing in the heart space, or as thoughts or emotions.

As with the mindfulness meditations, accepting whatever arises without judgment or striving is part of the loving-kindness practice. Only doing the practice is important, not getting a specific result during a particular meditation practice session.

Cultivating Equanimity and Composure: Sitting Mountain Meditation

The sitting mountain meditation is a mindfulness practice that incorporates visualization as a means to cultivate "equanimity," the capacity to remain fully present and unperturbed in the midst of change, disruption, chaos, or strife. (Note that a standing variant of the mountain meditation is available at the website for this book.) Equanimity may translate into not getting caught up in the emotional drama of a spouse or the acting out of a child but also not turning away or shutting down. It may also translate into remaining unperturbed in the face of a client's *transference test*—provocative, challenging, uncomfortable, or even scary behaviors that communicate unarticulated questions, such as *What do I have to do before you abandon me just like everyone else has?* or *Can I really trust you to stick with me when the going gets tough?* or *Do you have what it takes to stay with me, and be willing to connect, when I'm this depressed, anxious, suicidal, or otherwise symptomatic?* Equanimity may also translate into how you handle life when you feel like your plate is overflowing with challenges, but somehow life didn't get the message and continues to pile it on.

Equanimity is more than stress resilience. It also involves trust in yourself and life, rooted in embodied wisdom about impermanence and the constancy of change; skill in relating to change; and the ability and willingness to let go of attachments to outcomes over which you have no control. Equanimity incorporates the understanding that life is just what it is, and ultimately it is too precious to squander with upset or worry that accomplishes nothing.

Finally, equanimity involves a spacious perspective, the experiential understanding that we are all participants in the vast, unimaginably complex and interconnected "being" of the Earth. As the naturalist John Muir said more than a hundred years ago, "When we try to pick out anything by itself, we find it hitched to everything else in the Universe" (as quoted in Worster, 2008, p. 160). Paradoxically, this vast, spacious perspective is quite comforting and stabilizing, because it easily accommodates anything that arises within it without disturbance.

Exercise 6.8: Sitting Mountain Meditation

1. Sit comfortably in a relaxed, dignified posture, spine erect and upright without being stiff. Feel the sense of axial uplift as the spine rises up out of the sacroiliac joint, ascending to its insertion in the occipital opening of the skull. Do you trust the spine to support the weight of the head, or is there unnecessary tension in the neck and shoulders? Just investigate with awareness, noticing without judging.

2. Plant your feet solidly on the floor. Allow the hands to rest comfortably on your thighs or in your lap so that the chest is open and the belly soft. Let the eyes close, and feel the sensations of the body breathing, moment by moment. Just feeling breathing happening, each breath moment unique. Notice also any impulse or tendency to evaluate or judge the breath or the moment as good or bad, right or wrong. If you become aware of evaluating or judging, just note it and let it be without judging the judging.

3. Now visualize the image of a mountain in your mind's eye. It could be a mountain you've climbed, or hiked, or visited, or driven by, or seen in a photograph. Or it could be a mountain of your imagination. Whatever presents itself to your imagination, let that be the mountain for this meditation. See the mountain as clearly as you can. Is the peak jagged and barren, snow covered, or round and forested? Perhaps your mountain is a volcanic cone, a mesa, or desert ridge.

See the slopes of the mountain. Are they steep or gradual? Barren or forested? Are there streams and waterfalls? Animals and birds? See the base of the mountain. How large do you think the circumference is at the base? Could you walk or even drive around it in one day? Let your image be vivid and multisensory. Smell the smells. Feel the temperature, the dryness or humidity of the air, and the wind on your skin. Listen to the sounds of the mountain, and to its silence.

4. Now let the image of the mountain drop down into your body. Allow your head and neck to become the peak of the mountain; your shoulders, arms, and torso the slopes; and your pelvis, legs, and feet the mountain's base, rooted firmly in the earth. Letting yourself become the mountain in your mind's eye. Experience sitting like a mountain, massive, imposing, present, solid, and unshakable.

5. After ten or fifteen minutes of practicing in this way, begin to expand the field of awareness to include sensations throughout the body. Again, avoid right or wrong and good or bad judgments. Just notice sensations coming and going, neither reacting nor trying to not react. Just as the mountain witnesses the cycles of day and night and the larger cycles of the seasons, accommodating all change without preference or resistance, let sensations come and go without preference or resistance.

6. After five or ten minutes of practicing this way, expand the field of awareness once again to include hearing. Noticing sounds as events—how they arise, change, and pass away.

7. Imagine the mountain teeming with the activities of life. Continue to sit in the midst of all the changes, bearing witness but remaining unperturbed. Notice how the majesty of the mountain is not just its size but its formidable silent presence. Can you experience that same quality of presence in your own being as you continue to practice? Sitting like a mountain with an imposing, silent presence, abiding continuous change yet remaining immoveable and unperturbed.

Final Reflections on Sitting Mountain Meditation

In the sitting mountain meditation, we intentionally set out to develop an embodied, experiential metaphor for equanimity in the form of the mountain you visualized. Hopefully this experience will allow you to use the mountain image you embodied to reconnect with the experience of equanimity whenever you'd like. Are there other personally meaningful images that you could develop and embody as experiential metaphors for mindfulness in your own life?

Many people frequently use the image of a still mountain lake as an experiential, embodied metaphor for cultivating equanimity (Kabat-Zinn, 1994). The image of sky is useful for cultivating spacious awareness. Watching billowing clouds pass through a vast, open sky, and identifying not with the clouds but with the blue vastness may connect you with the space of awareness itself, within which everything else arises and passes.

Summary

This chapter elaborated on facet A of level 1—the therapist's formal mindfulness meditation practices—of the mindfulness pyramid model. The chapter included introductions to an eating practice, a breath-awareness practice, a body scan meditation, a mindful movement practice, a sitting meditation, a walking meditation, a loving-kindness meditation, and an equanimity practice called sitting mountain meditation, along with detailed instructions and additional reflections on each practice.

If you are new to mindfulness meditation, I strongly encourage you to choose one or two practices that particularly resonate with you, to do one practice every day, to record your practice in your mindfulness practice log, and to journal about your practice as well. More than anything else, formal meditation practice will develop the necessary experiential foundation and embodied understanding required to successfully incorporate mindfulness in your clinical work. Please visit the website for this book (http://www.newharbinger.com/32752) to avail yourself of the guided meditation recordings for the practices in this chapter. I also encourage you to seek formal instruction in mindfulness-based stress reduction or mindfulness-based cognitive therapy courses, and to consider an intensive, residential vipassana retreat (also known as insight meditation). See "Mindfulness Meditation Resources" in appendix A.

Chapter 7

Therapist's Practice: Skills, Inner Capacities, Attitudes, and Perspectives

This chapter examines specific mind-body skills (cognitive, behavioral, and emotional), inner capacities, attitudes, and perspectives that support, and can be developed and strengthened through, formal mindfulness meditation practice. Together, these elements comprise the second face, facet B, of the mindfulness pyramid model. Dialectical behavioral therapy (Linehan, 1993a), acceptance and commitment therapy (Hayes et al., 2003), mindfulness-based cognitive therapy (Segal et al., 2002), and the many other mindfulness-based therapies modeled after mindfuness-based stress reduction (originally developed by Jon Kabat-Zinn in 1979 at the Stress Reduction Clinic of the University of Massachusetts Medical Center; see Kabat-Zinn, 1990), pioneered time-limited psychotherapeutic interventions, which help clients identify and understand the causes of their suffering and intentionally develop and strengthen the skills and attributes necessary to alleviate it.

Mindfulness Pyramid Facet *B*—Skills, Inner Capacities, Attitudes, and Perspectives

Skills	Inner Capacities	Attitudes	Perspectives
Concentration	Distress tolerance and stress resilience	Nonjudging	Present moment, wonderful moment
Attention		Nonstriving	
Mindfulness	Affect tolerance	Beginner's mind	Can't change the present moment, only how we respond
Shifting modes of mind	Equanimity	Trust and confidence	
Allowing/letting be	Joy and humor	Unconditional friendliness	
Turning toward the difficult and opening to the unwanted	Authenticity and genuineness	Interest and curiosity	Neither thoughts nor other mental formations are facts, especially the ones that insist they are.
	Warmth	Letting go	
Radical acceptance and willingness	Patience		
	Cognitive flexibility		Change is the only constant.
Emotion self-regulation			Pain is inevitable in this life. Suffering is optional.
Disidentifying			
Empathic attunement			Reacting with aversion to the present moment leads to suffering. Clinging to the present-moment pleasure or happiness leads to suffering.
Mindful listening			
Discerning wisdom			
Compassion			
Being with, without fixing			Living in ignorance, denial, or delusion leads to suffering.
Optimal responsiveness			
Self-care			Happiness doesn't come from getting what you want; it comes from nonwanting.

Skills

The *skills* of third wave cognitive behavioral therapies are defined as specific behavioral responses to experience, both inner movements of mind and actions in the world, that allow us to reduce or avoid adventitious suffering and to optimize happiness, vitality, and well-being.

Concentration

From the perspective of mindfulness, *concentration* refers to the ability to gather up awareness completely so it is not partial or divided but focused completely, 100 percent, on the chosen object of focus in the present moment. Rather than being driven by the energy of effort or straining, concentration is driven by the energy of friendly curiosity and interest, even fascination, and the genuine desire to know its focal object.

If you're thinking that sounds like mindfulness, you're nearly right! In the context of mindfulness practice, nonjudging, nonstriving, friendly, curious, and interested awareness strengthens concentration, which in turn strengthens mindfulness, which further strengthens concentration in a continuous positive feedback loop. Such concentration cannot be "efforted" in the conventional sense but only allowed, generated through nondoing, or "being mode of mind" (see Segal et al., 2002).

Attentional

Attention refers to the ability to focus present-moment awareness precisely on what you want to pay attention to and in the way you want to pay attention. The first skill is noticing that you can choose what to attend to and how to attend to it. Next is learning to deploy attention where you want it, like pointing a camera at what you want to photograph, and then learning to move the attention from one focal object to another or following or not following a moving object.

You can also learn to strengthen skillful qualities of attention, such as alertness, accepting, nonjudging, and nonstriving, and to be aware of, and disidentify with, unskillful qualities, such as judgmental, dismissive, irritated, impatient, distracted, or spacey. By "skillful" I mean qualities of attention that heighten and clarify awareness and perception, increase acuity, and reduce distortion. "Unskillful" describes qualities of attention that actually reduce clarity and acuity of awareness and distort perception.

A final set of attentional skills involves shifting perspective in the sense of being able to zoom in for a very circumscribed, close-up (microscopic or telephoto) view of an object and to zoom out for a more inclusive, wide-angle view. I discuss a different kind of perspective shifting in the section "Disidentifying," later in this chapter.

Mindfulness

Mindfulness skills are those that help you to be in and fully experience the present moment without conditioned, emotional reactivity or judgment.

In a very real sense every element in the list of skills, inner capacities, attitudes, and perspectives is a mindfulness skill. However, as used here the term refers to becoming familiar with the experience of being present; skills for sustaining present-moment focus; and how to deal with the inevitability of the mind wandering, including noticing when you're not present and bringing the attention back to the present moment again and again.

Can you recall a time when you received 100 percent of someone's calm, accepting, totally interested, loving attention, with no agenda other than to understand you and really know you? It is a profound and powerful experience. Being the recipient of this kind of attention is itself transformative and healing (Rogers, 1966). Being the giver of such attention is also profound and transformative; it's one of the privileges of being a therapist. I talk more about this aspect of concentration in chapter 10.

Shifting Modes of Mind

Segal, Williams, and Teasdale (2002) coined the phrase "shifting modes of mind" to describe moving between doing mode of mind and being mode of mind. *Doing mode* is conditioned, habitual, automatic, and characterized by relentless judging and striving, and it's often triggered by fight-flight-freeze reactivity. *Being mode* of mind, synonymous with mindfulness, is the mode of simply experiencing each moment as it arises, with interest and curiosity, and without judging, expectations, or striving to attain or accomplish. Doing mode involves striving to accomplish or attain some goal or objective, even if only in our thoughts.

Doing mode of mind is not conscious of itself. Only being mode of mind can be conscious of doing mode of mind. When we experience emotional distress from feeling threatened, pressured, overwhelmed, or depleted, we automatically fall into conditioned, habitual doing modes of mind in an effort to alleviate the emotional distress. Unfortunately, since emotions are not problems that can be solved, and the thinking mind is oriented to problem solving, our default modes of mind either do nothing to alleviate emotional distress or make it worse.

Shifting into being mode of mind allows us to observe conditioned, automatic thinking, as well as the default mode of mind that generates it, as events. Noticing our default doing modes of mind (for example, worrying, obsessing, ruminating, or judging) and learning to shift out of them into being mode of mind (noticing, allowing, and letting be) allows for decentering from, or disidentifying with, conditioned, reactive thinking. Thought is experienced as an event rather than in identifying with its narrative content or story line.

Shifting from doing mode to being mode involves shifting our relationship to thought itself, from being caught up in automatic thoughts (*I am thinking*) to noticing thinking as an event in awareness (*Thinking is happening*). Shifting from doing mode of mind to being mode of mind is an important skill, not just for therapists and clients but for anyone who wants to experience peace of mind that is not contingent on circumstance.

Allowing/Letting Be

Segal, Williams, and Teasdale, developers of mindfulness-based cognitive therapy for depression, coined the phrase "allowing/letting be" (2002, pp. 218–243). It refers to the skill of not automatically reacting to painful or distressing sensations, feelings, thoughts, or unpleasant experiences by trying to get rid of them, fix them, or change them. Instead, we learn simply to notice the distress, allowing it simply to be present, understanding from the formal meditation practice that everything arises and passes by itself, and resistance only increases the distress.

Turning Toward the Difficult and Opening to the Unwanted

"Turning toward the difficult" and "opening to the unwanted" (Segal et al., 2002, pp. 269–271) are skills based on the embodied understanding that conditioned, reactive efforts to avoid, get rid of, or fix psychological distress and emotional pain actually *are* the distress and pain—both in terms of constituting distress and pain and perpetuating them. Understanding that experiential avoidance is not only ineffective in reducing distress, but actually constitutes most of it, makes it possible to do what feels deeply counterintuitive but essential: turning toward the distress and opening to it. Doing so offers the opportunity to see clearly what's actually happening and to respond creatively and skillfully.

Turning toward the difficult and opening to the unwanted requires concentration, attention, mindfulness, shifting modes of mind, radical acceptance, willingness, decentering and disidentifying, empathic attunement, and self-compassion. In reality these skills operate together in a nonlinear fashion and are interdependent. Bernie Glassman, a well-known American Zen teacher and social activist, describes turning toward the difficult and opening to the unwanted as "bearing witness" (1998). In psychotherapy, the act and process of bearing witness incorporates all the skills, inner capacities, attitudes, and perspectives that compose facet B of the mindfulness pyramid.

Bearing witness disrupts the escape-avoidance-escalation cycle and challenges the often unconscious assumption that life is never supposed to be painful, unhappy, or difficult (see Hayes et al., 2003, pp. 3–12). Bearing witness challenges the implicit belief that all psychological distress and pain are, by definition, bad, and thus should be avoided or discarded. Bearing witness also allows for a truly compassionate response, not just reactive avoidance or attempts to get rid of or fix the distress.

Radical Acceptance and Willingness

Radical acceptance describes the quality of mindful awareness that embraces each moment with equal appreciation, enthusiasm, and love. It doesn't discriminate between pleasant and unpleasant moments. From the perspective of radical acceptance, each moment is uniquely precious and of inestimable value. In this context, radical acceptance is similar to the concept of "willingness" in acceptance and commitment therapy (Hayes et al., 2003, pp. 132–138).

In Buddhist psychology, radical acceptance is called *metta*, another Pali word that is usually translated as "loving-kindness." In explaining what he meant by *metta*, the Buddha used similes, comparing it to the way the sun shines on the earth and the way that an adoring mother loves her only child.

These similes are instructive for understanding radical acceptance, which is unconditional, constant, and completely receptive while making no demands. Radical acceptance in this sense is similar to the quality of "unconditional positive regard" that Carl Rogers (1957) described as the first of his "necessary and sufficient conditions for therapeutic effectiveness."

A simpler way to describe radical acceptance is the willingness to embrace each moment, however it is, regardless of its feeling tone or content. Willingness can be developed and cultivated as a skill in the formal mindfulness meditation practice. Radical acceptance, willingness, and the attitudinal corollary "nonjudging" are technical requirements of mindful awareness. Conditioned, reactive judgments and preferences distort perception and disturb and contaminate the field of awareness, making it impossible to perceive and experience the moment clearly.

Think of mindful awareness as an absolutely still, clear mountain lake that mirrors everything surrounding it and above it, yet is also transparent, revealing everything beneath the surface. Judgments and preferences are like big rocks thrown into the lake. The surface of the lake, now disturbed and agitated, no longer mirrors. The depths, now churned up, muddy, and murky, no longer reveal.

Not being aware of judgmental and evaluative thoughts *as just thoughts*, it's impossible to perceive the moment clearly. We end up relating more to our thoughts about life than to life itself.

It follows that radical acceptance is a technical necessity of mindfulness practice. Without it, it's impossible to perceive the moment clearly. This doesn't mean we have to stop reactively judging. Such habitual, conditioned thought patterns are almost completely automatic and beyond our control. Nor are they worth trying to control. Instead, we simply notice that judging is happening and relate to it as an event in awareness without getting caught up in or identifying with the content. We can relate *to* the judging thoughts rather than *through* the judging thoughts.

Along the same lines, we don't need to stop liking and disliking, which is impossible in any case. Just notice liking and disliking as events in awareness without getting caught up in or identifying with the content.

Exercise 7.1: Cultivating Radical Acceptance

1. Notice what's happening right now with your sensations, emotions, thoughts, and mind states. As best you can, let it all be exactly as it is in each moment, even the unpleasant and unwanted elements of experience.

2. Begin to notice the sensations of breathing and the reliable support and strength of the breath. Notice how the breath has no agenda for itself other than breathing.

3. You needn't have an agenda for the breath either. As best you can, let go of agendas for the breath and trust the breath to breathe itself. Rest in the breath as it is, moment by moment.

4. Notice any agendas you might have for yourself without judging them or trying to change them in any way. What are they? Would you prefer to have or not have particular sensations, thoughts, emotions, mind states, or life circumstances? Just notice.

5. Now allow the awareness to saturate the belly-breath sensations, illuminating them from the inside out, moment by moment, without judging or striving. Take a few minutes to settle into the moment to moment awareness of breathing.

6. When you are ready, like a whisper in the background of awareness, begin to silently say the word *yes* on each in-breath and *thank you* on each out-breath.

7. Continue to practice in this way for the next five to ten minutes. Greet the sensations of each in-breath moment with warmth and hospitality, along with a silently whispered *yes* in the background of awareness. Then, with great care and tenderness, feel the sensations of each out-breath moment while saying a silent, background *thank you*. Be sure not to lose contact with the bare sensations of breathing in each moment, or the accompanying feelings of openhearted receptivity, appreciation, and gratitude invited by the words.

8. When, in your own time, you come to the end of the exercise, consider the possibility of living each breath, and every moment of your life, with appreciation and gratitude—a life of yes and thank you. Imagine what it might be like.

9. Finally, let yourself feel *encouraged* by your openhearted acceptance of each moment and each breath in the exercise. Be encouraged that you can allow yourself to trust life, can be confident about your ability to embrace each moment fully, and can respond skillfully. Allow the feelings of encouragement to saturate your being as you proceed with your day.

Emotion Self-Regulation

Clients often come to therapy because of difficulties with emotion self-regulation (Linehan, 1993a, 1993b; Epstein, 1995; Spradlin, 2003; Hayes et al., 2004). Problems with emotion self-regulation involve the general inability to tolerate strong emotions; to modulate emotions; or to experience specific emotions such as anxiety, hurt, shame, or anger without feeling overwhelmed, fragmented, or compelled to express them inappropriately. Often problems with emotion self-regulation accompany fears of abandonment, a vulnerability to narcissistic injury, and a general sense of fragility.

Effective emotion self-regulation begins with developing mindfulness of emotions and the capacity to radically decenter from and disidentify with emotions, as well as the thoughts that drive and sustain them. Emotion self-regulation also requires learning healthy self-soothing skills. Self-soothing skills in mindfulness involve anchoring awareness in the present by connecting to the physical sensations of the body and breath. They also involve expanding to a more spacious awareness of the distressing emotion, which allows for changes in the perspective of the difficult emotion and makes it easier to let it be without trying to suppress or get rid of it.

Paradoxically, emotion self-regulation through mindfulness requires turning toward painful and distressing emotions rather than reactively avoiding, suppressing, or avoiding them. Being with difficult emotions mindfully yields the insights that emotions change constantly, and that resistance to painful emotions is the problem rather than the emotions themselves.

Emotion self-regulation is an important personal and professional skill for therapists. Embodying emotion self-regulation skills in sessions helps clients to experience, understand, and internalize the skills for themselves. As therapists we are called upon to remain authentically present, calm, and unperturbed in the face of our clients' emotional distress, as well as our own, in order to provide a *safe container* or *holding environment* (Winnicott, 1984) for our clients. Our own emotion self-regulation skills are essential for inspiring confidence in our clients that we are capable of helping. Particularly when clients feel emotionally overwhelmed, it is important to embody the skill of emotion self-regulation by staying empathically attuned, engaged, and responsive rather than being emotionally reactive and overwhelmed.

Disidentifying

Disidentifying has two meanings as a therapeutic skill. The first is disidentifying from conditioned, automatic thoughts and feelings and instead perceiving them simply as events in awareness that don't necessarily reflect intrinsic truth about who you are or what your situation in life is (Segal et al., 2002). Disidentifying is an important skill for therapists because it is the basis for the therapeutic mode of action of mindfulness for clients. We need to experientially understand and embody disidentifying as a skill in order to teach it to our clients effectively.

Disidentifying as a therapist involves stepping outside of yourself and just being with your clients without intruding with your own personality formations, agendas, and expectations or interjecting your own attitudes, beliefs, and perspectives. Disidentifying also allows us to engage compassionately with our clients without buying into the perspective that their distress necessarily means that something is wrong. Disidentifying as a skill helps you keep in perspective that your therapeutic job is not necessarily to help your client avoid or get rid of distress. Depending on the circumstances, you may need to help your client open to and feel distress. When we disidentify from thoughts and emotions, we can relate to them simply as events in awareness that come and go and don't necessarily have intrinsic meaning. As long as we don't identify with thoughts and emotions, they aren't problems. We begin to see that the most intense emotional distress often arises from identification with particular thoughts and feelings in the form of resistance to experiencing them.

Disidentifying also connotes the ability as a therapist and a person to decenter from the everyday sense of self-experience and identity as solid and constant. In this sense, disidentification is the recognition and understanding, usually developed through intensive meditation practice, that even your sense of identity and personality is just a deeply conditioned pattern of memory, thought, emotion, and sensation about "I, me, mine, and myself" that doesn't accurately describe the truth of who you are.

The same goes for how you view your clients. Allow for the possibility that what you think you know about your clients—from theory and professional training, from history and past interactions—is not even close to the whole story. Instead, let yourself experience personality and sense of identity, both your own and your client's, as potentially significant and useful but also as narrative fiction, totally constructed and dependent on point of view.

This second meaning of disidentification suggests that taking our personalities and senses of identity too literally or seriously is constricting and self-limiting. It is much wiser to hold such concepts lightly, acknowledging them simply as stories we tell about ourselves and our lives to try to make sense of them; some are useful, others not. From the perspective of mindfulness practice, who you and your client really are in any moment of the therapeutic encounter, even the reality of this moment as you read these words, is far richer, more fluid, more surprising and mysterious than any description or story about it could ever be. When this understanding is experientially anchored through your meditation practice, it is a powerful source of therapeutic optimism in even the most difficult circumstances.

Empathic Attunement

Mindfulness meditation cultivates both empathic attunement and compassion. Empathic attunement as a mode of knowing is systematically refined and cultivated through disciplined mindfulness meditation practice, first as a means of tuning into, knowing, and understanding our sensations, perceptions, thoughts, and emotions. From the perspective of practicing mindfulness, *empathy* can be described as "passionate nonattachment." There is a sense of friendliness, care, tenderness, poignancy, closeness, even intimacy with experience, without making it "mine" or "myself."

Mindfulness meditation develops and strengthens intimate, precise empathic attunement as a skill. When you also develop sufficient concentration to be fully present, moment by moment, with the intrinsic suffering of the human condition (having a body that gets uncomfortable and feels pain and a mind that experiences distress), and you are able to observe how we routinely intensify this unavoidable suffering through our conditioned efforts to avoid it, your heart's natural response is compassion. I deliberately use the word "heart," because the languages of the Asian cultures in which Buddhism developed don't separate the words for "mind" and "heart" as Western cultures do, and the experience of compassion is often literally a sensation of the heart opening, or expanding outward, within and from the chest.

Thus empathic attunement and compassion become conjoined in mindfulness practice. Compassion is the natural response to the insights about suffering that arise from the facet-C aspects of practice in the mindfulness pyramid model—mindfulness as method of inquiry and investigation and mode of knowing. Although empathic attunement and compassion can also be considered inner capacities, I prefer to think of them as skills that we can learn and cultivate through practice and then apply in our own lives and with our clients.

More precisely, empathic attunement to our selves and to our clients gives rise to insight, and subsequently compassion. In other words, compassion is a mind-body experience evoked by empathic attunement to suffering, anchored by interoceptive awareness. It is a natural capacity, but it can be developed intentionally as a skill, like playing harmonics on the strings of a guitar or violin. If you play one string in a certain way, all the other strings vibrate in harmony with the string played. Spontaneous harmonics are always possible, but you can learn to evoke harmonics intentionally by striking the strings in just the right way.

I am certain there are other ways to describe this process equally well or better. Nonetheless, I think it's important to attempt descriptions based on experience that don't necessarily fit preconceived psychological categories. The mindfulness practices being described here come from cultures in which concepts of mind-body dualism and scientific materialism didn't exist, and in which understanding of consciousness and the mind was quite advanced (Khempo, 1997; Thurman, 2005). By resisting automatic tendencies to reduce mindfulness practice to conventional psychological and scientific terms, the convergence of mindfulness meditation and psychotherapy may help identify those areas of Western psychology and cognitive neuroscience where the scientific materialist paradigm is inadequate and might need to be revised.

Mindful Listening

Listening is a foundational skill in psychotherapy and a mindfulness practice in and of itself. In clinical social-work training, listening was referred to as "attending to process." As trainee therapists we wrote numerous process recordings of our sessions with clients and watched videotape after videotape in which we were encouraged to tune in to what was happening in the moment with our clients and with ourselves. However, I don't recall specific training in listening as a technical skill. The building blocks of good listening—concentration, beginner's mind, decentering, interoceptive awareness, empathic attunement, and compassion—are all developed and strengthened by mindfulness practice.

Concentration is required for skillful listening because, first and foremost, it is essential for calming and stabilizing the listening mind. When the listener's mind is not focused, it is prone to noise, static, and lack of clarity and precise attunement, like when radio reception is poor because the radio isn't properly tuned to the transmitting frequency. As therapists, we are called upon continuously to work with our own minds to let go of the experiential residue of the last session, the last phone call, the last conversation with a colleague, and our personal lives in order to receive our next client with beginner's mind. Of course we bring the sum total of all our past experiences into the present moment. But mindful listening as a practice requires us to allow past experience to be in the background of awareness and to receive our client in each moment with beginner's mind.

This requires that the therapist be capable of *decentered listening.* To practice decentered listening, your experiences, needs, and desires take a backseat to the primary job of understanding, as closely and precisely as you can, how it feels to be inside your client's skin in each moment of the therapeutic encounter. When appropriate, decentered listening also involves articulating your empathically attuned, compassionate understanding of the client's inner experience in a way that allows the client to feel deeply understood, supported, and safe.

I use the words "support" and "safety" in their broadest senses. An empathically attuned response might involve simultaneously appreciating the reasons for the client's experiential avoidance or cognitive and emotional patterns while still confronting the dysfunction. Truly compassionate, attuned confrontation, even when very strong, is always appreciative of a client's felt vulnerabilities and strengths, which the client may not yet perceive. Skillfully attuned, compassionate confrontation feels extremely supportive because clients feel not only known by you—sometimes better than they know themselves—but remain confident in their ability to change.

Clients feel "held in safety" by their experience of your caring, competent, confident presence. Not only can you articulate an empathic understanding of their dysfunctional behavior patterns, but you refuse to believe that their feelings of fear, shame, helplessness, and hopelessness reflect any objective reality. Your clients literally take courage from your willingness and ability to not abandon them, to vicariously feel and suffer with them while not buying into their shame—which arises from identifying with, and feeling accurately defined by, the distressing emotions. Your attuned presence, compassion, and personal capacity for distress tolerance literally encourage your clients to risk healthier, more adaptive behaviors, even when they are at first very uncomfortable.

The best operational definition of "empathy" I have encountered comes from my experience as a group-support facilitator in the Multicenter Lifestyle Heart Trial of the Dean Ornish Program for Reversing Heart Disease (Ornish, 1990). This was the first National Institutes of Health–funded, scientifically controlled study looking to see if coronary artery blockages could be reversed through lifestyle change alone. Group support was incorporated as one of the central program components, because research demonstrated that as a group, patients with coronary artery disease scored significantly lower in standardized measures of empathy and social connection than their healthier peers. My mentor, the director of psychological support services for the study, had formulated a concrete, operational definition of "empathy" to teach to support-group participants, many of whom were high-powered businesspeople, engineers, attorneys, and physicians who had classic type-A personalities; tended to be concrete, goal-oriented thinkers; and had little emotional self-awareness or empathy. For their benefit "empathy" was explicitly defined and behaviorally operationalized as a four-part listening process:

1. Listen carefully to the speaker's experience as communicated both verbally and nonverbally without succumbing to urges to give advice or propose solutions.

2. Imagine what emotions the speaker might have felt in the situation described.

3. Identify an experience in your own life in which you felt the same or similar emotions, as a way of more deeply understanding the speaker's emotional experience.

4. Share your understanding with the speaker as it relates to the speaker's experience, with the sole purpose of helping the speaker to feel supported and understood.

Through facilitating Ornish Program support groups I began to understand empathy as a *practice*. Each of the four parts of the practice requires mindfulness. I have since used this framework successfully in group, couples, and family therapy as a way to teach mindful listening.

Discerning Wisdom

Discerning wisdom refers to the ability to register distinctions without imposing conditioned biases and judgments, or preconceived categories. It also refers to insights and considered judgments based on mindfulness; clarity of perception; and a refined, experientially derived understanding of how life works and what is needed in the moment to restore harmony and wholeness. The opposite of discerning wisdom is prejudice, bias, or conditioned, reactive judgment. When I describe mindfulness as moment to moment, nonjudging awareness, it means awareness without conditioned, reactive judgment—which we experience as automatic, such as the automatic aversion to pain sensations or objects to which we have been negatively conditioned.

However, mindfulness does facilitate the considered judgments that arise from discerning wisdom. Discerning wisdom is actually one of the fruits of mindfulness practice, and it is an important skill for effective psychotherapy. Like mindful listening, it requires decentering, letting go of what you think you know and instead opening to what *is* with beginner's mind; being fully present without hope or expectation; and trusting the moment to reveal itself as it is, if you let go of conditioned preferences and judgments. Clearly, discerning wisdom is more easily said than done. Thus, we all need to practice it.

We can also think of the discerning wisdom aspect of mindfulness as passionate presence (Ingram, 2003). *Passionate presence* involves passionately experiencing each moment of "now" while remaining equally dispassionate about the content or outcome of the moment. We experience each moment with care, simply because each is a precious moment of life, never to be repeated. The natural responses to passionate presence are tenderness, appreciation, and gratitude.

Compassion

Compassion is the heart's natural response to suffering. It involves opening up to, being touched by, and taking action to alleviate suffering. It is the willingness to resonate with and be genuinely moved by suffering to the point that you want to move in closer in order to help end it, or at least lessen it. Although compassion is often confused with sympathy, with "sympathy" the heart moves in the opposite direction. Sympathy involves feeling sorrow for the pain of others while basically keeping them and their pain at a distance. In contrast, compassion involves moving in closer, feeling *with* ("com") passion ("compassion") the pain both in ourselves and in others, which evokes the aspiration to alleviate it.

We and our clients experience and respond differently to true compassion and sympathy. Letting ourselves respond with genuine compassion to our own and our clients' distress, to get close up and resonate in the heart space, even within the context of the professional relationship, is tremendously validating and encouraging. As therapists, our willingness to connect deeply penetrates the sense of isolation that many clients feel at the beginning of therapy. Our empathic attunement, respect for our clients' prior attempts to cope, and genuine curiosity and desire to know more about their inner experience encourages clients to adopt a less harsh, more compassionate way of relating to themselves as well.

Sympathy, on the other hand, feels like a polite or professional gesture behind which you distance yourself from your clients, hiding and protecting yourself from resonance or identification with their vulnerability and distress. Sympathy functions as a subtle or not-so-subtle message to your clients about what they can expect of you and what you expect of them. The existential, human dimensions of the relationship may seem to be off-limits, although they might also feel like the elephant at the dinner table that no one talks about. Instead, you stay within your clearly defined role as expert professional helper, and your clients understand that their role is to receive your expert help.

Mindfulness practice invites us to come out from behind our professional personas and masks, to the extent that we wear them, and to connect compassionately with our clients in our mutual vulnerability and hurt, as "wounded healers" (Santorelli, 1999), in the pathos of our shared human condition. I don't mean to belittle our professional training and expertise or to encourage inappropriate therapist self-disclosure or any other behaviors motivated primarily by the therapist's needs rather than the client's. I do mean that letting ourselves feel touched by our clients' emotional distress and vulnerability, and recognizing and understanding it not simply diagnostically, but also as part of our shared existential predicament, is as important as technical expertise. Our shared existential predicament was described by the Buddha as *dukkha*, or "unsatisfactoriness" (Goldstein, 1993, p. 11); by Steven Hayes (with regard to acceptance and commitment therapy) as "the theory of destructive normalcy" (Hayes et al., 2003, pp. 8–12); and by Jon Kabat-Zinn as the "full catastrophe" (2013, p. xxvi).

True compassion doesn't involve personal or professional agendas, such as wanting to feel good about ourselves, boost our egos, assuage our guilt, earn the respect of our peers, get ahead professionally, and so on. It is literally the heart's opening in response to suffering , moving out toward the sufferer based on empathic attunement to, recognition of, and identification with human suffering as universal. True compassion is a physical sensation in the chest, like melting, softening, releasing, or opening, while at the same time feeling exquisitely sensitive, very tender, somewhat sad, and experiencing and acting on the genuine aspiration to help alleviate the suffering. Chögyam Trungpa, the renowned Tibetan teacher, described this quality as "the genuine heart of sadness" (1984, pp. 42–46).

Hopefully you have many moments of unalloyed compassion; but compassion is frequently mixed with conditioned emotional reactivity (avoiding and distancing from pain) and professional concerns and ambitions. Accepting mixed feelings and motives as being simply human can deepen compassion and motivate us to be vigilantly mindful and humble in our work with clients. Self-compassion that arises from mindfulness practice encourages us to befriend and even honor our emotional wounds and vulnerabilities. These are "seed" experiences that, with sufficient empathy, self-compassion, and nurturing, can grow into deep sources of empathy, compassion, and healing for our clients as well.

Being With, Without Fixing

Years ago, when I was a graduate social work intern in psychotherapy training, most everyone in my training setting would have understood the importance of just being with a client's distress without trying to get rid of or fix it, and how important it was for therapists to be comfortable in that role. I trained in the outpatient clinic of a large, urban medical school's department of psychiatry. The clinical social work training in the department was well-known for its biopsychosocial perspective. The city's psychoanalytic institute was also very much involved in the psychotherapy training program.

Training included understanding the role of medications; psychoeducational and supportive therapy; cognitive behavioral therapy; time-limited psychodynamic psychotherapy; intensive, long-term psychodynamic psychotherapy; and both psycho-educational and process-oriented interpersonal group therapy. As a social work graduate student, I had the opportunity to train in all psychotherapeutic treatment modalities. In my interview to get the internship, I remember being asked by the interviewer, then a respected psychoanalytic psychotherapist, who is now, among other things, in charge of the large dialectical behavior therapy (DBT) program at the clinic, "What really heals in psychotherapy?"

I hadn't expected the question and fumbled around for an answer. I mentioned changing patterns of dysfunctional thinking and behavior, learning new relationship skills, changing dysfunctional family and marital behavior patterns, and teaching stress-management and coping skills. I'm not sure what else I said. The interviewer waited patiently and let me stew for a while. I knew I was missing something important. Finally, she rescued me. "It's the relationship," she said, "the therapist-patient relationship."

Over the next eighteen months at the clinic, I learned to appreciate and trust the healing power of the therapeutic relationship and to allow it to unfold at its own pace. That frequently meant learning to just *be* with my clients and their problems without trying to *fix* them or impose solutions.

An article that I read in the *American Journal of Psychiatry* early in my career, titled "The Uses of Hopelessness" (Bennett & Bennett, 1984), made a tremendous impression on me that has lasted to this day. The writers described experiences of doing family therapy at a clinic in Harlem as part of their psychiatric residency training. They saw multiproblem families who often lacked basic necessities, such as food, shelter, jobs, income, and access to decent educational and medical care. The social environment of many of these, was families plagued by high crime rates, drug and alcohol abuse, and violence. Many also felt the sting of racism and discrimination on a daily basis.

The authors felt ridiculous offering family therapy in these circumstances. Nonetheless, they met with the families assigned to them and listened as the family members talked about their lives, despite being certain that, as family therapists, they had nothing relevant to offer. These inexperienced psychiatric residents refrained from offering simplistic advice or fixes, and from psychologizing the overwhelming social oppression. They also imagined that most of the families wouldn't return after the first session. To their surprise, however, many families did come back, again and again. Even more surprising, for many who came back, life improved. Not a lot, but some.

Over the years my understanding and respect for the uses of hopelessness has deepened. On a number of occasions I have worked with the victims of violent crime as well as the family members of murder victims. In almost every instance, I have been shocked by the horror of the experiences, humbled by the strength and resilience of the surviving family members, and rendered mute by the horror of the circumstances. All I could do was bear witness to the experiences of these clients, and be present with them. Trying to "fix it" or "make it better" would have been profoundly disrespectful, as well as unempathic. I learned that bearing witness in such circumstances is the only appropriate therapeutic and human response. I now appreciate the simple act of bearing witness as a powerful, transformative therapeutic practice (Glassman, 1998).

In acceptance and commitment therapy (ACT), there is a moment called "creative hopelessness," when the client recognizes that all prior attempts to solve the problem (as understood by the client) have failed (Hayes et al., 2003, pp. 87–114). In ACT this is understood as a very fertile moment full of creative potential—thus its name. The patient recognizes the utter failure of solutions attempted in the past and is more open than ever before to accept a radically different perspective. Almost always, the problem is not what the client thought it was, and all along tried to avoid, but rather the experiential avoidance itself, along with all of the attendant anxiety and linguistic and cognitive traps that kept the "problem" system in place.

112

I now understand that surrendering to hopelessness, and letting go of hope, fear, remorse and regret, is simply a requirement for being fully present. "Hopelessness" in this sense doesn't imply despair. It isn't a negative experience. It simply means letting go of hope that either the present moment or past moments will ever be any different than they already are; it means remaining hopeless about the next moment because we have committed ourselves fully and completely to being present to this moment, now. It is simple, but far from easy.

I am still loosely affiliated with the department of psychiatry as a volunteer clinical instructor, and not surprisingly it's quite a different place now than it was thirty years ago. The department is world renowned for its research in biopsychiatry and neuroscience, which is also the major emphasis in training. The psychoanalytic institute has less involvement with trainees, and psychotherapy training emphasizes time-limited, evidence-based treatments, such as cognitive behavioral therapy, interpersonal therapy, and DBT. Emphasis on the therapeutic relationship seems to have diminished in the mainstream mental health professions generally, except in common factors research (Duncan et al., 2010), and clinically in the contemporary psychoanalytic, relational therapy, and attachment theory communities.

With increased pressure to produce quick, lasting, verifiable results and insistence on "evidence-based treatments" (ironic, since the therapist is the treatment as much as the procedures and the protocols), we seem far less comfortable just being with our clients' suffering, without actively doing something to try to get rid of it or fix it. For a wonderful story about this dynamic, see Segal, Williams, and Teasdale (2002, pp. 54–63). While under pressure of a mandate to develop a new, cost-effective cognitive behavioral treatment to prevent depressive relapse, the authors describe their personal odyssey as traditional problem-solving-oriented, cognitive behavioral therapists and clinical researchers who discover the healing power of mindfulness (particularly allowing/letting be as opposed to actively fixing) as a way to alleviate emotional distress

Optimal Responsiveness

"Optimal responsiveness" is a phrase that was coined by contemporary psychoanalyst, and intersubjectivity and relational theorist, Howard Bacal (1998, 2011). On its face, optimal responsiveness sounds simple: the therapist responds in whatever way is optimal for the specific client in the specific moment. But who decides what is optimal for the client? "Optimal" based on what criteria? According to whom?

What made Bacal's approach so unusual is how it embodied his primary commitment to his clients as unique individuals, rather than to a particular theory or technique. Bacal believed that clients could (on the whole) be trusted to use the therapist and the therapeutic relationship in the ways they specifically needed to remediate the symptoms and issues that led them to seek treatment, so long as the therapist made herself available to be used within the environment of a therapeutic relationship that felt safe to the client.

Optimal responsiveness from this perspective meant responding to individual clients in whatever manner gave them the needed psychological resources and helped them feel safe enough to move toward greater growth, development, mastery, and, more immediately, vitality and aliveness in each moment. Although the possibility of optimal responsiveness was informed by intersubjectivity theory, the practice itself was less so. I explain the mode of action of optimal responsiveness below.

Through a radically decentered, exquisitely sensitive attunement, the therapist brings mindful inquiry to bear on the intersubjective field of the therapeutic relationship. The therapist places the client's inner experience, both silently through empathic attunement and aloud through empathic and appreciative inquiry and dialogue, in the foreground of awareness. The inquiry is driven by two simple questions: What's happening right now (with the client and in the therapeutic relationship)? What's needed right now (for the client and in the therapeutic relationship)?

Optimal responsiveness is the capacity to respond appropriately and skillfully in each moment in the context of these two questions. Besides refined attunement and exquisite sensitivity, optimal responsiveness requires the therapist's trust and confidence in the power of mindfulness. If you can just get out of your own way, let go of trying, and allow yourself to be fully present, awake, and aware, the moment itself will evoke the optimal response.

In Buddhist psychology, the corollary to optimal responsiveness is the concept of *skillful means*. Skillful means originally referred to the hundreds of different ways that the Buddha taught the Dharma: customizing the teaching for the recipient, and the specific situation and context, with the intention of optimizing the power of the teaching to heal or liberate the listener from suffering (Conze, 1993).

Although skillful means is still used specifically in reference to teaching Dharma, it is now used in Buddhist circles in a more general sense as well. It refers to the benefits of creatively customizing or adapting the techniques, methods, and skills used in teaching, therapy, or other interactions with people in order to respond with the greatest wisdom, compassion, and efficacy for whatever the situation requires. Optimal responsiveness is always relationship- and context-dependent.

In teaching mindfulness, as in psychotherapy generally, optimal responsiveness, or skillful means, is a very important skill. Our students and clients have unique personalities, predispositions, sensibilities, and life histories. Their presenting complaints, needs, and treatment goals vary. In addition, we all share the common desires to be safe, happy, peaceful, and free.

Optimal responsiveness addresses both the unique and shared needs and desires of our clients. It is a manifestation of the intrinsic freshness and infinite creativity of mindfulness. Since every moment arises as a unique combination of causes and conditions, what constitutes skillful response in and to each moment is also unique. Conceptually, optimal responsiveness functions as an overarching, orienting factor for incorporating mindfulness in psychotherapy; as a skill and inner capacity that the therapist develops through all facets of his or her own meditation practice; and as a way of thinking about the practice of embodying mindfulness in each moment of psychotherapy.

Although many of the formal mindfulness-based interventions are manualized and highly structured, the experience of teaching mindfulness, especially in mindfulness-based stress reduction or mindfulness-based cognitive therapy, is more like jazz improvisation. Although there is an underlying chord structure and rhythm in jazz, these serve mostly as a foundation or scaffolding upon which to improvise, responding to the unique configuration of tone and rhythm in each moment. Improvisation is what makes the music come alive. My personal experience of teaching structured mindfulness-based groups and doing mindfulness-informed psychotherapy supports this view. The healing power of the interventions comes alive in the creative response of the therapist in each moment of the therapeutic relationship.

Self-Care

The therapist's discipline of mindfulness practice is central to therapist self-care in a number of ways. Most obviously, mindfulness is a powerful method of tending to your mind-body process, not only your capacity for mindfulness but also in the more general sense of caring for your health and well-being. I use the word "tend" very deliberately because of its relationship to "tender," which evokes gentleness, kindness, sensitivity, compassion, valuing, and even love. Mindful awareness is strongly informed by these qualities of tenderness.

In your own discipline of meditation practice, you are invited to be present to yourself with these same qualities of tenderness. Through your meditation practice you can nourish and replenish yourself by "resting tenderly," in an awareness characterized by gentleness, kindness, sensitivity, self-compassion, self-valuing, and love. This is nothing special, certainly not in the sense that you are different or more deserving or better than anyone else. It is simply an acknowledgment of your basic goodness as a human being (Trungpa, 1984).

Doing therapy is not an easy job. It is emotionally demanding, and it can be depleting. An established routine of self-care is essential, for the sake of your emotional and physical well-being and your professional satisfaction and longevity. Mindfulness practice can become the foundation for ongoing self-care. Ultimately, self-care is a reflection of your experience of your own basic goodness. I laugh as I write this, reminded of the saying "We teach what we need to learn."

There is a story I have heard many times about an incident that occurred at a meeting between the Dalai Lama and a group of Western Buddhist teachers and monks; they were discussing the unique challenges of teaching the Dharma in the West. *Dharma* is a Sanskrit word that has acquired multiple meanings, including "the way things are"; the law" or "lawfulness of how life works"; "the practice path" or "way of life," recommended by the Buddha based on his discoveries about how to end suffering; and the Buddha's teachings about the prior three meanings.

One of the teachers asked the Dalai Lama how to deal with the suffering of low self-esteem and self-hatred, which seemed fairly commonplace among her students. The Dalai Lama appeared puzzled, and he turned to his translator for assistance. It took a while for the translator to convey the concepts of low self-esteem and self-hatred.

When the Dalai Lama finally understood, he began to cry. He couldn't imagine that fellow human beings could have such low opinions of and so little compassion for themselves, phenomena quite unheard of in Tibetan culture. The idea that millions of fellow human beings actually felt that way moved him to tears.

From the perspective of mindfulness practice, human beings are basically good. This is not a Pollyannaish refusal to see the evil and violence in the world. Nor is it a denial of the genocidal nightmare that was the human experience in the twentieth century—and could easily be repeated to include the natural world in the twenty-first century if we fail to fundamentally change our ways. Nor is it denial of the greed, injustice, selfishness, hatred, and ignorance that permeate Western culture. This perspective is simply the empirical discovery through mindfulness meditation practice that it is not selfishness, hatred, fear, and violence that most strongly define who we are as a species, but rather the higher angels of our nature.

I once heard Peter Matthiessen, a Pulitzer Prize–winning novelist and nature writer who was also a Zen *roshi*, or master, give a keynote address to a group of several thousand people attending a conference on Buddhism in America. Matthiessen had just returned the day before from a five-day Zen *sesshin*, or intensive mindfulness meditation retreat, led by Roshi Bernie Glassman for about 150 people from Poland, Germany, Israel, the United States, Vietnam, and many other countries. The retreat was at the Auschwitz concentration camp, in Poland, inside the barbed-wire perimeter. For a few days the participants literally meditated inside one of the gas chambers in Birkenau, the extermination facility at Auschwitz. The purpose of the sesshin was for the participants to personally bear witness to what had happened there, without any expectations about what might happen as a result.

It was also the occasion for conferring the title of Zen priest on Claude Thomas, a Vietnam War veteran who, at age seventeen, began his military career as a helicopter door-gunner protecting troops dropped into combat zones and providing cover fire while airlifting returning combat troops, the wounded, and the dead. Thomas was himself wounded several times. The last wound ended his military career. Thomas figures that he alone personally killed several hundred people during his seven months in Vietnam.

Like thousands of other Vietnam veterans, he was unable to adjust to civilian life upon returning home. He got into drugs and alcohol and lived on the street for several years. Zen practice, both through communities connected with Thich Nhat Hanh and Bernie Glassman, helped Thomas get back on his feet.

When Matthiessen told the assembled crowd where he had been just a few days before, a profound silence enveloped the hall. Matthiessen was a physically impressive man, well over six feet tall with the lean, muscular frame of a mountain climber; angular features; and a full head of curly gray hair. But most striking were his face and eyes. When he spoke to us that day his face seemed illuminated, and I could see, even from the back of the room, that his eyes were burning fiercely.

He spoke a little about his experiences at Auschwitz: the horror, the grief, and the incomprehensibility of the place. Mostly, though, he spoke about what he had learned, which he summarized in two sentences at the end of his talk. Matthiessen said, and I paraphrase, "I learned beyond a shadow of doubt that we are animals. And I learned that we are more than animals."

If we are mindful, basic goodness (Trungpa, 1984) can be discovered even in the most horrific and dehumanizing contexts. Even in Auschwitz inmates shared their last scraps of bread and cared for one another (see Frankl, 2006). Some even managed to organize a resistance movement, and against all odds acquired explosives to blow up one of the crematoria and rifles to stage an armed revolt against their SS captors.

Seeing basic goodness in others helps us to see it in ourselves, and vice versa. Remembering our basic goodness can be a powerful motivator for us to take better care of ourselves. When you notice that your self-care has faltered, it might help to reflect on your basic goodness.

Inner Capacities

Inner capacities are emotional and psychological strengths and inner resources that are often innate but can also be cultivated and strengthened through intentional practice. These strengths and inner resources underlie, support, and potentiate the mindfulness skills described above.

Distress Tolerance and Stress Resilience

Emotional resilience in the face of crisis and the capacity to tolerate emotional distress are basic components of healthy, adaptive coping. These capacities are often poorly developed in clients who come to us for treatment. As therapists the requirements of our work challenge us to develop and strengthen our own capacities for resilience and distress tolerance; we need to be fully present with our clients, remaining empathically attuned and connected when they are in great distress, and we need to relate skillfully to the emotional demands of clinical practice all the time.

Distress tolerance and stress resilience are functions of realistic perspectives and attitudes about life (to be discussed at greater length in the coming sections) and specific, concrete psychological skills. We come by these capacities naturally, to a greater or lesser extent, by genetic disposition and socialization. All of us, however, can cultivate and strengthen these capacities through an ongoing meditation practice discipline.

I think of *distress tolerance* as the capacity to deploy the inner capacities and skills developed through mindfulness practice in order to cope with distress and crisis. *Resilience* refers to the same inner skills and capacities that have become so strongly embodied through an ongoing discipline of meditation practice that they are default responses to crisis and challenge.

Specific capacities include the ability and "willingness" (the term favored in acceptance and commitment therapy) to be fully present with unpleasant emotions and experience (described as "turning toward the difficult" in mindfulness-based cognitive therapy), often utilizing mindful breathing to make space for the distressing experience and to help yourself let go of resistance; the capacity to decenter and disidentify from distress, altering your relationship to distress so it no longer defines you; the capacity for healthy self-soothing, involving the ability to comfort yourself and be comforted by others in the face of grief, disappointment, hurt, and narcissistic injury; and the capacity to self-regulate emotions so you don't inadvertently intensify distress through unskillful attempts to avoid or get rid of it.

117

Affect Tolerance

Affect tolerance is similar to distress tolerance, except it is focused on the capacity to be fully present with intense affect and emotion, both your own and that of others. For therapists, strong affect tolerance is crucial. Our clients come to us almost universally because of painful affects and emotions that have become problematic or symptomatic because they have avoided them in dysfunctional ways. I don't mean to dismiss the role of genetics and biochemistry; these simply predispose some clients to a higher likelihood of certain kinds of painful affects or emotions (examples include major depression, bipolar disorder, and panic disorder) and greater challenges in coping.

If you as a therapist fear intense affect and emotion and seek to avoid them, your clients will not feel safe with you. They will consciously or unconsciously sense your discomfort and feel the need to protect you as well as themselves from their feelings. It becomes impossible to establish a working relationship in such a scenario, and therapy can't happen.

Mindfulness practice strengthens affect tolerance in the same ways it strengthens distress tolerance. In addition, as you again and again turn toward painful emotions and affects in your own formal meditation practice, simply allowing the emotions to be present without trying to avoid, get rid of, or fix them, you will gain confidence from your own experience that willingly being present with strong affect and emotion is actually less distressing than avoiding or resisting them. Mindfully turning toward and working skillfully with physical discomfort and pain or emotional distress in the sitting meditation (through acceptance and willingness) is a good way to develop tolerance. Marsha Linehan (1993b) has also developed mindfulness-informed cognitive-behavioral exercises to increase distress and affect tolerance.

Equanimity

Equanimity is stability, composure, and ease in the midst of life's storms. It's the capacity to experience life's inevitable difficulty and pain while remaining fundamentally unperturbed, and without being thrown off balance. True equanimity doesn't require that life be kept at a distance. From the perspective of mindfulness practice, equanimity isn't the product of circumstances being "just so." Rather, it's an unshakable sense of stability and ease that comes from the inside out, and isn't contingent on external circumstance.

I recognize that I have painted a rather idealized picture of equanimity. Like any other mind state, equanimity comes and goes, and waxes and wanes. Nonetheless, your equanimity as a therapist, to whatever degree you experience it, is profoundly important for both you and your clients.

For the therapist, equanimity is the capacity to stay empathically attuned and connected to your clients even in their most difficult moments. It allows you to maintain emotional stability and balance, and to stay present and connected, while still letting yourself be genuinely touched by your clients' pain, perhaps at times even shaken to the core by some tragic revelation: a molestation; a rape; a murder; the death of a child, partner, or spouse; the trauma of war; the violence of racism and sexism; and the less dramatic but still painful losses and disappointments that touch us all at different points in our lives. Equanimity allows us as therapists to keep our hearts open and to respond compassionately without literally drowning in our clients' pain or withdrawing or emotionally shutting down.

Equanimity incorporates the personal dimension of pain and tragedy, including yours and mine, in the much larger and more spacious context and perspective of life as a whole. Putting life into this perspective isn't meant to be a way to intellectualize or dissociate from personal pain; instead it helps us experience the connection to "life as a whole" as support; as a source of stability and strength; and as a way to hold the raw, personal experience of rage or grief in a more spacious awareness—as a human experience—so in the moment it feels less overwhelming.

When my oldest son, Zack, was a young boy he ran through a plate-glass door at a party and suffered severe lacerations, some of which were quite deep and required surgical repair. At the emergency room, Zack was examined and given sedatives and painkillers; then the physician proceeded to stitch him up, layer by layer. Even with sedation and anesthesia, it was very painful. I stood by his side feeling helpless, wishing it were me and not him on the table.

Just then I had a moment of recognition and insight. *This is how it feels to love your child and not be able to alleviate his or her pain.* In that moment I felt a kinship with the millions of parents around the world having similar experiences. I felt connected to the human experience in a way I had never before experienced. I also realized how fortunate we were to live in a city with a state-of-the-art children's hospital. I felt compassion for the children and parents who were dealing with much more serious injuries and illness and lacked access to good medical care.

This experience happened while I stood right next to Zack's gurney, holding his one uncut hand and being as present as I could be. The experience of connection to parents of injured children around the world and down through the ages was not distancing or distracting. Rather it was an expansion into a more spacious awareness. The expanded, more spacious perspective reestablished a sense of equanimity. It allowed me to be more present with Zack, even though my heart still ached for him, and all the other hurting children and their parents.

Joy and Humor

If a mindfulness-based stress reduction course, or a psychotherapy session informed by mindfulness, is on track and working well, the atmosphere is often light and humorous, even joyful, despite the client or class participants experiencing emotional or physical distress. It is a relief not to feel the need to hide or maintain a superficial façade of well-being and composure. It feels good to be able to connect genuinely with yourself as well as others. It is reassuring to know that human minds are tragicomically similar. What makes you special is not your psychopathology. You are special because of the never-to-be-repeated configuration of the human condition that you manifest as your own unique, creative genius.

It is comforting to understand that everyone suffers and struggles in life. You have your own type and measure of suffering, but it doesn't mean that there is anything wrong with you. Suffering just means you're human. That's not to say that you can't alleviate suffering. Rather, when you learn that pain is an inevitable part of life and discover how to experience and relate to it skillfully, it becomes possible to experience life's unavoidable pain without the additional suffering that results from attempts to resist or avoid it. You might even feel touched and inspired as you identify with the courage and determination shown by many millions just trying to get through their days. Although the perspectives described above can be developed through mindfulness meditation practice, they also fit the description of the curative factors in group therapy described by Yalom (1975, pp. 3–18).

The role of group effects in mindfulness-based treatment outcomes is an area needing further research. I have observed the same lightening up in psychodynamic therapy groups that I have seen in mindfulness-based treatment for groups, individuals, and couples. In light of Yalom's belief that nonspecific curative group effects are existential in nature, it makes sense that the lightening-up effect would be similar in psychodynamic, interpersonal therapy groups and the individual, couples, and group modalities of mindfulness-based treatments.

Mindfulness practice cultivates the capacity to open your heart fully to the intrinsic sadness and absurdity of life—without getting down about it—by disidentifying from the stories you tell yourself about your life, and life in general, and by anchoring awareness in the felt experience of the present moment. By fully inhabiting the present moment, we create the capacity for joy. In the fullness of the present moment, there is no past or future, there are no stories, there is only now. To paraphrase Charlotte Joko Beck (1993, p. 232), joy is the present moment with nothing added.

Mindfulness practice allows the therapist to develop the capacity to laugh at himself and to find the humor in the therapeutic situation. As therapy proceeds, clients are increasingly able to find humor in their own situations as well, an important element in the general lightening up that mindfulness practice seems to facilitate in therapy; lightening up is also an indicator that therapy is working. Finally, in developing a more nuanced and refined capacity for experiencing, mindfulness helps clients to connect with, and not miss, the moments of relative ease or joy—moments within experiences of overall pain or distress.

Authenticity and Genuineness

Think of a time when you were the focus of 100 percent complete, undivided, unconditionally loving and accepting attention from someone who palpably embodied a sense of peace, calm, and effortless ease as well as a powerful presence. What did it feel like to be the focus of that person's authentic care and concern, to experience that they had no other agenda than to be present with you, to know you and be known by you, moment by moment? Did you feel moved? Understood? Inspired? Did you feel encouraged to be more authentic and present as well?

Warmth

Warmth is the natural emanation of an unguarded, open heart. As a referent, think of the unalloyed, exuberant joy of a happy toddler. Warmth is our natural, energetic, and loving response to the world, undaunted by hurt or fear.

Patience

In *Full Catastrophe Living*, Jon Kabat-Zinn describes *patience* as "a form of wisdom." Patience expresses our understanding and acceptance of the fact that "sometimes things must unfold in their own time" (2013, p. 23). Patience as a form of wisdom in psychotherapy points to the importance of the therapist's respect for and attunement to process, and the understanding that each client's process, as well as that of each therapist-client dyad, is unique.

Cognitive Flexibility

Cognitive flexibility refers to the ability to step outside of automatic thoughts and to view them as events in awareness without getting caught up in their semantic content, allowing the freedom for creative responses. Steven Hayes, the developer of acceptance and commitment therapy, refers to this process as *cognitive defusion*, or "separating thoughts from their referents" (Hayes & Smith, 2005, pp. 70–86). Such cognitive flexibility requires understanding that thoughts are not facts, and that clinging to unworkable control strategies, such as experiential avoidance, is usually the result of some form of *cognitive fusion*, or not being able to separate thoughts from their referents.

Attitudes

Attitudes are beliefs or cognitive or emotional predispositions that inform perception and behavior.

Nonjudging

Often we relate and react more to our habitual, conditioned judgments about life than to life itself. How often do you miss out on experiencing the present moment because you're caught up in conditioned, automatic thoughts about the past or future—worrying, regretting, doubting, and, in particular, judging and criticizing?

When automatic thoughts are negative, judgmental, and self-critical, as is most often the case, not only do we miss out on the present moment, but our perception is distorted by self-criticism and judgment. Reactions to such perceptual and cognitive distortions can be debilitating, and in the long term they can cause or contribute to symptom formation and illness, both psychiatric and physical.

If, instead, we receive the present moment with an openhearted, nonjudging awareness, we are more likely to perceive it clearly and to respond skillfully in the next moment. Since conditioned, reactive judging is always about the past or the future, by anchoring awareness in the present moment we are less likely to be caught up in conditioned judgments based on preconceived prejudices and biases, anger and regret about the past, or fear and worry about the future.

Practicing nonjudging lets us perceive the present moment clearly. Then we are more likely to respond with skill and creativity to present-moment circumstances, whatever they are, and to more effectively navigate life's inevitable pain, difficulty, and hardship. If you pay close attention to the habitual discursive chatter of the mind, you may notice how ubiquitous and automatic judging is. It is the automatic default reaction to most experience—I like it or don't like it; it's good or bad, right or wrong, better or worse.

Most automatic judgments are based on whether experiences in the moment are physically or emotionally pleasant or unpleasant, which in turn is based on memory and conditioning from past sensory, cognitive, and emotional experiences that are similar. Automatic judging is conditioned and instinctual, anchored in the evolutionary survival adaptation of fight-flight-freeze reactivity.

The sympathetic nervous system activation, or fight-flight-freeze reactivity, happens faster than the cortex's ability to process potential threat data and decide on the reality of the threat. Often it happens so fast that we experience the cause of stress reactivity and emotional or physical distress more in retrospect, sometimes only in contrast to the relaxation that ensues when stress reactivity abates.

For most of us, automatic judging becomes habitual. Frequently it becomes so pervasive and unconscious that we don't even notice it. Imagine having your very own panel of political pundits inhabiting your awareness, making comments and passing judgment on your every action, perception, thought, experience, and behavior, each with his or own ideological agenda. Though uninvited and unwanted, they are loud and insistent.

Ultimately we may begin to relate more to our habitual, reactive judgments about life than to direct experience of life itself. This leaves us disconnected from what's actually happening in our lives and in a precarious position from which to respond to life's challenges skillfully and effectively.

Nonjudging is an attitude, as well as a skill, that allows us to see clearly what's happening in each moment, without the distortions caused by reactive judgments of right or wrong, good or bad. Instead of judging, we can learn to consciously substitute an attitude of unconditional friendliness and acceptance toward each moment. Then when we notice reactive judging happening, we just observe it with friendly interest and curiosity, like we would anything else that arises in awareness, without judging the judging.

Exercise 7.2: Cultivating Nonjudging Awareness

1. Ironically, one of the best ways to cultivate nonjudging awareness is to be mindful of reactive, automatic judging when it arises without identifying with it. In practical terms, this means catching yourself when you are already caught up in judgmental reactivity, identifying with the content and story line of the judging as true, and responding in one of two ways: either shifting awareness to noticing judging as simply a cognitive event, without identifying with its content—what in acceptance and commitment therapy is called "having a thought without buying a thought" (Hayes & Smith, 2005, p. 69)—or redirecting awareness to a focus on breathing or other body sensations. In either case, you are reconnecting with the direct experience of the present moment.

2. As you continue to practice mindfulness of judging, it might be helpful to use mental noting to stay focused on judging as an event, to avoid getting caught up again in the content or story line of the judging.

3. Remember that mental noting is like adding a silent verbal label in the background of the field of awareness that describes the focal object. Mental noting helps to aim awareness at the focal object, whatever it is in each moment. Keep the words simple and impersonal (for example, *This is judging*, or *Judging, judging*, or *Judging is happening*).

4. Noticing judging as an event and disidentifying from the content of a judgmental thought is in and of itself a very powerful therapeutic strategy. However, there is much more to learn, if you're so inclined. After a few minutes of simply noticing judging happening, begin to notice that most moments have a tone or flavor, either *pleasant* or *unpleasant*. (Some moments have a *neutral* tone, but these are more difficult to notice, so we begin with pleasant and unpleasant.) Use mental noting to label the pleasant moments *pleasant* and the unpleasant moments *unpleasant*. Without judging, be aware of impulses to label pleasant moments *good* and unpleasant moments *bad*.

5. You may notice bracing or stiffening against unpleasant sensations, as if you are trying to get rid of or resist them. Perhaps you notice tightening around or straining toward pleasant sensations, as if you are trying to hold on to or grasp them.

6. These sensations are often indicators that reactive judging is happening. We instinctually judge unpleasant sensations and emotions as bad, and tend to stiffen or brace against them. Similarly, we instinctually judge pleasant sensations and emotions as good, and we tend to grasp for and cling to them.

7. Continue to notice the quality or flavor of *pleasant* or *unpleasant* sensations in each moment. Notice bracing against unpleasant and clinging to pleasant without judging or trying to fix. Simply be with the clinging or pushing away moment by moment, silently asking yourself *What is this? What's happening?* Noticing the pleasant or unpleasant flavor of each moment; the reactive tensing,

stiffening, and bracing against unpleasant and reaching for, grasping at, and clinging to pleasant. Just noticing with curiosity and interest, and without judging the judging.

8. What, if anything, do you notice about the relationship between judging thoughts and physical reactions and sensations?

Nonstriving

Our culture celebrates and rewards relentless striving. "Nonstriving" may sound like being lazy, just cruising, or doing the minimum. But "nonstriving" doesn't really refer to doing or not doing. It is more an attitude or mode of mind than a measure of action.

Nonstriving refers to letting go of focus on goals and agendas in the present moment—letting go of trying to accomplish something, or get somewhere. In fact, it means letting go of *trying*. Instead, we experience *nontrying*, or nonstriving. We move out of doing mode of mind into being mode of mind. You can still be very productive within an attitude of nonstriving. The determining factor is whether you are showing up and engaging fully with each moment as it arises, or focusing on achieving a future goal and missing the moment you are in. An attitude of nonstriving lets you experience ease and stillness in the midst of doing. In contemporary psychology, this is called "flow" (Csikszentmihalyi, 1990).

Pop culture often associates mindfulness meditation with Buddhism, Taoism, and other Asian spiritual traditions. But all major world religious traditions feature and venerate mindfulness practice. In the Abrahamic traditions of Judaism, Christianity, and Islam, the central mindfulness practice is the Sabbath. Beyond the ritual observance, the spirit of the Sabbath is ceasing from striving, and delighting in just being (Heschel, 1951; Muller, 2000). Remember the Sabbath, the fourth of the Ten Commandments, was clearly considered as important as don't murder, don't steal, don't lie, don't covet, and so on.

A. J. Heschel, the great American Jewish scholar and mystic, described the Sabbath as its own unique dimension of time, different from conventional, linear time, which consists of past, present, and future. The Sabbath, which Heschel described as the experience of eternal time, or sacred time, is accessed experientially through the complete cessation of striving, and instead just being present. Anger and fear, the emotions of fight-flight-freeze reactivity, fall away, being dependent on past (memory) and future (apprehension or anticipation). The spirit of the Sabbath involves stepping outside of linear time and resting in the eternal now of the present moment.

I find it useful to think of mindfulness as Sabbath mind. Particularly in Western cultures, it reinforces the universality and importance of mindfulness as a way of being and relating. I have found it particularly helpful as a way to frame mindfulness that feels safe and nonthreatening for devout Christians, Jews, and Muslims who worry that mindfulness may be a Buddhist or Eastern religious practice and go against their religious beliefs.

Beginner's Mind

Beginner's mind (Suzuki, 1996, pp. 21–22), or what Korean Zen master Seung Sahn called "don't know mind" (Mitchell, 1994, pp. 3, 76–78), is the attitude of experiencing each moment as if for the first time, which, of course, is actually true, since each moment is brand-new and has never before happened. Beginner's mind requires shifting out of doing mode of mind into the mode of just being without expectation or agenda, receiving the moment with an enthusiastic interest and curiosity that comes from not knowing, and a genuine desire and willingness to know the moment by allowing it to reveal itself to us as experience.

Our clinical training prepares us to evaluate and respond to our clients' symptoms and suffering in a manner that might seem the antithesis of beginner's mind—that is, with powerful, organizing theoretical frameworks and filters and preconceived contextual-analytical schemes that guide intervention and treatment. If you've had good training, you know how important and useful a good theory can be if it's understood and used wisely. At other times, however, even good theories can prevent us from genuinely seeing and knowing the suffering human beings with whom we sit in our therapy offices.

Our clients come to us to alleviate pain and distress. Where would we begin without an initial, orienting theoretical understanding and frame of reference? Particularly in difficult or confusing moments in therapy, when you aren't sure what's happening or how to respond, you can fall back on theoretical understanding and empirically derived knowledge for clarification and direction. However, as clinicians, we need to understand not only the value but also the limitations of both theory and evidence-based clinical knowledge, and we also need to understand that scientific *knowledge* is not the same as "truth" or "wisdom."

Our theories constrain while they empower, defining what constitutes knowledge and thereby setting limits on what's considered interesting or even knowable. And since most clinical theory, and all scientific evidence-based clinical knowledge, reinscribes the paradigm within which it was created, it casts an ever-larger shadow over what can be known thereafter. As a colleague of mine, Steve Pashko, was fond of saying, "Even the best solutions have only limited life spans before they become hindrances."

Beginner's mind complements the more conventional modes of knowing in psychotherapy that are informed by theory and scientific, empirical research. It offers a way to be fully, authentically present without preconceived theoretical frameworks or evidence-based interpretive schemes and agendas for intervention. As a former clinical supervisor and highly respected, senior clinician once said to me, "Our theories are there for us if we get lost or confused, but beyond that they often get in the way" (Sanford Shapiro, personal communication). Clinical practice anchored in but not bound by theory requires that therapists be comfortable and flexible enough to move fluidly between doing mode of mind anchored in theory and being mode of mind grounded in mindfulness and the power of presence. It also requires an experientially grounded trust that the therapeutic relationship and process can be healing in and of themselves.

Beginner's mind in psychotherapy ultimately requires trust and confidence in the capacity for optimal responsiveness, which can only be developed through the therapist's repeated positive experience with optimal responsiveness in clinical practice, best had in the context of solid clinical training and supervision.

Appreciating the deeper implications of beginner's mind for optimal responsiveness in psychotherapy requires directly experiencing what acceptance and commitment therapy terms "self as context," or "contextual self." This is the radically decentered experience that beyond self-centered consciousness—which is based on memory and autobiographical narrative—there is just knowing, awareness, and presence without a *knower* (Epstein, 2008). We will explore this more deeply in chapter 10.

Trust and Confidence

As your practice of mindfulness grows stronger and deepens, you will find that your trust in the practice of mindfulness, and your confidence in your capacity to bring mindfulness to bear in the moment, also grows. Trust and confidence in the practice don't grow in an upward, linear progression. More than likely there will be a series of ups and downs: growth spurts and plateaus; breakthroughs followed by reversals; and moments of frustration, discouragement, and doubt as well as insight, appreciation, and gratitude.

If you continue to meditate over a number of years, you may begin to settle into a discipline and rhythm of practice that is integrally woven into the fabric of your life. As you realize that you always already had what you sought to attain, and where you wanted to get to was exactly where you have always been, you may also come to accept that there truly is nothing to attain and nowhere to get to with the meditation. You may notice yourself holding the experiential ups and downs of practice with a lighter touch and with greater acceptance, equanimity, and ease.

Unconditional Friendliness

Couples and family therapists new to the field commonly make the mistake of taking a stance of impartiality in their attitudes toward and interactions with the participating partners and family members. Rather than being impartial, I have found a stance of *multidirectional partiality* (Boszormenyi-Nagy, 1987), or being equally partial to each partner or family member, essential for creating a safe, facilitative environment for therapy. Multidirectional partiality, in family and couples therapy, parallels in mindfulness practice the *unconditional friendliness* with which we receive each moment of experience and every element of each moment.

Interest and Curiosity

The energy and effort that drive concentration in mindfulness meditation are not the conventional energy and effort of straining and striving, but rather the energy and effort of curiosity, interest, and wonder, which are self-generating and effortless. From the perspective of mindful awareness, each moment of human experience is utterly unique and precious. If we miss one, it's gone forever. In addition, each of us has only a finite number of moments to be alive. Any moment could be your last. You know for certain that one will be. You just don't know which one.

How is it possible then, if you really pay attention, to not be enthusiastic about and fascinated by each moment? Only the taken-for-grantedness of life allows for boredom, which is surely a sign of not paying close attention. A client in one of my mindfulness-based stress reduction courses, who suffered from chronic-pain syndrome, slipped me a note card as a way of thanks, on the last day of class, with the following written on it: "If you could open your heart fully to each moment of your life, your pain would seem no less wondrous than your joy."

In a similar vein the famous physician and essayist Lewis Thomas wrote the following: "Statistically, the probability of any one of us being here is so small that you'd think the mere fact of existing would keep us all in a contented dazzlement of surprise" (1974, p. 141). Reconnecting with curiosity, interest, and the sense of wonder can be as simple as being mindful of the sensations of breathing or noticing how the morning sunlight illuminates the dust motes dancing in the windowpane.

Interest and curiosity increase energy and concentration. Energy and concentration increase mindfulness. Mindfulness increases interest and curiosity. And so on. Once you get going in the right direction, mindfulness is a positive feedback loop.

Energy and concentration can also give rise to bliss and joy. The trick is to enjoy the bliss and joy (if they happen) while being vigilantly mindful, not allowing yourself to get attached, caught up in, or seduced by bliss or joy, and understanding that like everything else, bliss and joy come and go. Receive the experiences of bliss and joy (just like any other experience) with an open heart, without judging or striving, and let them go with appreciation and gratitude when they depart. If instead you attempt to hold on to bliss and joy (or any experience for that matter) or try to get them back once they are gone, I can promise you it won't be fun.

Letting Go

Perhaps in your own meditation practice you are beginning to notice the natural tendency to avoid, brace against, or push away unpleasant experiences and to reach after, grasp, and attempt to cling to pleasant experiences. This, once again, is an evolutionary adaptation. Generally, pleasant sensations and experiences were associated with survival and procreation—eating nourishing food, sex, dominance, high status, and so on. It made sense to reactively grasp and cling. Unpleasant sensations and experiences, such as bitter tastes, bad smells, fear, physical pain, and low status, were associated with threats to survival and procreation. It made sense to avoid and resist.

Now social evolution has far outpaced biological evolution, and language further complicates the whole mess (Hayes et al., 2003, pp. 26–44, 51–76). Our instinctual tendencies to grasp and cling to pleasant experiences and to brace against and avoid unpleasant experiences are no longer so adaptive. They tend to create adventitious suffering when mobilized in situations where there is no survival imperative.

Consider Alison, a woman whom I had seen in successful therapy for a number of years at the beginning of my career; I stopped working with her when she and her husband moved out of the area. She called me recently after many years without contact, requesting a session when she was in town to see family. In the session, Alison, now forty-seven, told me that her husband of twenty-five years had died not quite two years earlier of sudden cardiac arrest. He had had no prior symptoms and had appeared to be in excellent shape. Alison was devastated. She had tried to date about a year after his death, but mostly she had just talked about her deceased husband. She also felt reclusive, had withdrawn some from family and friends, and was still frequently tearful.

Fortunately, I knew Alison well from her past therapy. She tended to be very impatient with painful emotions. She had significantly reinforced and strengthened her distress tolerance and emotion self-regulation capacities from what they had been at the beginning of our therapy sessions, but she still wanted to be done with painful emotions before they were done with her. Sadly this was also the case with Alison regarding the death of her husband.

Although Alison had a history of depression, and there did seem to be bereavement complications related to a mood disorder—for which I encouraged her to seek treatment when she returned home—mostly she was simply tired of grief, hurt, and loss and wanted to be done with them. Reality testing her expectations about grieving the loss of her husband of twenty-five years, giving her permission to grieve, and also encouraging her to push through her isolation in order to socialize more was really all that Alison needed.

For Alison, the pain of avoiding her grief was more severe than the pain of grieving, but the grief was too overwhelming for her to process on her own. Alison tried to avoid grieving by telling herself that she ought to be over it, which of course only made it worse. In addition, Alison needed and sought out the reliable empathic container that she had constructed for herself with me more than twenty years earlier. "I called you because you know me so well, and you know my heart," she told me.

Perspectives

Perspective designates more general points of view, often underlying attitudes and beliefs that inform and shape one's orientation toward perceiving and experiencing. The following statements represent some of the more important perspectives that can be developed through mindfulness practice.

Present Moment, Wonderful Moment.

"Present moment, wonderful moment," written by Thich Nhat Hanh, (1991, pp. 9–11), encapsulates the notion that the present moment is the only moment we can actually live and experience. As such, it affords both an anchor (connecting to present-moment experience is how we can ground ourselves) and a refuge (since anger and fear require memory and anticipation for their existence, they fall away in the present moment). Even more, being alive is itself precious, and the direct experience of aliveness is accessible only in the present moment.

Can't Change the Present Moment, only How We Respond.

The present moment has always already happened. This statement is worth repeating because understanding it is truly important. We cannot change the present moment or any prior moments. Railing against them is pointless and just creates suffering. How we respond to the present moment can change the next moment and all moments thereafter. This is true with regard to habitual, conditioned behaviors that cause us suffering as individuals as well as social injustice and other crises that cause suffering at a societal and global scale.

Neither Thoughts Nor Other Mental Formations Are Facts, Especially the Ones That Insist They Are.

Thoughts are not facts. Neither are emotions, moods, attitudes, or beliefs. Yet we tend to identify more strongly with thoughts and other mental formations than even with our own bodies and physical sensations. In acceptance and commitment therapy, this identification with thoughts is called *cognitive fusion*, and it is one of the primary drivers of psychological suffering. *Cognitive defusion*, or disidentification, is separating from thoughts as facts and instead recognizing them simply as events in awareness; it is essential for alleviating psychological suffering and, ultimately, societal suffering.

Change Is the Only Constant.

This is a restatement of what is called the first noble truth in Buddhist psychology. It essentially means that everything that comes into existence continuously changes, eventually dying, or ceasing, to be. This includes people, relationships, possessions, creatures, the Earth, and the universe itself. Understanding and embracing this truth is essential to living with ease. Grasping anything with the expectation that it won't change, and that it will endure forever, is the recipe for suffering.

Pain Is Inevitable in This Life. Suffering Is Optional.

Being mortal, we all age, get sick, and die. Ultimately, this means we lose everything in our lives that we cherish. This is the normative emotional and physical pain of life, and it cannot be avoided. Attempting to avoid it is a recipe for unnecessary suffering, that which is in addition to the unavoidable pain of life. If we are willing to embrace the unavoidable, normative pain of life, we don't also have to add the pain of suffering to the intrinsic pain. In Buddhist psychology there is a poignant metaphor in which a man is shot with an arrow, and in an effort to escape the pain of the first arrow he asks to be shot with a second arrow in the same spot. This is the classic example of how not accepting the inevitability of pain leads to adventitious suffering.

Reacting with Aversion to the Present Moment Leads to Suffering. Clinging to Present-Moment Pleasure or Happiness Leads to Suffering.

Reacting with aversion to the present moment leads to suffering. Clinging to present-moment pleasure or happiness leads to suffering. This perspective elaborates on how change is the only constant; that we can only change how we respond; and how, if we are willing to accept the inevitable pain of life, we don't have to suffer. Some moments are unpleasant, and our instinctual reaction to them is aversion and pushing away. Other moments are pleasant, and our instinctual reaction to them is desire and clinging. When we are mindful of both pleasant and unpleasant from a radically decentered perspective, without getting caught up in the content of experiencing, we can avoid, or free ourselves from, adventitious suffering.

Living in Ignorance, Denial, or Delusion Leads to Suffering.

If we remain unaware of pleasant and unpleasant moments and our automatic aversion or clinging to them, we are doomed to create unnecessary suffering for ourselves. Suffering is inevitable when we forget or deny that all moments are transient and we are seduced by the content or flavor of moments, grasping after pleasure and resisting unavoidable pain. So by trying to cling to pleasure, we often turn it into suffering; and in trying to avoid pain by resisting it and pushing it away, rather than simply letting it be, we turn it into greater suffering. See if you can think of a time when you found yourself caught up in such a cycle. Now recall a client or clients who were caught up in cycles of aversion to the unpleasant, or grasping after the pleasant.

Happiness Doesn't Come from Getting What You Want; It Comes from Nonwanting.

We live in a culture that glorifies consumption. We are told that happiness comes from getting what we want. For a while I taught mindfulness-based stress reduction in a very affluent community. In order to evoke an experiential understanding of the intrinsic happiness of nonwanting, and the intrinsic dissatisfaction and suffering of wanting, I would sometimes ask if anyone in the class had recently purchased a new car. Almost inevitably someone had, usually an expensive luxury car. Together we would carefully investigate and inquire into the emotional process and experience of purchasing the car: thinking about it, researching, shopping, deciding which car to buy, buying it, receiving the key, putting the key in the ignition, and driving the car off the lot.

We reflected on and inquired into each moment of the process in order to discover which moment was the happiest. Inevitably, it was the first moments of taking possession of the car, usually receiving the key and turning on the ignition.

Prior to that, the moments were a mixture of agitation, angst, and excitement, and following that moment were moments of concern about not wanting to scratch or dent the pristine body. The moment of receiving the key and turning on the ignition was a great relief. It was a moment of nonwanting. Reflect on the happiest moments of your own life. Notice if they also embody this quality of nonwanting, of being enough just as they are. If we receive and embrace each moment however it presents itself, happiness and ease cease to be contingent on circumstance.

Summary

In this chapter we explored the therapist's mindfulness practice as a set of skills, inner capacities, attitudes, and perspectives, or facet B of level 1 of the mindfulness pyramid model. These same skills, inner capacities, attitudes, and perspectives can also be deployed in the therapeutic relationship (facet B of level 2) and be taught both implicitly and explicitly to clients (facet B of level 3).

In chapter 8 we will explore the therapist's mindfulness practice as method of inquiry and investigation and mode of knowing, facet C of level 1 of the mindfulness pyramid model.

Chapter 8

Therapist's Practice: Method of Inquiry and Investigation and Mode of Knowing

In this chapter we'll explore facet C of level 1 of the mindfulness pyramid model, or mindfulness as method of inquiry and investigation and mode of knowing. Mindfulness as *method of inquiry and investigation* involves deploying mindfulness in formal meditation practice and in daily life as an instrument and method of phenomenological inquiry and investigation into how we construct subjective experiencing in each moment. In particular, it takes into account how we construct suffering and happiness in each moment through the ways we perceive and react (or respond) to the moment. In other words, we do not register experience as passive recipients. Rather, how we perceive, and then react or respond to our perception of the moment, determines how we experience the moment. Mindfulness as *mode of knowing* refers to understandings and insights generated through such direct experiential observation.

Mindfulness as method of inquiry and investigation and mode of knowing is the formal mindfulness meditation practice most closely related to Buddhist *insight meditation*, or *vipassana* (a Pali word often translated as "clear seeing"), which was brought to North America and Europe in the mid-1970s from India, Thailand, Burma, and Sri Lanka and remains hugely popular today. The Zen practice of *zazen* attention, or *bare attention*, is similar and refers to experientially registering each moment as it arises with sensitivity, care, and precision and without conditioned reactive judgment or striving. The entire field of awareness in each moment is the focal object. Nothing is excluded.

The following excerpt from "Aphorism 109" of Franz Kafka's *Blue Octavo Notebooks* (Kafka, 2004) is an evocative description of the practice of bare attention and mindfulness as inquiry and investigation and mode of knowing.

> You do not need to leave your room. Remain sitting at your table and listen.
> Do not even listen, simply wait. Do not even wait. Be quite still and
> solitary. The world will offer itself to you to be unmasked. It has no choice.
> It will roll in ecstasy at your feet.

In his initial instructions to not leave the room and to remain sitting and listening, Kafka implies that whatever you are looking for is not outside. Just "sitting at your table" will be enough. Both vipassana and Zen practitioners frequently call the practices of insight meditation and bare attention "just sitting." At Zen and vipassana meditation retreats, there are long hours of meditation each day in which retreatants just sit in the same spot in the meditation hall. As a ritualized mindfulness meditation, retreatants even eat in the same spot where they sit. The message, like Kafka's, is that there is no need to go anywhere else. Whatever you are looking for is right here, in this room, at this table, in this moment.

Kafka refines and simplifies his instructions even more in the third, fourth, and fifth lines of the aphorism. First he contradicts himself and tells us to not even listen, but simply to wait. Finally he says, "Do not even wait. Be quite still and solitary." It's as if he is passing along the instructions in the order that he discovered them for himself. This sounds like the experience of someone doing systematic phenomenological inquiry, paying close attention to each moment of experience as it arises without judging or striving. Just being.

In letting go of listening and waiting, and simply being "quite still and solitary," Kafka invites us to shift completely out of doing mode into the mode of just being—wakeful and aware without goals, preferences, or striving. In the next three lines Kafka makes an extraordinary, even audacious, claim about being quite still and solitary without even waiting: "The world will offer itself to you to be unmasked. It has no choice. It will roll in ecstasy at your feet."

Kafka describes poetically but precisely the experience of mindfulness as method of inquiry and investigation and mode of knowing. The experience requires shifting completely out of doing mode into just being mode. Kafka recognized that even listening and waiting contained subtle elements of doing and striving. So waiting and listening are let go in favor of simply being still and solitary.

This requires trust. Trust in nondoing, in awareness, and in our senses. Trust that if we are simply still and solitary (as well as patient), the world will actually disclose itself and present itself to our senses (including the sense of awareness) to be known experientially. Trust that there really is no need to do anything. On the contrary, doing distorts perception and awareness with desire, aversion, beliefs, preconceptions, conditioned reactions, and identifications. Sustained, nondoing awareness eventually allows (temporarily at least) conditioned, habitual judgments and reactions to fall away. For even a moment, if we experience just being without judging or striving, the world has no choice other than to "offer itself to you to be unmasked." Because we are not different, or separate, from the world. We just think we are.

Mindful inquiry and investigation can potentially lead not only to experiencing each moment clearly (and even ecstatically), as in Kafka's poem, but also to experientially grounded understanding and insight into how subjective experiencing itself is constructed. Specifically, mindfulness as inquiry and investigation and mode of knowing can yield powerful, transformative insights into how we construct needless suffering through our attempts to avoid unavoidable pain or to hold on to pleasant experiences. Through mindfulness-based, experiential insight, we can also learn how to alleviate or even completely deconstruct suffering through nonaversion, acceptance, and willingness; through learning to embrace each moment with friendliness and hospitality, even those moments that are quite painful and distressing; and then letting go—allowing and letting be.

Concentration in Mindful Inquiry and Investigation

As commonly used in behavioral medicine and psychotherapy, *mindfulness meditation* refers to a combination of two types of formal meditation practice that traditional Buddhist psychology views as separate and distinct. In addition to being a formal meditation practice, in contemporary psychotherapy and behavioral medicine mindfulness is also viewed as a set of skills, inner capacities, attitudes, and perspectives (as discussed in chapter 7), and as a way of being and relating to experiencing (see chapter 9). *Concentration meditation*, sometimes referred to as the practice of "one-pointedness" or "calm abiding" (in Pali, *shamatha*), was viewed as a prerequisite for practicing mindfulness or insight meditation (in Pali, *vipassana*). In contemporary secular usage, the term mindfulness meditation refers to a practice that incorporates elements of both concentration and awareness practices.

The practice of vipassana meditation, or mindful inquiry and investigation, traditionally requires very strong concentration and stability of attention. Such intense concentration states usually only develop over the course of several days during an intensive, residential meditation retreat, in which participants are totally silent and do some form of meditation practice for twelve to sixteen hours or more per day.

However, mindfulness practice in behavioral medicine and psychotherapy settings, as initially developed and introduced by Jon Kabat-Zinn, included emphases on both formal meditation practice and informal or daily life practice. The dual emphasis on formal and informal practice has evolved further with mindfulness-based cognitive therapy (MBCT), mindfulness-based eating awareness training, and dialectical behavior therapy, the latter of which incorporates more intensive cognitive behavioral therapy exercises and mindfulness-skills training approaches.

The emphasis on mindfulness in daily life and mindfulness-skills training, as well as formal mindfulness meditation practice and the incorporation of cognitive behavioral inventories, behavioral home practice, yoga and mindful movement, and poetry has, in my experience, greatly enhanced the inquiry and investigation and mode of knowing facet of mindfulness practice in clinical use. In the course of teaching MBSR and MBCT courses, and doing mindfulness-informed psychotherapy, I have been repeatedly surprised and moved by the deep, experiential insights of course participants and therapy clients into how adventitious suffering is constructed, and how it can be deconstructed or avoided. I believe this relatively quick transformation is an example in which the cross-fertilization of Eastern and Western understandings of mind and therapeutic practices has greatly benefited both.

I have practiced vipassana in a variety of Western Buddhist retreat centers and have taught mindfulness to several thousand clients (MBSR, MBCT, and mindfulness-based individual therapy) and hundreds of therapists (in professional training groups).

It's clear to me that the insights accessible through the method of inquiry and investigation and mode of knowing facet of mindfulness in mindfulness-based therapies, though perhaps not as powerful experientially, can be as transformative as those accessible in a seven-day, silent vipassana retreat because they are often more readily integrated into daily life.

Inquiry, Investigation, and Insight

Inquiry in mindfulness meditation is as much an attitude as it is an action. It involves bringing an attitude of friendliness, curiosity, and interest to the awareness of each moment of experience so that awareness itself is imbued with a spirit of curiosity and a wanting to know the present moment intimately. Inquiry as friendly, curious, interested awareness can be focused on the present moment as a whole or on a particular aspect of the present moment.

What Is This? What's Happening?

Let's say I have been sitting in meditation practice for a while and begin to notice pain radiating out from under my left shoulder blade. In a spirit of friendly interest and curiosity, I begin to inquire into the pain with the question "What's happening?" I begin to notice that I am judging, avoiding, and bracing against the unpleasant sensations, resulting in my shoulder stiffening and my breathing tightening. The thought *pain* is already a negative judgment. It communicates more about the implied negative judgment than about the specific sensations. In a continuing spirit of interest and friendliness, I continue to inquire into the shoulder sensations, opening to a more precise awareness of what's happening—burning, tightness, tensing, judging (*don't like this*), fear, and a feeling of energy vibrating under the shoulder blade. As I let myself become more and more interested in, friendly toward, and curious about what's happening with the shoulder sensations, I notice sensations of softening and opening to the unpleasant sensations, and sensations of loosening and letting go. I then ask the questions "What is this? What's happening?" I notice fear about releasing the tension in my shoulder blade, as well as anger. I continue to pose the two basic questions to the sensations in my shoulder blade, over and over again: "What is this? What's happening?" There is no need to ask the questions aloud. The questions simply permeate the awareness field into which the unpleasant sensations arise, inviting the sensations into the foreground.

The questions are meant to be very concrete and literal. I experience the responses as physical sensations, emotions, thoughts, and sometimes experiential knowing or insight. I silently label the sensations—*shooting, tight, burning, stiff*—in the background of the field of awareness as a way to focus more acutely on the shoulder sensations. You can think of inquiry as the spirit of friendliness, interest, and curiosity embedded in the questions "What is this?" and "What's happening?"—both of which are focused on the present moment as a whole, or on a specific element or elements of the present moment.

Now investigation begins. Interest and curiosity intensify into something like fascination. Although the questions are still the same, there is a sense of the inquiry intensifying as awareness—imbued with friendly interest and curiosity—rubbing against the sensations, or saturating, penetrating and being intimate with the sensations. Obviously these words are metaphors, but they convey the felt experience of holding the sensation in this instance, or any other object, in mindful awareness.

As you might imagine, there are moments, or longer periods, of tightening and resistance. Patience is key. Time is on your side. Continue to investigate each moment of sensation as it arises, realizing that there is no adversary. You can also breathe into the area around the intense sensation, softening and making space for it to be there. Avoid battle. You are interrogating you. Continue to use mental labeling, perhaps also noticing movements of the mind-body process in addition to sensations. Sharp. Intense. Shooting. Pushing away. Bracing against.

Audio of the following exercise is available at http://www.newharbinger.com /32752.

Exercise 8.1: Mindfulness as Method of Inquiry and Investigation and Mode of Knowing

1. Settle into a sitting posture that is erect, upright, and relaxed and embodies wakefulness, dignity, and presence.

2. Let your awareness drop down into the torso, connecting with the sensations of breathing in the belly. Allow the awareness to concentrate itself in the breath by letting yourself become curious and interested in the sensations of each breath moment.

3. If you notice that awareness has wandered away from the breath sensations, gently let it settle back into the breath sensations as they are now. Notice how the breath sensations are constantly changing from moment to moment.

4. Be fully present in each breath moment, as if your life depends on that breath. (It does.)

5. When it feels like the concentration is fairly steady and stable, if you'd like expanding awareness to include the entire body as a field of sensation.

6. Use mental noting to observe each moment of sensation, noticing pressure, contact, warm, cool, aching, throbbing, itching, burning, and so on. If you'd like, also notice and label the feeling tone of pleasant, unpleasant, and neutral in each moment.

7. If a particular sensation in the body becomes strong or intense, allow the awareness to focus in that area of sensation.

8. Let your awareness be suffused with a sense of curiosity and interest that expresses these questions: "What is this? What's happening?"

9. Direct your awareness toward the focal sensation, continuing to hold the questions in awareness.

10. Now let the awareness begin to saturate, penetrate, or rub against the focal sensation using whatever word or image describes the felt sensation of investigating the area of interest.

11. Noting feeling tone (ex., pleasant or unpleasant) and the reaction to feeling tone: judging, aversion, wanting, grasping, bracing against, and so on.

12. Investigating each moment by being fully present, still, and solitary; letting the moment disclose itself to you to be known, without needing to do anything.

13. Perhaps also noticing moments of experiential knowing, or insight, as they arise during the mindful investigation of strong sensation, in the form of responses to the questions "What is this? What's happening?"

14. Finally, resting in the breath for a minute or two before ending the exercise and refocusing in the room.

15. Take a few moments to reflect on your experience in the exercise.

16. Journal about your experience, being as precise as possible about what you observed, anything you learned, and any insights that arose.

Meditative Insight: How Suffering Is Constructed and Deconstructed

Read the next paragraph with care, as it makes possible a potentially transformative insight that can help liberate you and your clients from suffering. Every moment has a basic "flavor," or "feeling tone"—pleasant, unpleasant, or neutral. When we experience pleasant, we usually like it, tend to judge it as good, and instinctually cling to or try to get more of it. When we experience unpleasant, we usually dislike it, usually judge it as bad, and react with aversion and a pushing away or a bracing against. When neutral moments arise, we tend to space out or not notice. The basic feeling of pleasant, unpleasant, or neutral in each moment can be hardwired or conditioned.

Negatively judging (I don't like this) and bracing against or trying to resist an unpleasant sensation is quite normal, but it intensifies the unpleasantness of the sensation. It makes it worse. Repressing anger or grief intensifies painful emotions or may cause psychosomatic symptoms.

If you have ever pulled a muscle in your back, reflect on the experience. After the initial injury the muscles surrounding it tighten up instinctually to protect the injured area (what's called the "guarding reflex"). Unfortunately, this tightening intensifies the pain, which causes the surrounding muscles to tighten even more, which further intensifies the pain, until perhaps you can barely walk or even stand.

137

In order not to suffer, you must be willing to experience the intrinsic pain that your suffering intensified or masked. "If you're not willing to have it, you will," is the acceptance and commitment therapy aphorism that describes the relationship between pain and suffering (Hayes & Smith, 2005, p. 44). Intentionally opening to the pain of losing a spouse, or to feelings of powerlessness in a relationship in which a spouse makes all the decisions, requires both willingness and courage to fully experience the intrinsic pain in order to avoid the adventitious suffering caused by avoidance of the intrinsic pain.

Inquiry and investigation, and the spontaneous experiential insights that arise (mindfulness as a mode of knowing), can free you from unnecessary suffering by clearly revealing that trying to avoid life's intrinsic pain only intensifies that pain and causes additional adventitious suffering. It hurts less just to feel it. That's the human condition. You can feel unpleasant emotions and sensations without judging them. Or if you judge, by being mindful of judging you can avoid the suffering of unconscious, automatic aversion and experiential avoidance.

Mindfulness of unpleasant and pleasant gives you great freedom. If you notice judging happening (often taking the form of liking and disliking or, after the fact, grasping and aversion), you can backtrack to notice the pleasant or unpleasant feeling tone being judged. If you notice desire or aversion happening in reaction to liking or disliking, you can backtrack to liking and disliking (judging) and then to the feeling tone (pleasant or unpleasant) being judged.

If you notice grasping or pushing away, you can backtrack through noticing desire or aversion, then through judging (liking or disliking), then through the feeling tone of pleasant or unpleasant, and then to the actual moment of experience. There is always the possibility of freeing yourself from the tangled web of suffering, starting in the present moment with whatever you notice happening. It's easier if you have some experiential insight into how suffering works. Developing such insight is ultimately the purpose of mindfulness as method of inquiry and investigation and mode of knowing.

Guided audio for the following exercise is available for download at http://www .newharbinger.com/32752.

Exercise 8.2: Noticing Feeling Tone and Reactions to Feeling Tone

1. Settle into a comfortable posture, either lying on your back or sitting on a couch or chair.

2. Allow your awareness to drop down into the torso and to settle in the belly.

3. Begin to notice the sensations of breathing in the belly.

4. Allow the belly to directly register the belly breath movements as sensations. No need for thought. Let thinking come and go in the background of the field of awareness. Let the sensations registered by the wakeful belly be in the spotlight.

5. Notice the feeling tone in the belly-breath sensations moment by moment. Is it pleasant, unpleasant, or neutral?

6. If you'd like, use mental noting to label the feeling tone in each belly-breath moment as *pleasant, unpleasant,* or *neutral.*

7. Is the feeling tone in each successive belly-breath moment constant or changing?

8. Is the feeling tone of the in-breath the same as the feeling tone of the out-breath?

9. Notice reactions to pleasant, unpleasant, and neutral, such as judging, like and dislike, desire and aversion, or grasping and pushing away. Label them when they arise with a mental note.

10. After a few more minutes, let go of noticing feeling tone and just rest in the physical sensations of breathing for several minutes. Then, when you are ready, let your eyes open and notice seeing happening as you bring your focus back into the room.

11. Journal about your experience noticing feeling tone and your reactions to feeling tone. What did you observe? Did anything surprise you?

12. As an informal exercise, you might periodically ask yourself if the moment you are experiencing is pleasant, unpleasant, or neutral. Pay attention to if or how noticing the flavor of the moment changes your perception or experience in any way.

Summary

In this chapter we examined the therapist's mindfulness practice as a method of inquiry and investigation and a mode of knowing. We explored how, just by being still and solitary, the world reveals itself to our awareness because we are part of, not separate from, the world. We looked at how each moment of experience has a feeling tone of either pleasant, unpleasant, or neutral and how the automatic reactions to these three feeling tones are desire or grasping (pleasant); aversion, resistance, or bracing against (unpleasant); and ignoring or spacing out (neutral). These automatic reactions lead to suffering. But when we are mindful of feeling tone or our reaction to it, it's possible to disidentify from the experience and to free ourselves from the continuing spiral of reactivity that leads to greater suffering.

In chapter 9 we will explore the therapist's mindfulness practice as a way of being and relating to experience. Similar to chapter 8, the discussions and exercises in chapter 9 apply as much to clients as they do to therapists.

Chapter 9

Therapist's Practice: Way of Being and Relating to Experience

In this chapter we will explore facet *D* of the mindfulness pyramid model, mindfulness as a way of being and relating to experience moment by moment in daily life. We'll begin with level 1, the therapist's mindfulness practice. The practices and exercises in this chapter are equally useful for both therapists and clients.

Mindfulness as a way of being and relating to experience is where the rubber hits the road clinically. Therapists and clients must deploy, moment by moment in everyday life, the skills, inner capacities, attitudes, and perspectives they have developed in the formal meditation practices in order to live more skillfully, with greater joy and ease, and with less suffering. Mindfulness meditation is transformative because it is not just about doing formal meditation practice; it is also about transforming your way of being in the world and how you relate to experience in daily life, moment by moment. This chapter explores how to do this and presents informal, daily practices that can help therapists and clients to incorporate mindfulness as a way of being and relating.

Mindfulness in and of itself is transformative because present-moment awareness without conditioned reactivity or judgment allows for perception that is undistorted by preconceptions and preferences and behavior that is not automatic, habitual, or conditioned. No longer caught in the cycle of stress reactivity, therapists and clients are free to choose more creative and skillful responses.

Present-Moment Awareness and Wise Discernment

Have you noticed there are sometimes days when you can't remember what you did, what you ate, with whom you spoke, or what you said and heard? For most of us, functioning on autopilot is our default mode, especially when pressured or stressed.

When caught up in thoughts about where you are going, where you have been, what you have done, and what you still need to do, you miss the present moment. The present moment is the only moment in which you can experience being alive and aware, in which you can be conscious of intention and choice, and in which you can respond intentionally or with spontaneous creativity to the circumstances that present themselves. It's also the only moment in which you can register where you are putting your wallet, purse, or keys.

Informal mindfulness practice involves bringing mindfulness to bear on the mundane activities of daily life, anything from washing the dishes to taking out the trash to showering and brushing your teeth. Informal practice focusing on daily life experience moment by moment also involves noticing when you have slipped into autopilot mode of mind and then consciously bringing awareness back into the present moment, focusing once again on fully experiencing what you are doing, moment by moment; it also involves sustaining present-moment focus from moment to moment, as best you can.

Another element of informal mindfulness practice or moment to moment mindfulness in daily life is the cultivation of *wise discernment*, or the capacity to accurately distinguish among the different elements of mind-body experience, including sense perceptions, thoughts, emotions, mind states, feeling tone, reactions, intentions, actions, and mindful awareness itself, without identifying with any of them as "myself." The informal mindfulness practices and exercises in this chapter will help you incorporate into daily life the skills and insights developed in the formal meditation practices.

Hopefully you will discover that life as a whole can be a seamless mindfulness practice. Whether you are engaged in formal meditation practice, getting ready for work, talking with a friend, shopping for groceries, or embracing a loved one, you can experience each moment with care; fully present, wakeful, and engaged; not caught up in reactive judgment or conditioned, automatic behaviors, and conscious of intention, choice, and action.

Informal Mindfulness Practices

Any activity can be a mindfulness practice if you are fully awake to the activity moment by moment, and engage in the activity with clarity of intention and discernment. Therefore, activities of daily life, especially the ones that we tend to do automatically, can be wonderful informal mindfulness practices. Through these informal practices we can incorporate mindfulness as a way of being and relating in daily life.

The exercises below describe a variety of daily life practices. I encourage you to try them all. Discover which ones resonate with you, and incorporate them into your daily routine. As you practice each of these exercises over time, record your observations and insights in your journal. You might find it more convenient and practical to journal about each day's informal practice as a whole at the end of the day. (Audio versions of exercises 9.1 and 9.2 are available for download; visit http://www.newharbinger.com/32752 to access them.)

Exercise 9.1: Dropping into Sensations in the Body and the Breath

1. Tune into and feel the sensations of breathing for one or two cycles of in-breath and out-breath, five or six times per day, as a discipline of practice. The discipline is more about remembering to feel the breath rather than having to set aside time to do so.

2. Anytime you notice being caught up in automatic behavior, ruminative worry, planning, memory, or fantasy, drop into the physical sensations of breathing, letting mindfulness of the breathing sensations in each moment concentrate and stabilize awareness.

3. Whenever you want to call yourself into the present moment, let awareness drop down into the sensations of pressure and touch associated with your posture. For instance, if sitting, feeling sensations of pressure and touch in the soles of the feet, heels, toes, buttocks, and the backs of the thighs. If standing, feeling sensations of pressure and touch in the soles of the feet, toes, and heels as well as any other sensations in the feet caused by socks or shoes.

4. To anchor attention in the present moment, redirect your attention to the breath sensations in the belly: expanding and releasing, rising and falling, filling and emptying.

5. Focus on the sensations that are most prominent in your experience. Be aware of each belly-breath moment as it arises, one moment after the next, noticing that each moment of belly-breath sensation is different.

Exercise 9.2: Take a Body Awareness Break (or Get Out of Your Head and into Your Body)

1. Periodically throughout the day, let your awareness drop down into your body. Inhabit your body fully and consciously. Experience the body as a field of sensations, registering touch, pressure, temperature, moisture, pulsing, throbbing, vibrating, itching, pulling, burning, stretching, and so on.

2. Notice that each sensation has a specific intensity, shape, area, volume, texture, duration, and feeling tone—pleasant, unpleasant, or neutral. Notice that within the awareness field of the body as a whole, sensations are continually arising, changing, and disappearing moment by moment. In any moment sensations may become more or less intense or maintain the same intensity; textures can stay the same or morph and change into different textures; sensations expand or shrink, change shape or stay the same, occupy more or less volume, and involve a larger or smaller area.

3. Pay attention to the moment by moment unfolding of the life of the body as a flow of continuously changing sensations. This is the "being of the body," which we tend to ignore in favor of the "doing of the body."

4. Take thirty seconds or a minute to experience and honor the being of the body without asking the body to do anything.

5. What if anything did you notice about the impact of breathing on the sensation field of the body as a whole? Record your observations in your journal.

Exercise 9.3: Choose a Routine Activity and Do It as a Mindfulness Practice

1. Choose a routine activity that you mostly do on autopilot. It could be showering, brushing your teeth, loading the dishwasher or hand-washing dishes, cleaning the kitchen, vacuuming, dusting, putting on makeup, getting dressed for work, taking out the trash, or removing and putting in contact lenses. We do many tasks on autopilot, which then become opportunities to get lost in thought.

2. It's best if the activity takes no longer than five or ten minutes and you can do it daily for one week as a mindfulness meditation. This means you pay close attention when doing the activity. Experience each moment with care, noticing perceptions, such as seeing, hearing, smelling, tasting, and touch sensation, as well as cognitive phenomena, such as thoughts, emotions, intentions, choices, and even awareness itself.

3. If you notice that you've spaced out or gotten caught up in thought, notice where your mind went, and then firmly but gently bring it back to focus on the routine activity.

Being Fully Present: Living Life as a Mindfulness Practice

Remember "the wisdom of no escape" (Chödrön, 1991) from chapter 3? Whether we wish it or not, whether we pay attention or not, life itself is practice. In each moment we are either practicing mindfulness or something else. Below are a few activities that we often do on autopilot. Consciously altering even one or two details of an activity can make it easier to be mindful.

Exercise 9.4: Mindfulness of Driving

1. Set the cruise control (or just maintain your speed) at five miles per hour below the speed limit.

2. Don't listen to the radio or music or talk on the cell phone while driving. Just drive.

3. Be aware of what driving entails, the size and complexity of the machine you are operating, the potential risks, and the responsibilities to self and others to be safe.

4. Be conscious of your intention in driving. What are you doing, and why? Where are you going, and why?

5. Be aware of driving a gasoline-powered vehicle as participating in the fossil fuel economy, and acknowledge its effect on the planet.

Exercise 9.5: Mindfulness of Smartphone Use

1. Monitor how much time you spend using or relating to your smartphone, for any reason. What percentage of your time is spent interacting with the device in some way? Perhaps spend a day, or even a week, really paying attention, tracking your usage, and gathering data. I would encourage you to do a formal time study, tracking the actual number of hours and minutes and also usage as a percentage of waking time.

2. Once you've determined the actual percentage of time you spend interacting with your device, notice how you feel. Are you satisfied or dissatisfied with using your time and life energy this way? Are there changes you want to make? What simple changes could you make to reduce the time you spend with email and smartphones and online?

3. Before initiating a text or e-mail or actually speaking or video chatting using your device, pause and take two or three slow, mindful breaths. Take a few moments to reflect on what the purpose and intention of the call, text, or e-mail is. If someone calls you, don't answer until the fourth ring, using the first three rings to anchor awareness fully in the present moment by mindfully noticing breathing, other body sensations, thoughts, emotions, and mind states.

4. Remain conscious of breathing and body sensations as you speak and listen. When listening, just listen. As best you can, refrain from thinking about your response while the other party is speaking. Avoid multitasking. If you made the call, be aware of your intention for the call. If you are receiving the call, be aware while listening of your reactions and your intention in responding.

Exercise 9.6: Mindfulness of Transitions

Common transitions in daily life frequently go unnoticed. Choose a transition that you often do on autopilot and make it a mindfulness practice.

1. Moving from sitting to standing or standing to sitting or lying down.

2. Walking from one room to another.

3. Initiating a conversation or responding to what someone says.

4. Beginning to eat, noticing tasting, chewing, and swallowing and putting down the fork between bites to notice if you feel full or are still hungry.

5. When arriving home, before entering the house and greeting loved ones, sit in the car or just stay outside and allow yourself up to five minutes of mindful breathing to decompress and focus on letting go of work and being home.

6. Arriving home, immediately change out of your work clothes.

7. Grasping a doorknob or handle, stop and feel one or two cycles of in-breath and out-breath before going through the door. This is a particularly useful practice before opening the door to greet your next client.

Exercise 9.7: Mindful Touching

1. Make an appointment with your spouse, partner, or yourself for a mindful touching session.

2. Before beginning the touching session, practice mindful breathing for five to ten minutes (with your partner or by yourself if alone), letting yourself come into the present moment and settle into stillness.

3. Give your undivided attention to the person you are touching. Clarify (with your partner or yourself) how the person you will be touching would like to be touched.

4. Clarify what you want your touch to communicate. As you begin to touch, let what you want to communicate to your partner or yourself flow through in the quality of your touch.

Exercise 9.8: STOP

STOP is the acronym for a brief, four-step, structured practice that lets you uncouple from stress reactivity on the spot.

S. <u>Stop</u> whatever you are doing, and for one minute settle into just being.

T. <u>Take a deep breath</u>, inhaling deeply and fully. Exhale slowly and completely

O. <u>Observe</u> what's happening in and around you.

P. <u>Proceed</u> skillfully based on what you observed.

SAGE and CARE are brief mini-mindfulness meditations inspired by practices called the three-minute breathing space and the coping breathing space, which Segal, Williams, and Teasdale (2002, pp. 184, 241) developed as part of mindfulness-based cognitive therapy. The acronyms reflect my intentions for the exercises, which are designed not only to bridge the gap between the formal meditations and the informal mindfulness practices in daily life, but also to emphasize the possibility of acting with and cultivating both wisdom and compassion in daily life. (Audio versions of both practices are available for download at http://www.newharbinger.com/32752.)

Exercise 9.9: SAGE

S. <u>Stop</u> whatever you are doing and shift into being mode of mind.

A. <u>Accept and open to</u> the present moment exactly as it is.

G. <u>Gather</u> and concentrate the awareness in the belly-breath sensations.

E. <u>Expand</u> awareness around the belly-breath sensations to include the body as a whole, breathing.

Exercise 9.10: CARE

C. <u>Connect</u> experientially with what's happening in the moment by dropping into the body.

A. <u>Accept</u> the moment exactly as it is. If the moment is unpleasant or distressing, imagine inhaling around the sensations of distress to make space for the distress to be present.

R. <u>Refocus</u> awareness in the belly-breath sensations. Concentrate awareness in the breath.

E. <u>Expand</u> awareness to include the body as a whole, breathing. If the distressing sensations or emotions are still present, repeat reassuring phrases to yourself silently, in conjunction with the breath: *It's okay, I can be with this. It's okay, I can let myself feel this. It's okay. It's okay.*

Exercise 9.11: PRN Prescriptions

The PRN prescriptions are mindfulness-based practices designed to address burnout prevention and self-care at three levels: of the moment (level 1); of the person and the individual's life as a whole (level 2); and of the collective, including family, community, organizations, institutions, society, nation state, and the planet and planetary life as a whole (level 3).

Exercise 9.11a: PRN Prescription Level 1 (the Moment)— Pause, Release, Notice

This instant coping skill takes sixty to ninety seconds to complete.

<u>Pa</u>use: Stop whatever you're doing and drop into being mode.

<u>Re</u>lease: Let go of agendas and striving and allow any tension or holding in the body to melt away, as best you can.

<u>N</u>otice: Be fully present in each moment, one after the next, just noticing what's happening. Then let the moment itself evoke a skillful response.

Exercise 9.11b: PRN Prescription Level 2 (the Person)— Practice, Retreat, Nourish

This practice is an ongoing discipline and guiding orientation at the level of the individual's life as a whole. If we lapse or fall away from our personal practice, we can return to it and reestablish it again and again.

<u>P</u>ractice: Establish your own daily discipline of formal mindfulness meditation and incorporate informal mindfulness practice into your everyday life.

<u>Re</u>treat: Make time for periodic mindfulness meditation retreats. They can be formal structured retreats at meditation retreat centers, or simply blocks of time (a day, a weekend, or longer) during which you set aside work and other routine activities of daily life for nondoing—just to be and experience.

Nourish: Participate regularly in relationships and activities that nourish mind, body, spirit, heart, and soul: loving, intimate relationships with family and significant others and close friendships; nourishing community involvements, sports, exercise, immersion in nature and wilderness, music, literature, and cultural and intellectual pursuits; mind-body practices such as mindfulness and other meditation practices, yoga, tai chi, and chi gung; preventive health practices that might include meditation, yoga, tai chi, and chi gung; regular exercise, following a healthy diet, and getting enough sleep; and spiritual practice or a sense of connection with a larger life beyond the egoic self, which may include cultivating qualities of gratitude, generosity, empathic connection, compassion, and forgiveness, among other virtues. Also, we have the choice to nourish either the seeds of wisdom, compassion, joy, and awakening, or the seeds of suffering (Nhat Hanh, 1991, p. 73). Nourish the seeds of wisdom, compassion, joy, and awakening.

Exercise 9.11c: PRN Prescription Level 3 (the Collective)— Possibility, Responsibility, Necessity

This practice addresses the organizational, institutional, and societal factors related to professional burnout as well as societal challenges and crises that we face as a species.

Possibility is the recognition that mindfulness and clarity about the systemic and institutional dynamics underlying organizational and societal problems allow for us to develop more skillful responses. As mental health professionals, such strategies include joining with like-minded people to address the problems in the mental health and health care systems as well as larger society; refraining from internalizing rage and feelings of powerlessness; refraining from efforts to personally compensate for system deficits and failures by overworking, transgressing professional and personal boundaries, or being overly responsible or demanding with clients and colleagues.

Responsibility comes from recognizing that our mental health and health care systems are broken, and it is our collective responsibility to fix them. Part of healing from the systemic and structural failures that contribute to burnout is to be proactive in the repair of the system of care. Many years ago I learned a simple equation from an activist friend that has been a source of inspiration ever since: vision + action = hope. It applies to addressing all sorts of problems, from the level of the individual to society as a whole.

Necessity points to the understanding that it's up to us as professionals and citizens to work together to reclaim our profession and fix our broken health care and mental health care systems. More than anyone else, as mental health professionals we bear witness on a daily basis to the suffering of clients denied appropriate care due to increased demand and decreased funding for services. We also bear witness to and experience the increasing incidence of burnout in our peers and ourselves.

Mindfulness is not just about *self*-awareness. It is an all-encompassing awareness that allows us to experience the truth of interdependence, or *interbeing* (Nhat Hanh, 1988a, 1988b), and to see through our collective delusion that as individuals we are separate from each other and the rest of life.

When we experience in this way, it becomes clear that it is up to us to repair our broken health and mental health care systems, and to address other societal and global crises such as income inequality and climate change. No one else will do this for us. There is no one else. We are the ones we have been waiting for.

Summary

In this chapter we looked at facet D of level 1 of the mindfulness pyramid model, mindfulness as way of being and relating to experience in daily life. We explored a variety of exercises for incorporating mindfulness practice in daily life. This chapter was the last of the chapters (5 through 9) that explore level 1 of the mindfulness pyramid model, the therapist's practice, which is the foundation for viably incorporating mindfulness in psychotherapy. Chapters 10 to 12 explore levels 2 and 3 of the mindfulness pyramid model—the therapeutic process and relationship as practice, and the client's practice.

Chapter 10

Doing Therapy as a Mindfulness Practice

In chapter 10 we will begin to explore level 2 of the mindfulness pyramid model, how the therapist's mindfulness practice informs doing therapy and the therapeutic relationship. Specifically, chapter 10 looks at the ways we can use mindfulness practices to support and enhance the therapeutic relationship.

Doing psychotherapy has a number of features that make it well suited for being a mindfulness practice for the therapist. The first involves motivation.

Certain basic motivations support mindfulness, and vice versa. Mindfulness practice cultivates the same motivations that support its development. For example, wanting to benefit others; wanting to avoid causing harm; valuing compassion and caring; wanting to be of service; interest in human psychology, particularly the psychological mechanisms that give rise to happiness and suffering; and wanting to help alleviate suffering and increase happiness are all motivations that support the development of mindfulness. They are also important for doing psychotherapy.

Remember "the wisdom of no escape" (Chödrön, 1991) from chapter 3? It's the insight that arises from seeing clearly in your own experience of practice that every moment conditions the moment that follows, which means there really is no such thing as not practicing. There are no vacations or breaks, no time off. Whatever we do in each moment, and the quality of attention that we bring to it, is our practice (Kabat-Zinn, 1994, pp. 160–161). What you practice in any moment, and how it shapes and conditions the next moment, depends a great deal on your intention and the qualities of awareness, presence, relatedness, discipline, and commitment that you embody. In that sense, doing therapy as mindfulness practice is no different than doing anything else in your life mindfully.

There are specific ways the therapist can understand and work with the therapeutic relationship and process as a mindfulness practice that enhance the therapy experience for both therapists and clients and also improve therapeutic outcomes. In the rest of chapter 10, I elaborate on what's involved in doing psychotherapy as a mindfulness practice and offer specific exercises and meditative practices to help incorporate each of the four facets of mindfulness, represented by the four faces of the mindfulness pyramid, at the level of the therapeutic relationship and process, level 2 of the pyramid.

Mini-Mindfulness Practices to Prepare for Working with Your Client

What follows are mindfulness practices in the form of contemplative exercises. They will help you prepare your physical space and attitudinal and psychological set to provide an optimally safe psychological container or holding environment (Winnicott, 1984), for your clients. I encourage you to try each practice at least once; then choose one or two that feel particularly useful and experiment with them in your clinical practice.

Exercise 10.1: Creating the Physical Container

1. Do this exercise while you are sitting in your office or consulting room—wherever you see clients. Sit where your clients usually sit. Look around. See the room with beginner's mind, as if seeing it for the first time, the way a very observant new client might see it.

2. How does it feel to be sitting in this seat, in this setting? Is the seat comfortable? Is the environment warm and inviting? Is it orderly? Does it feel lived in? Does it feel safe?

3. Notice if you like being in this environment. Based solely on your experience of the environment, if you were a first-time client, would you want to come back? If so, why? If not, why not?

4. What might you change about the physical environment and setting of your office, if anything, to make it warmer and more comfortable for your clients or for yourself? In your journal, make a list of the changes you might make. If you wouldn't make any changes, write in your journal about what you have already done to create a physical space that feels inviting, comfortable, and safe.

5. If you made a list of desired changes, divide the list into three groups: changes that can be done immediately, changes to be done in the intermediate term, and changes to make over the long term. Choose a change that can be done immediately and make it. For instance, as I was writing this on my laptop, sitting where my clients often sit on a couch in my office, I noticed a bookcase that was disorderly. I straightened it. Look out at the room again, aware of the change you made, noticing if and how it alters your experience of the setting, and imagining what if any impact it might have on your clients.

6. Go back to your list of possible changes and choose one from the immediate, intermediate-term, and long-term lists. Form an intention to make the changes, and then schedule them as mindfulness practices. After you complete each change, sit again in your client's seat and notice if and how it alters your experience of being in the physical space.

Exercise 10.2: Creating a Safe Emotional Container: Preparatory Exercises

The next five exercises are designed to be on-the-spot, informal mindfulness practices to help you create a sense of safety and to function as a safe container for the client you are about to see.

Exercise 10.2a: Dropping into Being

1. Before opening the door to greet your next client, sit quietly; just be still for a minute or two.

2. Let your awareness drop down and settle into the physical sensations of sitting and breathing. Just experience the physical sensations of sitting and breathing happening.

Exercise 10.2b: Setting Intention

1. Take a minute to set your intention for the session in general terms. This could be forming an intention to listen mindfully to your client, to be aware of what isn't being said as well as what is, to be sensitive to how safe your client feels, or to resolve to understand what might help your client feel safer. The intention could also involve working with your own reactivity or practicing loving-kindness for your client during the session.

2. By setting an intention you incline your mind toward a particular way of being in the session. It's like creating a guiding principle or orientation. If you stray from the intention, just remembering it will bring you back.

3. Setting intentions is not a substitute for reviewing clinical notes, reflecting on a prior session, or making formal preparations for a particular mindfulness-based stress reduction or mindfulness-based cognitive therapy session.

Exercise 10.2c: Touching Loving-Kindness and Compassion

1. Loving-kindness (unconditional acceptance) and compassion (which involves opening the heart to suffering, letting yourself be emotionally touched and moved toward a deeper, more empathic understanding) are basic elements of healing presence. This exercise cultivates and strengthens capacities for loving-kindness, compassion, and empathic attunement.

2. Sit in a comfortable, wakeful posture. Become aware of the sensations of breathing, feeling the breath flow into and out from the heart space. Imagine a sensa-

tion of comfortable warmth in the heart space as you feel the breath flowing in and out.

3. Now place an image of yourself in the heart space, and imagine with the in-breath you are saturating yourself with the energies of loving-kindness. On the out-breath, allowing all toxins, tension, and holding to flow out of your body with your breath.

4. Repeat phrases that embody the energies of loving-kindness, either the phrases from the formal loving-kindness practice in chapter 6 or any other phrases that appeal to you and embody the energies of loving-kindness. Direct the intentions of the phrases toward the image of yourself in the heart space, wishing yourself well.

   May I be happy and peaceful.

   May I be safe from all internal and external harm.

   May I be free from emotional and physical suffering.

   May I live with joy and ease of being.

5. Now letting go the image of yourself from the heart space, and replacing it with an image of your client. Feeling the sensations of warmth and comfort bathing your client in the energies of loving-kindness, and directing the intentions of the phrases to the image of your client in the heart space as you silently repeat them again.

   May I be happy and peaceful.

   May I be safe from all internal and external harm.

   May I be free from emotional and physical suffering.

   May I live with joy and ease of being.

6. Now let your own image rejoin that of your client in the heart space. Allow the energies of loving-kindness and warmth to envelop you both as you complete the practice with a final repetition of phrases.

   May we both be happy and peaceful.

   May we both be safe from all internal and external harm.

   May we both be free from emotional and physical suffering.

   May we both live with joy and ease of being.

7. Finally letting go of the images of you and your client from the heart space; and for the last minute or two of the exercise feeling the energies of loving-kindness continue to flow into the heart space with the in-breath and then out into your consulting office with the out-breath, until you can imagine your office saturated with the warm glow of loving-kindness.

Exercise 10.2d: Touching Beginner's Mind

Just as we have touched the attitudes and capacities for loving-kindness and compassion, we will also touch beginner's mind, that quality of childlike wonder and enthusiasm for discovery and learning in which each moment is brand-new, without preconceptions, and full of the pure joy of being alive.

1. Bring an image of your client into your heart space. Simply notice any thoughts and emotional reactions that arise, without judging. Let the image of your client be in the background, and let your thought stream and emotions come into the foreground.

2. Notice in particular any thoughts and emotional reactions that incorporate pre-conceived ideas and beliefs about the client. Just letting each of the thoughts and emotions come and go.

3. Allow the image of your client to come into the foreground once again, and let the stream of thoughts and emotions be in the background. As best you can, see your client as a total mystery, the mystery far outweighing any beliefs, precon-ceptions, or knowledge you might have.

4. While you're at it, why not see yourself that way as well. Imagine the two of you sitting down together in your next session, both of your brains firing away, one hundred billion synapses each, galaxies within galaxies, parallel universes. Unfathomable. Amazing. The mystery of simply sitting together. What could you possibly know compared to what you don't?

5. That's okay. Even better than okay, it's wonderful. Let yourself embrace not knowing, and celebrate mystery.

Exercise 10.2e: Greeting Your Client and Tuning In

1. Greeting your client can be a mindfulness practice. First, form an intention to practice mindfulness of greeting your client. You might begin with a deep, cleans-ing breath; then be mindful of walking to the door, and be aware of grasping the doorknob, turning it, and pulling the door open. Notice sensations, thoughts, and emotions as you greet your client and invite her in.

2. What form does the greeting take? What is said? If appropriate, is there any physical touch? A handshake or a hug? If touch does not seem appropriate, what is the reason? If there is a physical greeting, do you initiate it, or does your client? Does your client appear happy to see you? Are you happy to see your client?

3. Does seeing your client bring a genuine smile to your face? Do you smile spon-taneously from deep down in your toes, radiating out from behind your eyes? Does your smile generate warmth as well as light? Perhaps you prefer to main-

tain a professional reserve. Perhaps you don't feel comfortable with this client. If not, can you pinpoint why? Is there something you instantly become aware of when you greet your client? Do you pick up on something about your client after you both sit down?

4.   Now that you are both sitting, as best you can, let all self-centered thought fall away. Let yourself attune to your client's inner life. This is much like the practice of inquiry and investigation and mode of knowing in your personal meditation practice. Except in this instance, mind is in the room, in the intersubjective space of the therapeutic relational field as well as the intersubjective spaces between partners in couples therapy, family members in family therapy, and group members in group therapy, where each subjectivity evokes the other or others, contingently co-arising and together coming into being. You as therapist consciously choose to function as the mindfulness of the intersubjective relational field.

Listening as Healing Presence: Being the Mindfulness of the Relational Field

Although listening is usually considered the most basic psychotherapeutic skill, the term *mindful listening* is paradoxical and somewhat misleading. Mindfulness is a mode of being and experiencing that involves ceasing from striving, or nondoing, while listening is conventionally thought of as making a conscious effort to hear someone or something. The word "listening" connotes an action that requires effort. This is quite far from the lived experience of being mindfully present with and attentive to a client in therapy. Recall these lines from Kafka (2004):

> You do not need to leave your room. Remain sitting at your table and listen.
> Do not even listen, simply wait. Do not even wait. Be quite still and
> solitary. The world will offer itself to you to be unmasked. It has no choice.
> It will roll in ecstasy at your feet.

What happens in the therapeutic relationship is both much more and much less than listening. I prefer the terms *therapeutic presence* or *healing presence* to describe the therapist's stance in the therapeutic relationship. I say "stance" because healing presence is a mode of being rather than an action. Healing presence includes hearing and might resemble listening, but it is neither. It is not something you do. Rather, it is an expression of nondoing and an exquisitely sensitive, receptive quality of being that the therapist embodies in the therapeutic encounter.

Healing presence is also less than listening. It is a process of subtraction, not addition, of letting go of even the least hint of doing or striving, and instead just being. Kafka made this clear in his prose, which describes precisely this experience of subtraction (letting go) and receiving.

First Kafka subtracts leaving his room, and just remains sitting at his desk. Then he subtracts listening, and he simply waits. Then he subtracts even waiting. When Kafka finally lets go even of waiting, the last gasp of the doing mind, and surrenders to the experience of being still and solitary, of just being, the world offers itself to him to be "unmasked." It has no choice. It even "rolls in ecstasy" at his feet.

Through letting go of doing and shifting into the mode of just being still and solitary, also known as nondoing mode of mind, Kafka is healed in the most basic sense of the word; he is restored to wholeness (Kabat-Zinn, 1994, 2005). He no longer feels alienated and separate, caught up in individual self-striving, but rather experiences himself as integrated and whole and simultaneously an integral part of the world. The world not only offers itself to him to be unmasked, but it dances ecstatically for him. Kafka describes his new connection with the world in terms that are joyful, intimate, and even erotic in the sense of the vital energy of life, which he can now fully experience (Macy, 1991).

The process that Kafka describes as "unmasking," in which you trust and feel safe enough in relationship to let yourself be seen as you really are, and then experience your authentic self being mirrored and reflected back in the experience and through the eyes of the trusted other, is at the heart of the therapeutic relationship. The therapist's contribution to this process is healing presence, in a very real sense choosing to function as the mindfulness of the therapeutic relational field.

Healing Presence, Affect Resonance, and Empathic Attunement

We know from affective neuroscience, infant-development, and attachment research that we all have *mirror neurons*, specialized brain cells (Siegel, 2007, 2012) that are a major component of the neurobiological capacity for *affect resonance*, which involves literally sensing another's emotional vibrations and vibrating on the same wavelength, similar to the harmonic resonance between the strings of a perfectly tuned guitar. When you play one string, the strings that are harmonically tuned to the same note also vibrate.

Affect resonance is the neurobiological precursor and foundation of *empathic attunement*, which is the developmental capacity to recognize, identify with, and vicariously experience the emotional experience of another. Affect resonance and empathic attunement, in the unshakable stillness at the center of present-moment awareness, together comprise the listening function of healing presence.

The therapist embodying healing presence can empathically attune to even the most distressing and painful experiences and emotions without shutting down or being overwhelmed. Healing presence remains openhearted, close, and connected, yet also solid, stable, unshakable, and composed. These attributes help the client feel safe.

The therapist's mindfulness also functions as an invitation, always implicit and sometimes explicit, for the client to join in with the collaborative mindful inquiry and investigative function of the relational field.

Unconditional Friendliness, Curiosity, and Interest

Unconditional friendliness, curiosity, and interest, joined with empathic attunement, drive mindful inquiry and investigation. Unconditional friendliness, curiosity, and interest suggest a more energetic attitude than the therapist quality described by Carl Rogers as "unconditional positive regard" (Rogers, 1980, pp. 95–103). In addition, unconditional friendliness, curiosity, and interest refer to a way of relating to *moments* of the therapeutic relationship and process (for example, this client moment, and then the next, and the next) rather than to the client, the therapeutic relationship, or the therapeutic process as a reified whole.

Far from being impartial, unconditional friendliness, interest, and curiosity require being equally partial to each moment as it arises and require sustaining high levels of mindfulness and loving-kindness in each moment, which may at first seem daunting. However, genuine curiosity and interest effortlessly focus the mind and drive concentration, and once firmly established become self-sustaining. Effortless concentration then generates energy, which enhances and sharpens awareness, which further intensifies interest, curiosity, and concentration in a self-reinforcing positive feedback loop.

Being the Mindfulness of the Therapeutic Relational Field

Ultimately, doing therapy as a mindfulness practice involves consciously choosing to function as the mindfulness of the intersubjective relational field of the therapy. Functioning as the mindfulness of the intersubjective relational field of the therapy requires experiencing the therapeutic relationship as the emergent co-arising of client and therapist subjectivities in each moment of the client-therapist encounter. In a very real sense client and therapist call each other into being from within the intersubjective relational matrix of their encounter in each moment.

The primary focus of the therapist's relational mindfulness practice is inquiry into and investigation of the client's self-experience. This involves empathic attunement to and engagement with the client, including registering the nuances of client affect, speech, and behavior and sensing their meaning and significance. Empathic attunement to the client's inner experience, as well as the emergent co-arising of each moment of the therapeutic relationship, requires the therapist's exquisite sensitivity to her own inner experience, and serves as the therapist's primary tool and guide, the basis for the therapist's optimal responsiveness in each subsequent moment.

Doing Therapy as Mindfulness Practice for the Therapist

Doing therapy as a mindfulness practice requires the perspective, anchored in experiential understanding, that "mind is in the room" (Minuchin, 1974), not between the ears. Mind exists as an emergent property of the intersubjective field in any relationship. Doing therapy as a mindfulness practice means self-consciously choosing to function as the mindfulness of the intersubjective field of the therapeutic relationship.

Functioning as the mindfulness of the intersubjective field of the therapeutic relationship requires radically decentering from one's own self-experience and focusing on being friendly toward, and curious about, the client's self-experience as it arises, moment by moment, as an emergent quality of the intersubjective relational field of the therapeutic encounter.

The Therapist as Mindfulness of the Intersubjective Relational Field

As the mindfulness of the intersubjective relational field, the therapist brings all of the qualities of healing presence into the intersubjective context, including unconditional acceptance, nonjudging, empathic attunement, compassion, warmth, friendliness, interest, curiosity, trust, patience, courage, authenticity, and optimal responsiveness.

Mindful inquiry and investigation of the client's self-experience is driven by friendly curiosity and compassionate interest, which are embodied in the three simple questions:

What is this?

What's happening?

What's needed?

Therapeutic *optimal responsiveness* is a form of wise insight, based on the therapist's mindful inquiry and investigation into what's happening with, and what's needed by, the client in each moment of therapy in order to move the therapeutic process forward. Therapeutic optimal responsiveness is similar in couples, family, and group therapy as well, but the intersubjective mind in the room is more complex.

Just as in practicing any formal mindfulness meditation, for instance focusing on mindfulness of breathing sensations when practicing breath-awareness meditation, or mindfulness of body sensations when doing the body scan, for the therapist doing therapy as a mindfulness practice, the therapist focuses on mindfulness of the intersubjective relational field. However, because the intersubjective relational field of the therapy comprises at least two subjectivities, functioning as the mindfulness of the intersubjective relational field requires that the therapist be capable of radical decentering, or disidentification from, egocentric self-awareness.

What Is This? What's Happening?

Functioning as the mindfulness of the intersubjective relational field, the therapist, from a radically decentered perspective and oriented by two basic questions—"What is this?" and "What's happening?"—empathically attunes to, explores, investigates, and comes to understand the client's subjective experience of affects, memories, impulses, desires, and behaviors that are often feared, painful, shameful, or dysfunctional. The client's experience of the therapist's warmth, kindness, authenticity, accurate empathy, compassion, clear lack of personal agenda or imposed ego needs, and radically decentered perspective help the client to feel safe and implicitly invite the client to join with the therapist as the collaborative mindfulness of the relational field. The therapist, though serving as mindfulness of the intersubjective relational field and focused on the client's self-experience, is still called on to be authentic and transparent, so that the client feels safe enough to be willing to engage in the therapeutic process.

What's Needed?

In addition to the two basic questions that drive mindful inquiry and investigation in formal mindfulness meditation practice ("What is this?" and "What's happening?"), doing psychotherapy as a mindfulness practice involves a third question that arises from the therapist's professional role of helper and healer and the therapist's compassionate concern and genuine desire to alleviate the client's suffering. The third question is "What's needed?"

The question "What's needed?" is often implicit in the responses to "What is this?" and "What's happening?" And often what's needed is simply continuing to be mindful of the therapeutic process as it unfolds. Sometimes a more active intervention is called for, including further inquiry, interpretation, psychoeducation, role-play, or even providing specific information or suggestions.

In psychotherapeutic mindful inquiry and investigation, the question "What's needed?" can be a primary question as well, arising from the professional role and responsibilities of the psychotherapist as professional helper and healer. "What is this?" and "What's happening?" are similar, though "What is this?" is oriented more to objects, and "What's happening?" is oriented more to processes. You can use just one of the questions or both interchangeably according to your preference.

"What's needed?" focuses on resonance with and attunement to the client as a whole from the perspective of fulfilling treatment goals; meeting the client's developmental needs; developing client strengths; and understanding the risks, opportunities, and contingencies of that particular moment of the therapy. The question "What's needed?" is driven by the therapist's compassionate concern, mindfulness of the intersubjective field of the therapeutic relationship as it unfolds moment by moment, and desire to be optimally responsive.

Exercise 10.3: Practicing Mindful Inquiry and Investigation as Therapy—What's Happening? What's Needed?

1. Recall a moment in therapy with a particular client. Allow yourself to not know what's happening, and instead imagine attuning to the moment with beginner's mind.

2. As best you can, instead of trying to figure out what's going on, let yourself not know what's happening; let the moment disclose itself to you and tell you about itself. Then, as best you can, get out of your own way, and from a radically decentered stance imagine the moment itself eliciting the most skillful response.

3. If you can experience yourself as not separate from the moment but as one with the moment, you might experience an intuitive insight into what the moment requires in order to unfold into the next moment in a manner that will be of benefit. It could be that nothing is required, or that nothing is required of you except your listening presence, or that it would be helpful for you to say something.

4. This experience requires tremendous clarity and trust in your own inner wisdom as cultivated in your personal mindfulness practice discipline. It's best to practice this first in your own meditation practice, then in personal life situations, then in doing therapy.

The Importance of Functioning as the Mindfulness of the Intersubjective Field

Clinically, allowing yourself to function as the mindfulness of the intersubjective field of the therapeutic relationship is vital, because it allows you and your client together to collaboratively "see into" (perceive, experientially know) and explore how and why the client gets stuck in adventitious suffering, and it illuminates for you and your client together how your client can get unstuck. Functioning as the mindfulness of the intersubjective field of the therapeutic relationship is the foundation for the therapist's optimal responsiveness in the moment by moment unfolding of the therapeutic process.

Collaborative mindful inquiry within the therapeutic relationship depends on accurate attunement and an "empathic-introspective mode of investigation" (Shapiro, 1995, pp. 36–41). The empathic attunement of the therapist in each moment, as well as the therapist's willingness to take responsibility for empathic failures, encourages and supports the client's willingness to explore, understand, and repair empathic failures and to attempt behavior changes. Functioning as the mindfulness of the intersubjective field of the therapeutic relationship, in the form of moment to moment empathic attunement, is the basis of the therapist's understanding of what's needed for the client's growth and healing.

Summary

In this chapter we explored how therapist mindfulness functions within the therapeutic process and relationship, as well as how doing therapy can be a mindfulness practice for the therapist. We also looked at the attitudinal factors comprising the therapist's healing presence and implications for the therapist's listening and responding.

Chapter 10 also presented a variety of mini-mindfulness exercises that you can use as preparatory practices prior to welcoming your clients into session. Most significantly, we explored how the therapist can intentionally function as the mindfulness of the intersubjective relational field of the therapeutic encounter in a way that supports the therapist's optimal responsiveness and enhances the necessary conditions for client insight and behavior change.

Before exploring the client's mindfulness practice, we need to account for one more element of the mindfulness pyramid model: the intersubjective diamond (see figure 9 in chapter 4). The intersubjective diamond represents the emergent, intersubjective relational field of therapy. In chapter 11 we will explore and experience the underlying foundation of intersubjectivity in the therapeutic relationship, what Thich Nhat Hanh refers to as "interbeing" (1988a, 1988b). Experientially understanding intersubjectivity, that the fundamental context of subjectivity is relational (Stolorow & Atwood, 1992), is what allows the therapist to function effectively as the mindfulness of the relational field.

Chapter 11

The Intersubjective Diamond: Accounting for Interbeing

In this chapter we'll explore the *intersubjective diamond*, the element of the mindfulness pyramid model that depicts the self as contingently co-arising, not separate, and examine the intersubjective diamond's implications for psychotherapy. In the present moment there is no experience of separate self. We construct our sense of separate self with narrative, which requires past and future constructed from memory and fantasy. Without past and future, our separate self-identity, the story we tell ourselves about who we are, falls away. There is just what is, in the present moment.

Charlotte Joko Beck, founder of the San Diego Zen Center and the Ordinary Mind Zen School (Beck, 1993; Beck & Smith, 1989), along with a senior student, dharma heir, and cofounder of Ordinary Mind, Elihu Genmyo Smith, and another student, poet Allen Kaprow, wrote beautifully about the experience of separate self, and the reality of interbeing, in their rendition of the Buddha's Four Noble Truths, which is recited daily in Ordinary Mind Zen centers:

> Caught in the self-centered dream, only suffering. Holding to self-centered thought, exactly the dream. Each moment, life as it is, the only teacher. Being just this moment, compassion's way.

Ayya Khema, a famous Theravadan Buddhist nun and mindfulness meditation teacher, said in a similar vein, "In the beginning mindfulness takes away worries and fears about past and future and keeps us anchored in the present. In the end it points to the right view of the self" (Khema, 1987, pp. 167–172).

Exercise 11.1: Guided Reflection on Intersubjectivity and Interbeing in the Therapeutic Relationship

Guided audio for this exercise is available at http://www.newharbinger.com /32752.

1. Call to mind a client you are currently treating, or have treated in the past. See this person vividly in the mind's eye.

2. As you hold the image of this client in awareness, recall a particular therapy session; better yet, focus on a particular moment in the session.

3. Use the power of your imagination and sense memory to revivify the felt sense of the session and moment. Make the moment palpable again.

4. Notice and feel the quality of your presence and attentiveness with the client.

5. What words best characterize the quality of your presence and attentiveness?

6. What do you observe about the client? What do you empathically intuit or sense about the client's experience?

7. What qualities of presence, attentiveness, and responsiveness are called for—and called forth—by the client or the moment as a whole?

8. How clear, confused, alert, dull, composed, balanced, at ease, grounded, solid, centered, distressed, shaky, uneasy, or uncertain do you feel in the moment?

9. How does this affect your behavior, your relationship toward your inner experience, and your attitude toward the client?

10. Continue to observe the client closely. What is the client doing now? What reactions do the client's behaviors evoke in you? What reactions do your presence and attentiveness seem to evoke in the client?

11. Reflect on and journal about how you experienced the client in and through the exercise and about your experience doing the exercise.

12. Repeat the exercise with two more clients. With each client, notice what the client calls forth in you and how your presence affects the client. In addition, during the next week do the exercise in real time with several different clients during therapy sessions. Notice how you are with each client. How does each client call you into being in a different way? How does each client respond differently to you and evoke different responses from you?

Intersubjectivity refers to the idea that who we are is completely dependent on the relational, situational, and historical context in the present moment. Self-experience, in particular, is shaped and determined by its relational context. From the perspective of intersubjectivity theory, relationship is the context of being and the foundation of all subjective experience; thus all subjective experience is actually intersubjective (Stolorow & Atwood, 1992). Self-experience (subjectivity) cannot be extracted from its relational context. Also, self-experience is subject to change because relational contexts are always changing. Through noticing how our way of relating to the moment shapes the experience of the moment, mindfulness practice experientially gives rise to similar insights.

Narcissistic Injuries and Disjunctions in the Therapeutic Relationship

Human relationships are complex and subtle; therapy relationships even more so. Often our clients are emotionally fragile and easily hurt (*narcissistically vulnerable* in self-psychology and intersubjectivity terms), either due to acute distress or as part of a longer-term characterological problem. Depending on the context and the client's vulnerability, even subtle lapses of attention or misunderstandings on the part of the therapist can cause narcissistic injuries and disjunctions in the therapeutic relationship (Wolf, 1988; Epstein, 1998; Bromberg, 1998, 2006; Shapiro, 1995).

The client might experience confusion, dissociation, anger, or hurt and react outwardly with hostility, sarcasm, silence, or dissociative spaciness. He or she might also shut down emotionally, becoming circumstantial or tangential, or use other forms of defensive distancing, thus retreating to a less vulnerable level of connection.

Unintended injuries and disjunctions occur inevitably in all intimate relationships, not just in psychotherapy. The capacity to repair such injuries and hurts is a central feature of healthy relationships. It requires the ability to tolerate distress, to decenter and disidentify from thoughts and emotions, to attune empathically, and to take the perspective of the other. Working through such injuries and successfully repairing the disjunction strengthens a relationship and often leads to increased closeness and intimacy.

In psychotherapy, particularly in psychodynamic therapies that focus on the experience of the therapeutic relationship, unintended narcissistic injuries, relationship disjunctions, and empathic misattunement, are all opportunities for growth, development, and healing for the client, the therapist, and the therapeutic relationship. They also can cause lasting negative impacts that affect the client's sense of trust and safety in the therapeutic relationship, as well as the outcome of therapy. The impact of injuries and disjunctions in the therapeutic relationship is rarely neutral. Whether the impact is positive or negative depends largely on the therapist's response.

Mindfulness in the Breach

The therapist's level 1 practice (personal mindfulness meditation practice) and level 2 practice (consciously doing therapy as a mindfulness practice) systematically enhance the therapist's ability to recognize and respond skillfully to narcissistic injuries and relationship disjunctions. Practice at these levels cultivates and strengthens the therapist's capacity to perceive, experience, and respond therapeutically (and optimally) within the intersubjective context of the relationship.

For example, if the therapist is doing therapy as a mindfulness practice, he experiences each moment of the therapeutic relationship from a radically decentered perspective. The therapist perceives, experiences, and participates in the relationship, moment by moment, as contingently co-arising relational space. The therapist commits to being the mindfulness of the space, with everything that implies about the quality of the therapist's presence and relatedness in each moment.

In response to a disjunction, the therapist might be curious, interested, compassionate, and concerned; and he would likely inquire empathically into the client's experience of the disjunction, wanting to understand what he said or did that was hurtful to the client in the intersubjective context in order to repair the breach and avoid similar hurts in the future. Empathic investigation of the injury can also give rise to new insights into old injuries and developmental derailments as they come into play within the intersubjective relational field of the therapy.

Not only do such relationship repairs permit the work of therapy to proceed, but they are also important aspects of the therapeutic work. Having strengthened capacities for distress tolerance, emotion self-regulation, and interpersonal skills, such as decentering and perspective taking (Linehan, 1993a, 1993b) in the process of repairing disjunctions, hopefully the client will be more likely to move beyond regressive defenses when appropriate, to be more open and vulnerable, and to trust the intimacy of the restored intersubjective context.

Self psychology (Wolf, 1988), intersubjectivity theory (Stolorow, Brandchaft & Atwood 1987; Stolorow & Atwood, 1992; Stolorow, Atwood & Brandchaft 1994), and other contemporary psychoanalytic approaches, including those based on attachment theory (Wallin, 2007) and evidence from neuroscience and infant-observational studies (Siegel, 2007, 2012), all view therapeutic relationship disjunctions as opportunities for restoration, reconstruction, and growth of a more adaptive, coherent, and resilient self-experience.

From an intersubjective perspective, the therapist assumes that she participated, at least coequally, with the client in any relationship disjunction or rupture, no matter how unintentionally. Furthermore, the therapist's compassionate curiosity, and the client's involvement in collaborative empathic inquiry into the causes of the disjunction, begins to develop a shared understanding of the disjunction that includes both therapist and client in the explanation. The therapist's optimal response to a disjunction in the therapeutic relationship simultaneously

1. repairs the disruption in the relationship;

2. soothes and heals the narcissistic injury that caused the rupture;

3. encourages compassionate awareness and insight into the narcissistic vulner-ability underlying the injury and the associated defensive behaviors;

4. cultivates self-awareness, insight, and compassion;

5. strengthens emotional resilience; and

6. reactivates and restimulates psychological development and growth where it had been shut down or derailed.

The following guidelines should be helpful when seeking to repair disjunctions in the therapeutic relationship:

1. Notice external signs of the disconnect in sudden changes in the client's behavior and mood, including irritability, withdrawal, avoidance of eye contact, other avoidant body language, change in content of therapeutic dialogue, or withdrawal into silence.

2. Tune into corresponding shifts in emotional tone in yourself. Ask yourself what's happening in you.

3. Empathically attune to the client's experience as well as to the relational context; stay with the client's experience in the moment. Don't get ahead of the client.

4. To avoid premature interpretations or conclusions about what the client is thinking or feeling, use general questions, such as "What just happened?" or "What's happening?" or "I sense you might be feeling some pressure or distress. What is your experience?" If there is no response, or the client denies anything is wrong, you might continue, "I wonder if you had a reaction to my saying or doing _____ (fill in the blank). What was your experience?" Avoid specific suggestions about what your client is feeling unless it is very clear.

5. Avoid defensiveness and projecting blame, especially if the client blames you or is defensive.

6. Instead, openheartedly investigate the intersubjective context of the slight with compassion and care. Empathically attune to both the anger and the underlying hurt.

7. As therapist, what did you do or say that was hurtful?

8. How did it feel to, and what did it mean to, your client?

9. What was your own inner experience when you said or did whatever caused the disjunction?

10. Together with your client, reflect on how it feels to investigate the relationship disjunction collaboratively.

Exercise 11.2: Further Exploration of Intersubjectivity

Guided audio for this exercise is available at http://www.newharbinger.com /32752.

1. Choose another client you are treating or have treated in the past, and vividly and palpably allow the image and feeling of that client to arise in the mind's eye.

2. Carefully note the nuances of your inner experience as your perception and experience of the client's presence inform and evoke your response.

3. Allow yourself to empathically sense the client's experience as well.

4. Can you experience the moment of encounter as "stepping into the space between" (Bromberg, 1998), in which your experience of self is an emergent property of the moment of encounter, co-arising with the client's experience of self, again and again in each moment?

5. See if you can re-create this experience again for yourself, right now.

6. Bring the image of another client to mind.

7. As best you can, recall a particular therapy session and a specific moment during the session.

8. Recall the quality of your attention and presence with that client. As best you can, re-create your inner experience—sensations, emotions, perceptions, and thoughts. Recall what you said and did, and how it felt.

9. What did you observe about the client's behavior? What was your sense of the client's inner experience?

10. What did you sense about the client's reaction to the quality of your attention and presence and to your inner experience and behavior?

11. What did the client's behavior, and your felt sense of the client's presence and inner experience, evoke in you?

12. How did the client's presence and your empathic attunement to it both evoke and inform your own self-experience and shape your response as you brought each other into "being" in the moment of encounter, in the "space between."

Do the same exercise with one or two more clients. Take your time, focusing on the experience of stepping into the space between.

1. Notice who "you" are with each client, both in terms of your self-experience and your behavior.

2. Who is the self, the "I," that each client evokes? How does it feel?

3. How do these "I's" experience themselves? Are the self-experiences the same, or do you notice differences?

Reflect on your experience of exercise 11.2 as a whole. Hopefully you noticed how each client evoked a slightly different quality of presence and responsiveness specific to his or her needs in a particular moment and context. If the therapist has an intersubjective perspective, she can perhaps more easily understand, and allow the client to elicit, the relational experience required for healing.

Often the elicitations of the client are nonverbal, coming in the form of enactments and systemic paradoxical binds that the therapist needs to understand and respond to creatively from outside the system. Examples include, "If you love me, don't love me," or "If you really knew and understood me, you would be disgusted, and since you're not disgusted, you don't really know and understand me." Such systemic paradoxical binds are more often not articulated but rather enacted by the client with the therapist within the crucible of the therapeutic relationship. In my experience, my personal mindfulness practice has enhanced my ability to clearly perceive, appreciate, and respond compassionately to the client's needs without getting trapped in the paradoxical bind being enacted. This can often be as simple as verbally appreciating the wisdom of the defensive system as an emotional (and sometimes physical) early survival adaptation in an untenable situation.

Such was the case with my client Oliver, who at times seemed so dissociated and disconnected that I wondered if he suffered from schizoid disorder or severe autism. When we first met, he almost completely avoided eye contact. Oliver spent many hours each week in interactive computer games and role-playing games. He took great pleasure in designing intricate strategies and characters and then sharing them with me in session. Surprisingly, in spite of his social anxiety and avoidance of direct emotional connection, Oliver also had a sizable network of friends who cared deeply for him and with whom he made great effort to stay connected. He also had strong relationships with siblings and extended family, which he also attended to with care.

Oliver knew I taught mindfulness-based stress reduction and was interested in attending class. I was concerned that he needed a practice that would be less inwardly focused and more activating, but I decided to trust him (he had been my client for several years already), and he proceeded to take the course. To my surprise, the mindfulness practice as well as the group experience seemed to bring Oliver out of his shell. It grounded him, allowed him to experientially identify with me more closely, and allowed us together to explore the meaning of his extreme involvement with gaming from a more objective, decentered perspective.

Oliver came from an extremely chaotic family. The man he related to as his father was an alcoholic, and sometimes abusive and violent. Oliver's mother was loving but often ineffectual. The family moved frequently due to financial problems. Not until high school did Oliver live in the same house for more than a year.

In high school Oliver found teachers who took a personal interest in him. They mentored him and encouraged him to pursue his talent for computer programming. He also took refuge in role-playing games such as Dungeons and Dragons, in which he could connect with peers, imagine having supernatural powers, and escape from the chaos and sense of helplessness at home. With computer programming and gaming as anchors, as well as kind and caring mentors, Oliver became the first person in his family to attend college.

During the course of our work together, Oliver faced a number of serious situational and mental health crises. In each crisis he increased the time he spent gaming as a means of self-soothing and holding himself together. As I came to understand and then appreciate and admire aloud the ingenuity of using role-playing and interactive computer games as psychological survival adaptations, Oliver began to come out of his shell, make more direct eye contact, and make himself more available for emotional connection.

Both mindfulness practice and the intersubjective perspective helped me relate to Oliver with beginner's mind. Although I had concerns about more serious underlying disorders that might have precluded individual psychotherapy, and certainly insight-oriented psychotherapy as treatment of choice, I was unwilling to commit quickly to those diagnoses. Instead I chose to see how Oliver responded to treatment. Although at first Oliver was unable to talk about gaming and dissociation, I trusted that the intersubjective relational context and Oliver's responses to my healing presence would inform appropriate responses from me.

Mindfulness, Intersubjectivity, and the Primacy of Relationship

In figure 9 (chapter 4), the diamond formed by the intersection of the client and therapist pyramids represents the intersubjective relational field of the therapy as an emergent property of the intersecting subjectivities of client and therapist. *Emergent property* means that the subjective experiences of client and therapist, though apparently separate and distinct, are actually mutually contingent and co-arising. The subjectivities of client and therapist evoke and call each other into being, coconstructing the experiential context of the therapeutic relationship as it unfolds from moment to moment.

Again, think about how you experience yourself with different clients. Each client evokes qualities of presence and responsiveness specific to his or her needs, defenses, and desires in that moment and context. For a seasoned and mature therapist, as well as for trainees who aren't too afraid to make mistakes, these responses may not be fully conscious or considered, but so long as you are solid, centered, clear, and well trained, they can usually be trusted.

My First Glimpse of Intersubjectivity in a Therapeutic Encounter

In September of 1978, a Boeing 727 collided with a small plane and crashed in a residential neighborhood of San Diego, California, killing all 135 people on board, the two men in the small plane, and seven people on the ground, including a family of four. The crash injured nine others on the ground and destroyed or damaged twenty-two homes. My training cohort was in its second semester of graduate internship. Our clinic held the mental health contract with the county for the area where the crash occurred, so it was our job to provide crisis services for survivors, including neighborhood residents, family members, and airline employees based in San Diego.

In addition to individual crisis-intervention sessions, we held several large community meetings in the neighborhood where the crash occurred. Anyone could attend. During these meetings, after several community leaders and our clinic leaders addressed the large group, we broke into smaller groups of eight to ten to give people a chance to talk about their reactions and feelings regarding the disaster. A senior clinician and an intern co-led each small group.

My group had an actively hallucinating member suffering from chronic schizophrenia who everyone in the neighborhood knew by sight. Being particularly vulnerable to the tragedy and disruption of the event, she was having trouble sitting still and listening, was muttering warnings out loud to herself and others, and was pacing around in the middle of the group. I looked to my cotherapist, the director of the outpatient clinic, but he looked baffled. The outpatient clinic did mostly psychodynamic psychotherapy with higher functioning patients.

Prior to graduate school I had worked for several years at a residential group-treatment facility for patients suffering from chronic schizophrenia, so I wasn't frightened by what was happening, though I had no conscious idea of how to intervene. Suddenly I found myself standing up in front of this terrified woman and gently but matter-of-factly asking her name. Norma, she said. Then I started pacing alongside Norma, speaking to her about what I sensed were her concerns, letting her know that we all shared similar concerns, and encouraging her to sit down with me to help with the work of the group.

In retrospect, I realize that I literally was "pacing" Norma, like an Ericksonian or strategic therapist, though I didn't realize it at the time. I physically paced her disruptive walking and normalized it by walking alongside her inside the group circle, making the pacing therapeutic for the group as a whole as a physical expression of the traumatic anxiety and horror that everyone was feeling but not exactly talking about. This helped Norma to reconnect with the group, and the group with Norma. The group members could now experience what had felt like a disruption as a useful contribution. Norma was a participating group member.

Also, during my work in the residential treatment facility I had learned to listen for underlying meanings and contexts in thought-disordered and delusional speech. So I verbally paced Norma's paranoid utterances with reality-based statements, affirming the perceptions and fears to which I sensed (and hoped!) her delusions referred while also reality testing their delusional content.

A tragic and horrific plane crash *had* killed many people and destroyed many homes, but the sky was not falling, the world was not ending, Jesus was not yet coming, and it was safe to stay in the building and in our group. In the group we were helping each other to cope with the trauma, sadness, and loss and to take steps to rebuild the neighborhood and our lives after the catastrophe. Within the group was not only a safe place, but a good place to be.

I had no conscious idea why I was doing what I did. I see now that I was responding to the need to protect the integrity of the group, and to protect Norma from herself while still including her in the group. Fortunately I felt relatively relaxed and confident, and I was able to trust myself and the moment (the internship was almost over and had gone well). At that time I had never heard the word "intersubjectivity" before, nor was I familiar with mindfulness meditation. In retrospect I can see how my experience and response were evoked by the intersubjective context of the group and the clinical training situation, and by the need to respond helpfully to what was happening and what was needed.

My response to Norma was based on implicit mindfulness and an unarticulated, experiential understanding of intersubjectivity. Rather than being afraid of Norma's psychotic process, I allowed myself to enter into it and implicitly invited her into my subjectivity as well. Her subjectivity (including what she needed) informed my experience and response, as mine did hers.

Intersubjective experiencing requires mindfulness, an acute awareness of and attunement to each moment through full engagement with the moment from a radically decentered perspective. Rather than focusing on self and other, the focus is on fully engaging and experiencing each moment as it arises. Though it may sound cliché, mindfulness means becoming one with the moment. If you can let go of primary identification with the experience of being me, myself, and I, and instead let your primary identification be with the relational field as a whole as it arises in each moment, then the moment itself will evoke a skillful response.

Trusting the moment to evoke a skillful response requires a solid foundation in quality training and supervised experience. In the example above, that foundation came from being at the end of a difficult but successful year of nearly full-time psychotherapy training; from several years of working in a residential treatment facility for people with chronic schizophrenia; and from several positive, personal therapy experiences, both individually and in groups.

Thich Nhat Hanh, the famous Vietnamese Zen teacher and popularizer of mindfulness around the world, puts it simply thus: "I am, therefore you are. You are, therefore I am" (1996, p. 87).

The subjective experiencing of both client and therapist contingently co-arise in every moment of the therapeutic encounter. An intersubjective perspective on experiencing helps us to understand how subjective experiencing is constructed.

The basic capacity for subjective experiencing depends on interpersonal relational development in infancy and beyond (Siegel, 2007, 2012; Wallin, 2007). The experience of each participant in the therapeutic relationship is contingent on that of the other participant or participants (Stolorow et al., 1987). In couples, family, or group therapy, the same emergent, intersubjective property of the relational field applies. However, the complexity of the relational field increases exponentially as the number of participants increases.

In sum, we call each other into being through the quality of mutual presence and connection in each moment, particularly in psychotherapy (Rogers, 1980; Stern, 2004; Siegel, 2007; Stolorow & Atwood, 1992). This insight in psychoanalysis gave rise to an entirely new way of thinking about the therapeutic relationship—that the analyst was not a neutral screen for the client's projections but rather an active participant in cocreating the relationship.

Many highly skilled therapists don't do formal mindfulness meditation practice, nor is their clinical work informed by intersubjectivity theory. However, I would argue that the best therapists still implicitly perceive and experience the therapeutic relationship intersubjectively. They attune to their clients with empathic precision. They are exquisitely sensitive to the changing context of the therapeutic process from moment to moment. And they allow the present-moment context to inform their clinical choices and responses to clients.

I would call this natural ability *implicit mindfulness*. Since mindfulness is an innate human capacity, for some therapists it may simply be a gift of temperament. Others who don't practice mindfulness explicitly learn through being supervised by, or being in therapy with, wise, seasoned clinicians, as well as through many years of consciously cultivating clinical wisdom.

My own experience, validated by the experiences of trusted mentors and colleagues who have practiced mindfulness for many years, is that mindfulness meditation, in addition to good clinical supervision and personal therapy, can be extraordinarily valuable to therapists in helping to refine and strengthen the psychological capacities and skills required for bringing about successful treatment outcomes.

Many therapists are now embracing a view that self-experience, and from a larger perspective "being" itself, is wholly contingent, contextual, and intersubjective (Stolorow & Atwood, 1992; Gergen, 1991). In other words, neither you, nor I, nor anyone else has essential self-existence. In traditional Buddhist psychology this is called "emptiness" or "voidness," and it is often misunderstood to mean that nothing exists. Rather it means that nothing, including the self, exists separately, or has essential self-nature, apart from everything else.

Thich Nhat Hanh puts it simply: "In order to understand anything as empty you have to ask empty of what? The answer is empty of essential self. If it is empty of essential self, then what is it full of? The answer is, it is full of everything else" (1988a, pp. 7–10).

Understanding the self as intersubjective and empty of essence allows us to let go more easily of fixed ideas and expectations about our clients (and ourselves). It is easier to hold theoretical constructs and clinical training with a light touch and to experience each moment of our clinical work with beginner's mind.

Experiencing the self as empty also helps us to understand the intersubjective diamond as the transformational crucible of the therapeutic relationship. The intersubjective diamond is the continually changing and unfolding relational present, within which therapist and client co-arise, are intersubjectively present for each other, and are healed together—in the root sense of the word *healing*, "restored to wholeness" (Kabat-Zinn, 2005, pp. 321–339; 2013, pp. 175–201).

Please don't think of experiencing the self as empty as being abstract or theoretical. It is actually experiential and very practical. I would argue that it is a concrete and literal description of the central mode of action of psychotherapy. It is very difficult to describe in words or to operationalize as a variable for quantitative research, but it can be understood experientially, both contemplatively and clinically, as well as researched using qualitative methods. I also believe that for us as therapists, even a glimpse of emptiness, whether through meditation or simply as an insight in the course of living, can enhance flexibility, creativity, optimal responsiveness, and ultimately therapeutic efficacy, as long as we hold the experience lightly and don't reify it, cling to it, or turn it into a position to defend.

Exercise 11.3: Glimpses of Intersubjectivity and Emptiness

1. Think of a turning point in the course of a therapy, when your client had a profound shift in understanding or glimpsed a new way of being as a real possibility.

2. Were you also aware of a simultaneous shift and emotional response in your own being?

3. Think of a therapy experience in which change was more gradual, but nonetheless significant.

4. Reflect on how your inner experience of being with the client, as well as your experience of the client's being with you, gradually shifted and changed over time.

The Intersubjective Diamond: Therapist and Client Healed Together

The therapist's healing presence is an essential precondition for therapeutic change. Healing presence can also be understood as fundamentally intersubjective and contingent, because it arises in a relational context, in the present moment, as an emergent property of the therapist-client encounter.

Therefore we can understand therapeutic change as the effect of the intersubjective co-arising of the therapist's healing presence and the client's subjectivity within the transformational crucible (represented by the intersubjective diamond) of the therapeutic relational field.

Healing presence initially addresses the client's hurts and needs, but ultimately it touches the therapist just as much. In the crucible of the intersubjective diamond, client and therapist are healed (made whole) together (Boorstein, 1991; Santorelli, 1999; Kabat-Zinn, 2005). As therapists we are called upon to let ourselves be healed again and again, with every client that we treat. It is both a challenge and a perk of our work.

Exercise 11.4: Meditation on Interbeing and No Essential Self

Guided audio for this exercise is available at http://www.newharbinger.com /32752.

1. Cut an apple into pieces and choose one. (An apple wedger works well if you are doing this exercise with a group.)

2. Look carefully and deeply into this piece of apple. Can you see the cloud in the apple? I mean this quite concretely. The moisture content in the apple derives from and is cloud in the most literal sense.

3. Can you also see the soil in the apple, the rich dirt in which the apple tree is planted? All of the mineral content in the apple is soil.

4. Can you see in the apple the labor energy of the farmers, the cultivators, the fieldworkers, the pickers, the packers, the truckers, the warehouse workers, and the grocers, all whose labor brought the apple to you, including your own or that of the person whose labor earned the money to purchase the apple? What about the labor energy of all those who fed, clothed, housed, and in other ways cared for the workers whose energy brought you the apple? What about the parents, grandparents, and ancestors of those people as far back as you can imagine, all part of a great chain of being culminating here and now in this wedge of apple, and in you? If you can't see it, look more deeply.

5. Can you see the sun in the apple, and experience the sun in yourself? Again, I mean this quite literally because the energy driving the process of photosynthesis, which ultimately created the apple, is solar energy. The life energy in you is also solar energy derived from plants and animals, and the sun's energy drives the carbon-oxygen and hydrological cycles that sustain all life on Earth. Reflect on the sun in the apple for a minute or two.

6. Now reflect on where the sun comes from, according to your best understanding of its origins. Can you think of one thing in the entire universe that you're not connected to through this piece of apple?

7. Eat the apple mindfully, experiencing each moment of eating with sensitivity and care, with all the senses awake, holding in awareness the question, "What is this experience we call 'eating'?"

8. When the eating sensations disappear, rest in the sensations of breathing in the belly. With each breath moment, experience yourself participating in the larger breath of the planet, the Earth's carbon-oxygen cycle. See if you can let go of experiencing your body as breathing separate from everything else, and instead feel yourself being breathed by the great forests, the oceans, and the

atmosphere, along with all other living beings. This isn't poetic metaphor—this is science.

9. For the last few minutes of this meditation, just let yourself rest in the sensations of being breathed by the larger breath of the planetary carbon-oxygen cycle. Feeling yourself being supported and cradled by the larger breath of the planet. Intuitively trusting it to breathe you.

10. Reflect on your experience of this meditation. How did you respond to the instructions to see a cloud, soil, labor energy, and the sun in the apple? What did you notice when asked to reflect on the origins of the sun? What thoughts or emotional reactions did you have?

This meditation focuses on the experience of interbeing as it plays out in one of the most commonplace activities in our lives—eating. It also highlights the power of mindful awareness, and the experience of interbeing, as an antidote to feelings of isolation and alienation by making clear our intrinsic connection to each other and all life.

Summary

In this chapter we explored two dynamics of interbeing and intersubjectivity in the therapeutic relationship: as the basis for the therapist's doing therapy as a mindfulness practice, and as another way the therapist's mindfulness practice can enhance therapeutic efficacy. In chapter 12 we will investigate level 3 of the mindfulness pyramid model, the client's mindfulness practice.

Chapter 12

The Client's
Mindfulness Practice

In this chapter we'll explore level 3 of the mindfulness pyramid model, the client's mindfulness practice. We will examine a variety of practices for our clients, what types of practice are beneficial for which clients, and indications and contraindications for explicitly teaching both formal and informal mindfulness practices to clients.

The pyramid shape recommended itself as a model for incorporating mindfulness in psychotherapy because it illustrated my belief that the depth of the therapist's personal practice and understanding, more than any other factor, determined the efficacy of mindfulness in psychotherapy, as much or more than explicitly teaching practices to clients. Just as clinical wisdom informs how we work with clients in deploying any psychotherapeutic technique or theory, the same is true for mindfulness meditation, only more so. With regard to incorporating mindfulness meditation in therapy, the therapist's experiential understanding is crucial.

This isn't to say that you shouldn't incorporate mindfulness in your clinical work if you don't have a long-standing mindfulness practice. Returning to the discussion in the introduction, I'm simply suggesting that you stay inside yourself. Teach what you know, and don't teach what you don't know. What follows are some case vignettes of clients with whom I incorporated mindfulness practice in therapy in various ways.

Any One of the Facets of the Mindfulness Pyramid Can Be Beneficial

Beth was referred to me for couples therapy by her psychiatrist, who was treating her for depression. Beth and her husband wanted to get pregnant, and she wanted to get off her antidepressant medications for the pregnancy without relapsing.

Beth and her husband, both medical professionals and very bright, had little regard for psychotherapy or behavioral medicine. In addition to having an underlying mood disorder, I soon discovered that Beth's marital-relationship dynamics were depressogenic, and neither spouse was interested in addressing them. When I suggested a conventional cognitive behavioral therapy treatment for depression with a focus on relapse prevention, she initially agreed but was very skeptical. In addition, I recommended that she attend my mindfulness-based stress reduction course. (Generally, I think it's best to refer clients to someone else for adjunctive MBSR, but at the time there were no other courses available, and I thought she could really benefit.)

Beth "completed" both the CBT treatment and the MBSR course, but, despite my encouragement and best efforts to understand her resistance, she was noncompliant with most of the CBT homework assignments and the MBSR home practice. She was disdainful of the CBT exercises, seeing them as silly and childish, and hated meditation practice, even though she could see intellectually how both could be helpful. She liked the yoga okay, but mostly as exercise. It seemed so uncomfortable for Beth to be still and to be with herself. She just did not want to go there. Despite Beth's noncompliance with homework, she attended her therapy sessions and seemed to benefit from the relationship. I wanted to establish a decent therapeutic alliance in case it was needed later.

I met with Beth several times for follow-up supportive therapy during her pregnancy, which she got through feeling good and without medication. Soon after the birth she went back on her antidepressants, but they didn't seem to work as well. Within nine months she had succumbed to a severe postpartum depression and was hospitalized. She returned to therapy briefly after discharge. I didn't see her for several years; then she called once again severely depressed. Again she was hospitalized. This time she went from inpatient to a cognitive-behavioral day-hospital program with a mindfulness component. Again she hated both the CBT exercises and the mindfulness practices.

Beth came back to see me in therapy after discharge from the day-hospital program. She had been on disability for a while and wanted to go back to work. We started to address her marital conflicts openly, her shame about her depression, and her fears about not being a good wife and mother. Although she still would not meditate, we were able to talk about how doing the CBT exercises and the mindfulness practices made her feel inadequate and "less than."

Beth liked to read the books I recommended about mindfulness. So we talked about ways to hold her shameful and self-doubting thoughts in awareness gently, without buying into them; how she could be more accepting and compassionate toward herself and others; and how she could use the attitudes and perspectives of mindfulness practice, such as allowing/letting be, nonjudging, loving-kindness, and compassion to self-regulate emotions and to disidentify from her harsh self-judging.

Although Beth never established a formal meditation practice discipline, she benefited greatly from our discussions of the mindfulness skills, inner capacities, attitudes, and perspectives (facet B of the mindfulness pyramid model). Together we came up with phrases she could say to remind herself that her thoughts and emotions were not factual reflections of life, or truths about herself. She would later report "hearing" these thoughts in my voice, reporting that the phrases were more effective when she could hear me saying them.

Eventually Beth started to come up with her own phrases and metaphors to amuse herself, including putting the phrases to Broadway show tunes and singing them. In retrospect, I realize now that this was an intervention right out of the acceptance and commitment therapy treatment manual, though I had no training in the method at the time.

Revisiting What's Happening? and What's Needed?

From a psychotherapeutic perspective, the practices represented by each of the four facets of the mindfulness pyramid model have potential benefits and risks, depending on the presenting symptoms and personality of the client.

Formal Practices

In my experience, formal mindfulness meditation practices are most beneficially used as a way of developing concentration and stabilizing the mind; decreasing anxiety; and strengthening the skills, inner capacities, attitudes, and perspectives of facet B. As a complement to psychodynamic, interpersonal, and cognitive behavioral psychotherapies, formal mindfulness meditation can potentially strengthen observing ego and capacities for self-awareness, insight, and distress tolerance, thereby enhancing the client's capacity to make use of and benefit from therapy; in addition, these capacities are therapeutic in and of themselves.

Mini-meditations and informal mindfulness practices are helpful in bridging the gap between formal practice and daily life. They highlight the skills, inner capacities, attitudes, and perspectives of facet B, and with the help of therapy, mini-meditations and informal mindfulness practices make it easier for clients to understand and apply experiences and insights from the formal meditation as ways of being and relating in daily life (facet D, way of being and relating to experience).

Some clients, like Beth, have an aversion to the formal practices; they resonate more with personalized metaphors and informal structured exercises, which they can use to learn mindfulness skills, inner capacities, attitudes, and perspectives and to apply mindfulness in daily life.

Mini-meditations and informal, on-the-spot practices are also extremely useful for clients who have a formal mindfulness practice that is compartmentalized and has not helped them cope with chronic depression or other long-term psychiatric illness or symptoms. These practices can serve as a way to connect experientially with their formal practice in daily life. In some instances, it may be necessary to teach additional formal practices that the client is not familiar with (for example, teaching the body scan or a mindful movement practice if the client has an established sitting meditation practice that has not helped alleviate his or her symptoms) or to "reteach" a practice by guiding it in a way that emphasizes a different experience or understanding (for example, incorporating elements of loving-kindness with perfectionistic, depressive clients who use their meditation practice as another club to beat themselves with).

For instance, William, a long-term Zen practitioner, presented with a lifelong history of major depression complicated by several very serious health concerns. He was interested in mindfulness-based therapy and came to me specifically for that reason. In doing the initial assessment, it became clear that William was very judgmental of himself and others. We did a simple breath-awareness practice together, adding some elements of sending loving-kindness toward himself.

I also suggested the informal practice of sending himself loving-kindness whenever he noticed he was being self-critical, and congratulating himself for noticing judging, explaining that self-judgment was most depressogenic when unnoticed. Finally I recommended that William send loving-kindness to random strangers he passed on the street.

I predicted that the longer he did the exercise, the more judging he would notice. I framed this positively, as an indication that the exercise was working, because the judgments William noticed would have less power to affect his mood. I also predicted that he would likely judge the judging, which I framed as a "wonderful catch"—even stronger evidence that the assignment was working. After each "catch" he was again to direct loving-kindness phrases toward himself or the person he had judged.

When it seems appropriate to recommend formal practice (a discussion of indications and contraindications follows later in the chapter), I discuss with the client why I think it could be helpful. If the client is willing, and there's enough time left in the therapy session, I guide the practice while doing the practice with the client; otherwise, I wait until the next session to introduce formal practice. The initial practice I choose to teach is based upon my own meditation practice experience, my clinical experience, my sense of the client and the client's personality, the client's therapeutic needs and goals, and my knowledge of the literature.

The initial practice is usually breath awareness or breath awareness and body scan, unless there are reasons to teach another practice first. I instruct the client to do the same practice daily using a guided meditation recording that I have made, and to keep a practice log as well as a journal if he or she chooses.

From then on, working with the formal practice, and introducing additional practices, is a collaborative process based on the client's experience doing the practice since the previous session (particularly what has seemed helpful or not helpful and why); the client's clinical needs and goals; and my assessment of the client's practice experience and what, if anything, could beneficially be added or subtracted to the formal practice.

Much of this process is based on my own mindfulness practice experience, clinical wisdom, and discernment. In prescribing practices for clients, it's most important to keep it simple and only prescribe practices that you know well from personal experience. The latter is key, because it means you have a personal basis for evaluating what the client's experience is likely to be, as well as what the likely benefits will be, and for anticipating potential negative reactions and obstacles.

Indications and Contraindications for Teaching Formal Meditation Practices to Clients

Although I am not aware of systematic research on the issue, based on my clinical experience I think it is safe to say that formal mindfulness practice is contraindicated for acutely psychotic or paranoid clients, clients in crisis, clients having a severe depressive or manic episode, and clients who are acutely intoxicated. Clients with borderline personality disorder can potentially benefit from regular but brief (five to ten minutes) periods of formal meditation practice (Linehan, 1993a, 1993b).

However, the issue of indications and contraindications for teaching formal mindfulness meditation is more complex than it first appears. It's important to understand the differences between the concentration and insight elements of what we now call "mindfulness meditation." In traditional Buddhist psychology, concentration meditation (in Pali, *shamatha*), sometimes called calm abiding, and mindfulness meditation (in Pali, *vipassana*), also called insight meditation, were actually completely different practices.

Mindfulness meditation in Buddhist psychology refers specifically to the "method of inquiry and investigation and mode of knowing" element of mindfulness as we know it in facet C of the mindfulness pyramid model. Mindful inquiry and investigation leads to clear seeing into the way things are. From clear seeing, spontaneous insights arise regarding how subjective experience (generally) and adventitious suffering (in particular) are constructed in each moment depending on how you react or respond in the moment before. Direct, experiential insights into adventitious suffering and the nature of subjectivity generate wisdom about how adventitious suffering can be ended and avoided and how joy and ease are most readily experienced.

Concentration meditation develops focus, energy, and one-pointedness, and stabilizes, calms, and strengthens the mind. It is both a beneficial practice in its own right and, traditionally, a prerequisite for effective mindfulness practice. In vipassana, as it is taught in North America and Europe—and from which the formal mindfulness meditation practices used in mindfulness-based stress reduction and its offspring are drawn—the differences between the concentration and mindfulness elements of the formal meditation practice are not emphasized. It's all considered mindfulness meditation. However, from the standpoint of traditional Buddhist psychology the meditations in MBSR and related therapies actually have significant elements of concentration practice, as well as mindfulness practice.

It's important to understand that it is the facet C (inquiry and investigation and mode of knowing) elements of formal meditation practice, as well as very intense and prolonged concentration practices, that pose the greatest risk of psychotic decompensation or severe dissociation for more severely disturbed clients if they are exposed unskillfully. I would also suggest that the risk for such clients increases with the duration of the practice period as well as with the type of practice. In my clinical experience, some clients with psychotic or borderline disorders can experience distress tolerance, anxiety reduction, and emotion self-regulation benefits from brief concentration meditations (for example, breath awareness or body scan, without an investigative component) for practice periods of five or ten minutes. However, longer periods of practice are potentially destabilizing.

Early formulations about using mindfulness meditation in psychotherapy generally considered psychotic, borderline personality, and severe dissociative disorder diagnoses to be automatic exclusions (Wilbur, Engler, & Brown, 1986). This was wise, because mindfulness meditation at the time was almost exclusively associated with the facet C (inquiry and investigation and mode of knowing) elements of practice, taking the form of residential silent vipassana or Zen retreats that lasted seven to ten days or more and included frequent formal meditation practice periods of forty-five minutes to an hour, from 5:30 or 6:00 a.m. until 9:00 or 10:00 p.m. For those lacking ego strength and solid reality testing prior to the retreat, retreats of this type really could, and sometimes did, precipitate decompensation.

The therapeutic conventional wisdom of the time was that you first had to have an ego (a healthy sense of self) before you could let it dissolve. You had to have a strong sense of self in order to see through it and let it go. The risk of decompensation is much less when clients experience concentration elements of formal practice in very small doses. My own clinical experience supports breath-awareness practice, emphasizing concentration, emotion self-regulation, and self-soothing, as being safe and often beneficial for clients with borderline personality disorder and chronic psychotic disorders in small doses of five to ten minutes in structured group settings. Marsha Linehan's seminal research with clients with borderline personality disorder strongly supports this claim also (Linehan, 1993b).

In my own experience in a day-hospital setting, working mostly with patients who had chronic schizophrenic, bipolar I, and severe personality disorders, the staff started each day with a five-minute silent meditation using the Benson relaxation response technique, a concentration practice involving breath awareness and repetition of a word. Many patients suffering from schizophrenia found focusing on breath sensations alone more soothing and less threatening than focusing on a word.

With one client who suffered from dissociative identity disorder, we decided together to begin our daily fifteen-minute, one-on-one contact sessions with a five-minute breath-awareness practice to help alleviate her initial anxiety and to facilitate the therapeutic process. Although this patient had many alters, and I never knew "who" would be showing up in my office, doing the five minutes of practice together helped both of us feel more integrated, whole, and connected. Interestingly, that brief five minutes of practice seemed to allow for the emergence of more alters, even though it also helped the client to feel safer, less anxious, and more "glued together." Although I am not aware of any confirmatory research, my clinical experience strongly suggests that brief duration of practice and emphasis on concentration rather than investigative or insight elements are both important for minimizing risk of decompensation and dissociation.

One of my fondest memories from my work in day treatment involves coaching the day treatment volleyball team, the Wooly Bullies. The patients had chosen our team name from the '60s hit song "Wooly Bully," by Sam the Sham and the Pharaohs. Naturally, it became our theme song, which we played, sang, and danced to after every practice and game. The culmination of our year was the county mental health day treatment volleyball tournament, in which about twenty teams from all over the county participated.

There was a role on the team for everyone. Anyone who wanted to could play. Patients who didn't want to play could help make the team banner or team shirts, take care of equipment, be in the cheering section, cue up the "Wooly Bully" song, be in charge of water, or do anything else they could think of that contributed to the team.

Nonparticipation was not an option. Nor was it an issue. We were all having too much fun participating, and the foundational norm of the group culture was participation. Both staff and patients were expected to participate as much as possible given their unique combination of skills, capacities, and limitations. As staff we made it clear that for the program to be therapeutically effective, we all had to be responsible, not just for ourselves but also for each other. We were all in it together. Each person participated, not only for himself or herself but also for everyone else.

It was understood that limitations were fluid, and that everyone (especially in a program for people suffering from chronic, severe mental illnesses) had good and bad days. So levels of individual participation of course waxed and waned. Patients trusted the staff to create and maintain a safe and supportive group environment within which each patient, no matter how ill, felt valued, appreciated, understood, and challenged to function at as high a level as possible, given the realities of the patient's inner capacities on any particular day.

We were a community. Each day began with a community meeting. After welcoming everyone, our first order of business was five minutes of breath-awareness meditation (based on the Benson relaxation response). The meditation helped the group to settle, and the communal silence, brief enough that it didn't feel threatening, helped everyone feel more connected. This was particularly useful (and perhaps even easier in the silence) with a population that was generally paranoid and avoidant. After meditation anyone who wanted to could check in with the community, and then the staff member in charge did an empathic summing-up focused on connecting all of that day's participants to each other and their common program goals. Then we reviewed the day's schedule and adjourned the meeting.

Volleyball in particular made it clear how much we depended on each other as a community. It is truly a team sport. No one could do it in isolation. The players depended on each other and on all of the nonplayers who had assumed other roles supporting the team. The community as a whole suffered when even one member was absent or not participating.

One of our participants, Martha, had sadistic, self-punitive, and cruel auditory hallucinations that were completely refractory to medications. She was also a very warm and caring person, a much-beloved and important figure in our community. She had a nursing degree, had been a licensed vocational nurse, and had worked for a few years in a nursing home prior to the onset of her illness in her early twenties. She was a devout Catholic, and her auditory hallucinations frequently had religious content.

Although Martha was certainly not a candidate for intensive meditation practice, mindfulness was an important part of her treatment. Through her relationships with staff, and in the safety of the day treatment community, she learned to recognize the auditory hallucinations as very painful, irrational thoughts caused by her illness. She learned that because she had schizophrenia, she heard the thoughts out loud, as if they were coming from another person speaking to her (or more likely screaming at her), and the content of the thoughts was not only crazy but often intensely negative, paranoid, cruel, and sadistic.

In more "benign" instances, Martha heard the voices whispering, and was sure that other participants and staff were saying negative things about her and laughing at her. The hallucinations with religious content were harsher and more painful. For instance, she heard the devil mocking her, screeching at her to kill herself because she didn't deserve to live, and telling her to hang herself like Judas because she was no less loathsome. We knew the hallucinations were particularly bad when Martha mumbled the rosary with a faraway look in her eyes, beseeching assistance and aid from Jesus and the Virgin Mary. One morning Martha showed us how she had carved the word "Jesus" into her arm with a razor blade because the voices taunting her told her that if she did so, maybe Jesus would finally come to her aid.

Eventually, we were able to teach Martha to radically decenter from the auditory hallucinations, first by recognizing and naming them ("That's an auditory hallucination") and then by reminding herself that the hallucinations were not true or factual, but rather symptoms of paranoid schizophrenic illness, a brain disease involving neurotransmitter imbalances. Having been educated as a nurse, Martha enjoyed medical language, and although the voices still felt real, it made intellectual sense to her that an experience so painful and powerful could be caused by very mixed up brain chemistry. In addition, we taught Martha that although many people with her illness could be helped with their auditory hallucinations by psychotropic medications, a not insignificant percentage were refractory to medications, and no one knew why or could predict who would or wouldn't be helped.

It was comforting to Martha to know that others were also refractory to medication, because she had always interpreted her symptoms being refractory to medication as an indication of her loathsomeness in the eyes of God. At first Martha felt guilty about taking comfort in the suffering of others, and we had to reassure her that she was actually taking comfort in knowing that she wasn't alone, and that anyone would do the same under the circumstances. Those familiar with treatment of the chronically mentally ill will recognize the psychoeducational approach we took with Martha, in particular the illness education approach spearheaded by the National Alliance for the Mentally Ill in the late 1970s.

So Martha began to practice radical decentering. Though that's not what we called it at the time, that's what it was. She learned to disidentify from the auditory hallucinations by naming them as soon as she noticed them. Then she reminded herself that hallucinations were not true or factual, no matter how real they sounded or how true they insisted they were, but simply symptoms of her brain disease. We also taught Martha that she needed to be particularly forceful with hallucinations that insisted they were true and factual, or even screamed disdainfully that they were, as unfortunately was often the case. Martha slowly learned not to argue or agree with the hallucinations, hide from them, or get involved in any way with their content, since they were simply the product of a neurochemical imbalance. She learned to shift her relationship to hallucinating, so instead of being caught up in the hallucinatory experience and content, she was able to identify and name the hallucinations as events—specifically, as symptoms of schizophrenia.

Martha's hallucinations were so powerful and relentless that she needed an ample tool kit of action techniques to help her to disidentify and shift her relationship to them without becoming panicked or overwhelmed. Just observing, naming, and reminding herself that hallucinations were caused by chemical imbalance and weren't factual wasn't always enough. So with the help of staff and other program participants, she developed an action plan of things to do when the hallucinations were particularly upsetting or distracting. These included calling a friend from the program, doing her crafts, taking a walk, talking to her husband, and so on. If she was attending day treatment that day, she might even shadow a staff member.

Although Martha's hallucinations continued, as treatment proceeded her mood brightened and she began to engage more actively in group activities, including volleyball. She was actually a very good player, except that when it was her turn to serve the voices ridiculed her about being a horrible player and an embarrassment to the team, among other things.

Martha reacted by freezing. She literally couldn't move, let alone serve the ball. After this had happened several times, we asked her what she might do about it. She paused for a long while, deep in thought, still standing on the baseline with the ball, ready to serve. At a certain point she lifted her head, turned to look over her shoulder, and then screamed literally at the top of her lungs, "SHUUUUUT UUUUPPPPPPPP!!!!!!!!!!!!" Then with a half smile on her face, Martha served the ball beautifully.

We all howled with laughter and appreciation and enthusiastically congratulated Martha on her courage and ingenuity. Martha laughed too. We celebrated after practice with our usual dancing and singing to "Wooly Bully." But that afternoon, the singing and dancing were particularly enthusiastic and heartful. It felt like we had really coalesced as a team and that our patients, many of whom had so often felt isolated and alone, had a sense of belonging to a loving, supportive community that they had never known before.

The Wooly Bullies won the day treatment volleyball tournament that year, and Martha's serve was an important part of the team's success. She screamed "shut up" at the voices whenever they became too loud or distracting, and also to put them in their place, because they were, after all, neither true nor factual. It put the other teams off balance as well, an added benefit.

Community and Connection as Context for Formal Mindfulness Meditation

In retrospect, I can see that mindfulness was a powerful component of what worked in our day treatment program, though only the director and I (two out of a full-time staff of four) had established formal meditation practices, and our clients did formal practice only five minutes per day. Yet mindfulness skills, inner capacities, attitudes, and perspectives were both implicitly taught and reinforced, and were interwoven and reflected in every element of the program. These included awareness of and compassion for self and others, as well as the importance of structure and discipline, which then safely allowed for flexibility and creativity when responding to difficulty and distress. The story of Martha and the volleyball team also illustrates generally the therapeutic importance and value of community and connection, and more specifically the value of community and connection as a context for teaching formal mindfulness meditation practice.

When I teach formal practices and guide individuals, couples, or groups through them in the context of psychotherapy, I always provide a guided meditation recording (that I recorded) that offers an initial sense of connection early on, even if only through my voice on the recordings. I also continue to include some formal practice in every session (even if only a few minutes at the outset), and I encourage clients who are interested to connect with a community of practice of some type. There are now mindfulness programs in many, if not most, major cities in North America and Europe, as well as many virtual practice communities online.

Introducing and Orienting Clients to Formal Meditation Practice

Formal mindfulness meditation offers many potential benefits for clients who want it. Motivation is key. When I first started teaching mindfulness-based stress reduction in a hospital setting, participants who completed the course would sometimes send a spouse, child, or friend, telling me that he or she "really needs to do this" or "could really use this." I learned from experience to be skeptical about such referrals. Even when self-referred to learn mindfulness meditation, I make it a point to clarify what the client thinks mindfulness meditation is and how it might be of benefit, and then I correct misconceptions.

I am as clear as I can be at the outset that formal mindfulness meditation is not a relaxation technique, can be stressful or difficult at times, and is not a panacea. I might even mildly discourage someone from beginning by describing mindfulness meditation as "the stressful approach to stress reduction" (Kabat-Zinn, 2005, 2013), both because it is true, and as a motivational challenge.

After describing the difficulty and potential discomfort involved in formal mindfulness meditation, I might wonder aloud with clients why people would voluntarily submit themselves to such a practice since it can be both stressful and unpleasant. I then pose the following questions: *If you could develop and cultivate a sense of resilience, ease, and well-being that was not contingent on circumstance, would that be of interest to you? How much discomfort would it be worth to develop such a capacity?* I want to be sure that clients understand the profound potential benefit, as well as the potential cost, before proceeding.

Indications and Contraindications for Formal Mindfulness Practice

Almost anyone, including clients with borderline personality disorder and even chronically mentally ill clients with underlying psychotic disorders, can benefit from very brief (five to ten minutes) breath-awareness practice, if the therapist or teacher has sufficient depth of understanding and sensitivity.

Mindfulness practice is contraindicated for clients who are in crisis, acutely psychotic, or intoxicated, or for clients with psychotic and borderline personality disorders who are unstable or fragile. When clients present to therapy in crisis, I might suggest some informal practices, such as diaphragmatic breathing or dropping into the breath and body, or other simple techniques to anchor awareness in the body. I wouldn't teach formal meditation practices until the crisis is resolved and the client is stable. In general, completing an initial assessment and observing the client's response to therapy are prerequisites to deciding whether to incorporate formal mindfulness practices in therapy, and if so, how.

Because it is a potentially transformative and powerful experience in its own right, it would seem inappropriate to introduce formal mindfulness meditation during the termination phase of therapy. It could potentially disrupt the termination process, and there would likely not be enough time for the client to integrate the mindfulness practice experience with the therapy experience as a whole. It would be more appropriate to recommend a mindfulness-based stress reduction, mindfulness-based cognitive therapy, or compassion cultivation course as a posttreatment resource, depending on the needs of the client.

Client Use of Logs and Worksheets

If the treatment plan involves the client doing formal meditation practice, guided meditation recordings are crucial for two reasons:

1. It's very difficult to learn to meditate on your own without guidance.

2. Formal mindfulness meditation is best practiced in a context of connection and community.

So it's best for your client if you guide in real time, in your office, any meditation you want him or her to do, and then to have your client practice that meditation daily with a guided meditation recording. It's best if the recording is in your own voice, to maintain a sense of connection to you and the therapeutic relationship during the home meditation practice. If that's not possible, use a recording that you have practiced with—perhaps one of the ones available at the website for this book.

Formal Meditation Practice Logs

Meditation practice logs are a simple way to track daily, formal mindfulness meditation (see the practice log in appendix B). I tell my clients that keeping a daily practice log is mostly a motivational tool for self-reinforcement and for monitoring progress. ("Progress" means doing the meditation practice regularly, preferably daily; the experiential content of any day's practice is far less important.) Keeping a practice log can also be useful for strengthening the ability to identify and differentiate physical sensations, emotions, thoughts, and other perceptions and mind states.

Mindfulness Practice Journals

I encourage clients who like to write to journal about their formal meditation practice immediately after each session. The object is simply to remember and recollect the actual subjective experiences (sensations, perceptions, emotions, thoughts, mind states, and so on) of the practice session and to describe them precisely without embellishment, evaluation, or judgment.

Mindfulness journals are also useful for reflecting on mini-mindfulness practices, informal practices, and mindfulness in daily life practice (facet D, mindfulness as a way of being and relating to experience). See the practice journal in appendix B.

The Client's Practice: Skills, Inner Capacities, Attitudes, and Perspectives

The skills, inner capacities, attitudes, and perspectives of facet B of the mindfulness pyramid model function as a useful *positive psychology* framework for identifying a client's strengths, resources, and vulnerabilities and to assist in formulating therapeutic goals. You can use the table in chapter 7 as a framework for informally assessing a client's psychological vulnerabilities and strengths. It can also help guide decisions about what to focus on in treatment and to formulate treatment goals. The table is particularly helpful for clarifying how best to integrate the enhancement of client strengths with the remediation of vulnerabilities.

For example, Jane was a highly successful senior executive in a biotech company who presented with *impostor syndrome*, the belief that she didn't really deserve her success, and that at any moment she might be discovered as a fraud and fired. She lived with severe chronic anxiety, which she mostly masked. Her remarkable capacity for distress tolerance was both a blessing and a curse. She had been in therapy several times but didn't stay with it.

After taking a history and sharing my impressions, I discussed with Jane how strengthening distress and anxiety tolerance through a combination of brief formal and informal mindfulness practices might be useful in therapy. I explained how the formal and informal practices could help her to tolerate just observing self-critical thoughts without trying to fix or change them. She could then learn to simply dis-identify from negative self-judgments and other automatic thoughts and relate to them simply as events in awareness rather than factual truths. I also interpreted Jane's family-of-origin dynamics as a basis for cultivating self-compassion and reality testing the contents of her self-judgments. I speculated out loud that harsh self-judgment might have been a useful psychological defense mechanism and survival skill while growing up.

As Jane became less preoccupied with self-judging thoughts, she was able to take in evidence that she was actually seen, liked, and valued for who she was. She began to see that she was hiding her anxiety and feelings of vulnerability, not her fraudu-lence. She also gained greater insight into the childhood origins of her impostor fears, how severe anxiety and self-judgment were less painful than either feeling invisible or being attacked, and how she had long interpreted the severe anxiety itself as evidence of her unworthiness. Jane has continued in therapy, and she is now beginning to take in and enjoy positive feedback about her accomplishments as being both genuine and deserved.

Teaching Formal Practices to Cultivate Facet B, Level 3 Mindfulness

You can use any of the formal mindfulness practices to enhance specific skills, inner capacities, attitudes, and perspectives of facet B of the mindfulness pyramid model. The breath-awareness, body scan, sitting meditations, and mindful movement practices develop all the elements of facet B in a general way.

As you gain experiential insight through your own formal meditation practice into how the formal mindfulness meditations systematically develop and strengthen specific skills, inner capacities, attitudes, and perspectives, you will organically begin to understand and gain insight into how to facilitate the development of specific skills, inner capacities, attitudes, and perspectives for your clients through what you focus on in guiding formal meditations, as well as through the language you employ to guide formal practices.

For example, in mindfulness-based cognitive therapy (Segal et al., 2002) there are specific sitting meditations that focus on opening to the unwanted and allowing/letting be. In sitting meditation the therapist guides clients to identify a distressing or emotionally painful situation; to notice body sensations, emotions, and thoughts associated with it; to imagine breathing into the area around the distress, as if the client is creating space around the distress in the body and making room for it to be there; to continue breathing into the space around the distress, expanding into a more spacious awareness; and to begin saying silently, along with the breathing, *It's okay, I can be with this. It's okay, I can let myself feel this*, and so on.

You can guide sitting meditation to emphasize self-forgiveness, acceptance, com-passion, nonjudging, nonstriving, equanimity, and curiosity—really any of the ele-ments of facet B, level 3 mindfulness that might be particularly beneficial to your client. Use your imagination. Guiding principles (pun intended) include focusing on the physical sensation of breathing and sitting to anchor awareness in the present moment; as best you can, incorporating breathing and/or body sensations into any instructions you give; and doing the practice along with the client so the instructions arise from your own meditation practice experience and your empathic attunement to your client. In this way, the client experiences that the two of you are connected through the meditation practice and are doing the practice together.

Using Paper-and-Pencil Inventories, Exercises, and Readings

All of the time-limited, mindfulness-based treatment protocols, such as MBSR, MBCT, DBT, and ACT, use paper-and-pencil logs, journals, inventories, and homework exercises in addition to the formal and informal home meditation practices. I have found a number of these practices to be very useful in individual treatment as well. I would encourage you to become familiar with these treatments and tools to adapt them to the needs of your patients.

Pleasant and Unpleasant Moments Calendars

After weeks two and three of mindfulness-based stress reduction and mindfulness-based cognitive therapy, instructors assign a pencil-and-paper exercise in two parts as part of the home practice. The two parts involve creating pleasant and unpleasant events calendars. The purpose of the exercise is to help clients experience clearly the differences between events, physical sensations, emotions, thoughts, and the experiences of pleasant and unpleasant. It also helps clients better understand their own reactions to events and to explore tendencies to conflate the various components of experience or to attend only to some and not others.

I have found it useful to modify the exercise to have clients identify pleasant and unpleasant *moments* rather than *events* as a way of beginning to deconstruct the sense of solidity and continuity of the narrative of the self. I ask clients to identify one pleasant moment per day for a week, then one unpleasant moment per day for a week. After identifying each moment, clients record the following information on a worksheet: the day of the week, a brief description of the moment, physical reactions to the moment, emotional reactions to the moment, and thoughts about the moment (see Kabat-Zinn, 1990; Segal, Williams, & Teasdale, 2012; and Williams et al., 2007 for sample worksheets). Frequently clients confuse sensations, emotions, and thought. The worksheets provide opportunities to clarify and work with the distinctions.

I also like to use the pleasant and unpleasant moments calendars to illuminate how we participate in constructing the pleasant or unpleasant flavor of each moment through the way we relate to the moment. After both calendars are completed, I ask clients to choose one pleasant and one unpleasant moment. We then explore together what made the pleasant moment "pleasant" (apart from any intrinsically pleasant flavor) and the unpleasant moment "unpleasant" (apart from any intrinsically unpleasant flavor). I ask questions such as Were you completely engaged with what was happening or also thinking about other things? Were you aware of being judgmental or critical? Were you aware of wanting things to be different than they were in the moment? Were you aware of comparing one moment with other moments? (See the table below for examples.)

Pleasant Moment—Watching a Sunset	Unpleasant Moment—Going to the Dentist
Completely engaged	Thinking about other things
Concentrated	Lack of concentration
Fully present in each moment	Not fully present
Not comparing	Comparing
Nonjudging	Judging
Nonstriving	Striving
Appreciation and gratitude	Aversion
Moment as it is: enough	Moment as it is: insufficient
Absence of desire; contented	Want it to be different; discontented

The final part of the exercise is crucial and involves the following two questions:

1. Can you imagine a circumstance in which watching a beautiful sunset might be unpleasant?

2. Can you imagine a circumstance in which going to the dentist might be pleasant?

These questions are designed for inquiry and insight (which has usually already begun) about how subjective experiencing works. The bottom line is that, in addition to the intrinsic flavor of pleasant or unpleasant in the moment, your attitude and reaction (or response) to the moment have great impact on how you experience it. For instance, you could be watching the sunset thinking, *I wish my partner were here to share this with me*, or *This is nice but that sunset in Hawaii was really beautiful*. There is nothing wrong with thinking these thoughts, but it's also useful to see how they decrease the enjoyment of the sunset.

For example, I actually experience going to the dentist as a reprieve from the hectic pace of daily life. *This is so great, for a whole hour I am captive in this comfortable, reclining chair, my mouth open wide and stuffed with cotton so I don't have to talk. And I get to see my warm and sweet dentist, who I have known for a long time and treats me like an old friend coming for a visit. Sometimes the physical sensations are unpleasant, but when I focus on the sensations with friendly curiosity, they are actually pretty interesting and useful for concentrating the mind. I wouldn't choose to have them if I had a choice. But since I don't have a choice, I will choose to have them, because aversion to the sensations makes them even more unpleasant.*

Client's Practice: Facet C—Method of Inquiry and Investigation and Mode of Knowing

The client can incorporate mindfulness as a method of inquiry and investigation and mode of knowing in three ways: 1) from its embodiment as an aspect of the therapist's healing presence and communication in the therapeutic process; 2) through direct experience of mindful inquiry and investigation embedded in the guided meditation practices; and 3) through explicit instructions for mindful inquiry and investigation, if appropriate, during the expanded sitting meditation practice or other practices.

As stated previously, it is the inquiry and investigation and mode of knowing aspect of mindfulness practice that is most often associated with client decompensation, along with long periods of formal meditation practice. If you are new to formal mindfulness meditation, it's better to err on the side of caution and focus on deepening your own practice before beginning to incorporate facet C practice with clients.

Experience with mindfulness as inquiry and investigation and mode of knowing may organically begin to inform how you do therapy in your embodiment of mindfulness in the therapeutic relationship as healing presence.

In the context of accepting and nonjudging presence, friendly curiosity and interest, empathic attunement, and genuine care and concern, the implicit questions "What is this?" "What's happening?" and "What's needed?" are the drivers of mindful inquiry and investigation, both in formal mindfulness meditation and in the therapeutic dialogue, particularly in how you, as the therapist, communicate with the client.

As a therapist with a formal mindfulness practice that informs your work with clients, you want to understand the client's subjective experience of self and life's circumstances as clearly and precisely as possible. How does it feel to be this client? To live inside his skin? Mindful inquiry and investigation are quite similar to therapeutic explorations driven by empathic attunement in contemporary self psychology, and relational psychoanalytic therapies based on intersubjectivity theory and optimal responsiveness, for example. Compassion, curiosity, concern, and care are the motivational engine, and empathic attunement directs and informs the therapist's interventions.

Collaborative Mindful Inquiry and Investigation in Formal Meditation Practice

When appropriate and indicated for the particular client, the therapist can incorporate collaborative mindful inquiry and investigation into guiding formal meditation practice, for example by focusing on noticing common unpleasant or distressing physical sensations, such as stiffness, rigidity, burning, tearing, stretching, and so on, or unpleasant emotions such as fear, anger, or grief. This might involve instructing your client in the guided meditation to "soften" around the unpleasant sensation or emotion, "making space for it" to be present, and even "embracing it," and then allowing the friendly curiosity embodied in the implicit questions "What is this?" and "What's happening?" to gently drive the inquiry and investigation of the unpleasant sensation or emotion, moment by moment, noticing constituent physical sensations, thoughts, and mind states.

Formal meditative inquiry and investigation is best done in the context of the expanded sitting meditation practice, and it requires extensive debriefing of the experience afterward, essentially a verbal continuation of the inquiry and investigation. This follow-up is vital for developing and integrating any insights that arose and for monitoring for negative therapeutic reactions.

Mindfulness as a Way of Being and Relating to Experience

The moment in which clients fully realize that mindfulness practice is a way of being and a way of life, rather than simply a formal meditation practice, is often a turning point in therapy. Sometimes it doesn't happen, but clients still benefit in many other ways from the formal practices and skills. Yet when the client does get it, that mindfulness is a way of being and relating as well as a formal meditation practice, it can be profound and validating, as was the case with Beth, the client I described earlier who never connected with the formal meditation practice.

Using Mini-Mindfulness Practices and Informal Practices with Clients

There are truly no exclusionary criteria or contraindications for informal mindfulness practices in psychotherapy, or life in general, except lack of interest or willingness.

Feeling the Breath for Two or Three Cycles of In-Breath and Out-Breath

Remember you are breathing, and feel the sensations of breathing for two or three cycles of in-breath and out-breath. Three times per day, see if you can remember that you are breathing in this way, and from there build up to six or eight times per day. This practice doesn't involve regulating the breath, but rather simply feeling breathing happening. You are breathing anyway, so it doesn't require additional time. All the practice requires is remembering to feel what's already happening.

Belly Button Breathing

I like to teach diaphragmatic breathing, or belly button breathing, as a mindfulness practice. This is a more formal, structured practice but very brief. Place the palm of your hand on your lower abdomen with your thumb in your belly button. Now inhale fully and deeply through your nostrils, breathing in until your hand moves, focusing on the physical sensations of each moment of the inhalation. Now exhale a long, slow exhalation, feeling each moment of exhalation as sensation in the belly, and feeling sensations of release and letting go as you allow any tension and holding to flow out of your body with the breath. Repeat.

Belly button breathing disrupts the positive feedback loop of the sympathetic nervous system by intentionally breathing fully and deeply. The lungs fill and expand, stimulating the stretch-receptor neurons in the intercostal muscles and diaphragm to send an "all clear" signal back to the brain, uncoupling us from fight-flight-freeze reactivity. That's why the out-breath, in particular, feels so good. You really are releasing tension and holding as the brain gets the message and sends out the signal *all clear, you can relax.*

Reinhabit Your Body

Another daily life practice that is absurdly simple yet profound is to reinhabit your body. Periodically through the day, allow awareness to drop down into the physical sensations of sitting, standing, walking, driving, typing, eating—whatever it is you're doing. This is another exercise that requires no extra time, just remembering to allow the body to feel itself as physical sensation. You may be so wrapped up in thinking or striving that you don't experience the physical sensations of being in your body for hours at a time. Dropping into physical sensations immediately brings us back into the present moment.

Stop, Be, and Notice

Stop whatever you are doing. Shift out of doing mode of mind into being mode of mind. Let yourself rest and be refreshed in just being. Before proceeding, notice what you're experiencing and what's happening.

Final Thoughts About Mini-Mindfulness Meditations and Informal Practices for Clients

All of the brief, structured mini-mindfulness practices presented as part of the therapist's practice in chapter 9, such as SAGE, CARE, STOP, and the PRN practices, as well as the informal mindfulness practices, such as mindful eating or choosing a routine activity of daily living and doing it as a mindfulness practice, can be just as beneficial for your clients as they are for you, if used with discernment and care.

Before prescribing a structured mini-meditation or informal practice, be sure to explain to your client how and why you think the practice will be helpful. If possible, do the practice with the client in your office first, allowing time for debriefing and questions and answers. If it's an informal practice, such as doing a routine activity mindfully (for example, brushing teeth or taking out the trash), have the client choose an activity while in session. Then discuss with the client some of the ways she might relate differently to the activity by doing it as a mindfulness practice (for example, slowing down, paying close attention moment by moment without judging, or focusing on the physical sensations of performing the action). Take care not to tell the client what she will experience, but only how she might relate differently to the activity.

Summary

In this chapter we discussed client mindfulness practice, emphasizing the various ways mindfulness can be incorporated in therapy as a client practice instead of, or in addition to, formal meditation. We looked at the specific benefits and risks of teaching formal meditation to clients, particularly those involving longer practice periods or a focus on the inquiry and investigation and mode of knowing elements of mindfulness (facet C of the mindfulness pyramid model). We also looked at the indications and contraindications for teaching formal practices based on client diagnosis, presenting problems and symptoms, and level of motivation and interest. Finally, we touched on how to incorporate specific structured mini-mindfulness meditations and informal practices in psychotherapy to address specific types of symptoms and client problems.

Conclusion

Mindfulness in Psychotherapy, Now and in the Future

In this book I've presented and elaborated on a model and clinical framework that illustrates how clinicians from any theoretical orientation or training background can incorporate mindfulness meditation in psychotherapy, beginning with the central importance and power of the therapist's mindfulness practice. Whether or not you explicitly teach mindfulness practices to your clients, your own mindfulness practice is expressed as healing presence in the therapeutic relationship, and it informs inquiry, investigation, and optimal responsiveness in the therapeutic encounter and dialogue.

In teaching mindfulness practices explicitly to clients, I believe it is your embodiment of the practice in your teaching, as much as the practice itself, that determines its therapeutic efficacy for your clients. In other words, your healing presence and embodiment of mindfulness *is* the teaching as much as any particular practice you might teach. This is true whether it's guiding a formal meditation practice, suggesting an exercise or informal practice to strengthen a specific mindfulness skill or inner capacity, or discussing your client's experience of home practice.

So the mindfulness pyramid model rests on the foundation of your own meditation practice and your commitment to it. Regarding developing your own mindfulness practice, it's okay to be patient. Your own mindfulness practice will inevitably begin to inform your clinical work, whether or not you are explicitly teaching mindfulness practices and perspectives to your clients. You can always recommend one of the self-guided mindfulness workbooks with guided meditation recordings, or use one of this book's guided-meditation audio files with your client, meditating together in the session. Then debrief the client, focusing on what was noticed and learned in the experience. This assumes you already have an established practice yourself.

You can also refer your client to a mindfulness-based stress reduction course or another mindfulness training course. Be aware, however, that all mindfulness-based interventions are operator dependent. Of course the content is important, but it's really more about the teacher, who either empowers the content and brings it to life, or doesn't.

Since mindfulness has hit the mainstream, many people say they teach mindfulness. If you are looking for a teacher either for yourself or a client, ask any potential teachers if they practice themselves, how long they have been practicing, who their teachers are, and where they received their teacher training. Check into the experience others have had with the teacher you are considering, as well as whether you personally feel comfortable with the teacher.

The Future of Mindfulness in Psychotherapy

Over the last fifteen years, to say that increasing numbers of respected neuroscientists, cognitive scientists, and clinical psychology researchers have taken on the scientific study of mindfulness and the mind and established mindfulness research programs at prestigious universities would be an understatement. It's no exaggeration to say that academic and scientific interest in mindfulness meditation has exploded. It's my hope that this increased interest in mindfulness might eventually lead to revisiting and reconsidering the strict criteria that define rigorous, empirical research in clinical psychology, cognitive science, and neuroscience, with an eye toward integrating rigorous, phenomenological-empirical methods for studying subjectivity and mind, such as mindfulness meditation, with scientific-empirical methodology. In this way the scientific study of mindfulness may afford an even greater opportunity to bridge the gap between the science and the art of psychotherapy, perhaps creating a new, more inclusive category of "knowing." This new category might equally value empirical science, which generates objective knowl¬edge and the power to predict and control, and phenomenological investigation, which cultivates awareness, insight and self-knowledge, wisdom, and compassion.

I predict that as global crises such as climate change intensify in the near future, there will be increasing need and demand for mental health services, and mindfulness-informed psychotherapies will evolve toward a stronger, more explicit emphasis on the experience of interbeing not only as it relates to the health and well-being of individual clients, but also to the urgent global crises we face, recognizing that individual well-being absent collective well-being is delusional.

We can no longer afford American culture's idealization of heroic individualism and strong identification with the self as separate and individual, each of us striving against and competing with the other. Species survival depends on moving toward a more expansive, ecological self-experience based on a deep understanding of interbeing (Macy, 1991). Mindfulness practice can potentially help to bring this about.

I sincerely hope you have enjoyed this book and found it helpful. All the best with your mindfulness journey. Ultimately, we are all journeying together. Please avail yourself of the guided meditation audio downloads and the worksheets for this book, available at the website for this book, www.newharbinger.com/32752.

Appendix A

Mindfulness Resources

Professional Training Resources

METTA Training & Consulting

Mindfulness education and tools for transformation and awakening

Steven A. Alper, LCSW

Mindfulness in psychotherapy professional trainings; mindfulness trainings for businesses, professional organizations, and nonprofits; and public MBSR courses

San Diego, CA

Phone: (619) 463–6387

http://www.mettaconsulting.com

Center for Mindfulness in Medicine, Health Care, and Society

University of Massachusetts, Worcester Campus

MBSR Teacher Training and Certification

Oasis Institute

55 Lake Avenue North

Worcester, MA 01655

Phone: (508) 856–1097

http://www.umassmed.edu/cfm/training

cfm.oasis@umassmed.edu

El Camino Hospital Mindfulness-Based Stress Reduction Program Awareness and Relaxation Training

MBSR teacher training and certification

2500 Grant Road, Mountain View, CA 94040

Phone: (650) 940–7000 ext. 8745

Bob Stahl, PhD

http://mindfulnessprograms.com

info@mindfulnessprograms.com

The Linehan Institute: Behavioral Tech

Dialectical-behavioral therapy training
2133 Third Avenue, Suite 205
Seattle, WA 98121
Phone: (206) 675–8588
http://www.behavioraltech.org

Oxford Mindfulness Centre

UK mindfulness-based cognitive therapy training
University of Oxford Department of Psychiatry
Prince of Wales International Centre
Warneford Hospital
Oxford OX3 7JX
http://www.oxfordmindfulness.org/train
omcadmin@psych.ox.ac.uk

The Centre for Mindfulness Studies

180 Sudbury Street, Unit C2*
Toronto, ON M6J 0A8
Phone: (647) 524–6216
Fax: (855) 344–9519
http://www.mindfulnessstudies.com
info@mindfulnessstudies.com

The Center for Mindful Eating

http://www.thecenterformindfuleating.org

Nancy Bardacke, CNM

Mindfulness-based childbirth and parenting; professional development and
    training program
Phone: (510) 595–3207
http://www.mindfulbirthing.org

Association for Contextual Behavioral Science

Acceptance and commitment therapy training
http://www.contextualpsychology.org

UC San Diego Center for Mindfulness

Professional training in MBSR, MBCT, MBRP, MBCP, and MSC
MBSR and MSC courses
La Jolla, CA
http://health.ucsd.edu/specialties/mindfulness/Pages/default.aspx

Mindfulness Meditation Resources

Insight Meditation Society

Vipassana Retreat and Practice Centers
1230 Pleasant Street
Barre, MA 01005
Phone: (978) 355–4378
http://www.dharma.org/ims

Spirit Rock Meditation Center

P.O. Box 169
Woodacre, CA 94973
http://www.spiritrock.org

Gaia House Meditation Retreat Centre

West Ogwell, Newton Abbot
Devon, TQ12 6EW
Phone: +44 (0) 1626 333 613
http://.gaiahouse.co.uk

Cambridge Insight Meditation Center

331 Broadway
Cambridge, MA 02139
Phone: (617) 441–9038
http://www.cambridgeinsight.org

IMCW—Insight Meditation Community of Washington, DC

P.O. Box 3
Cabin John, MD 20818
Phone: (202) 986–2922
http://www.imcw.org
meditate@imcw.org

InsightLA

1430 Olympic Blvd.
Santa Monica, CA 90404
Phone: (310) 450–1821
http://www.insightla.org

Insight San Diego

2640 Historic Decatur
San Diego, CA 92106
http://www.insightsd.org

Appendix B

Meditation Practice Log and Mindfulness Journal

Meditation Practice Log

Day/Date	Time of Day	Setting/Practices	Duration	Observations
Sunday				
Monday				
Tuesday				
Wednesday				
Thursday				
Friday				
Saturday				

Mindfulness in Psychotherapy Journal

Day/Date: _____

Daily life practice: (informal practices, experiences, observations)

_____

_____

_____

_____

Mindfulness in psychotherapy: (Did you notice your mindfulness practice informing your clinical work in the session? How have you thought about or related to your clinical work? If you explicitly taught mindfulness as part of the therapy session, what exactly did you teach, and for what purpose? What did you sense about how your client received the instructions?)

_____

_____

_____

_____

_____

_____

_____

_____

_____

_____

Bibliography

Bacal, H. A. (1998). *Optimal responsiveness: How therapists heal their patients.* New York, NY: Jason Aronson.

Bacal, H. A. (2011). *The power of specificity in psychotherapy: When therapy works and when it doesn't.* New York, NY: Jason Aronson.

Baer, R. A. (Ed.). (2006). *Mindfulness-based treatment approaches: A clinician's guide to evidence base and applications.* Burlington, MA: Academic Press.

Batchelor, S. (1994). *The awakening of the West: The encounter of Buddhism and Western culture.* Berkeley, CA: Parallax Press.

Batchelor, S. (2005). *Living with the devil: A meditation on good and evil.* New York, NY: Riverhead Books.

Beck, C. J. (1993). *Nothing special: Living Zen.* New York, NY: HarperCollins.

Beck, C. J., & Smith, S. (1989). *Everyday Zen.* New York, NY: HarperCollins.

Bennett, M. I., & Bennett, M. B. (1984). The uses of hopelessness. *American Journal of Psychiatry, 141*(4), 559–562.

Bien, T. (2006). *Mindful therapy: A guide for therapists and helping professionals.* Somerville, MA: Wisdom Publications.

Boccio, F. J. (2004). *Mindfulness yoga: The awakened union of breath, body, and mind.* Somerville, MA: Wisdom Publications.

Bodhi, B. (2005). *In the Buddha's words: An anthology of discourses from the Pali canon.* Somerville, MA: Wisdom Publications.

Boorstein, S. (Ed.). (1991). *Transpersonal psychotherapy.* Stanford, CA: JTP Books.

Boszormenyi-Nagy, I. (1987). *Foundations of contextual therapy.* New York: Brunner/ Mazel Publishers, Inc.

Boyce, B. (Ed.). (2001). *The mindfulness revolution: Leading psychologists, scientists, artists, and meditation teachers on the power of mindfulness in daily life.* Boston, MA: Shambhala Publications.

Brach, T. (2003). *Radical acceptance.* New York: Bantam Books.

Brantley, J. (2003). *Calming your anxious mind: How mindfulness and compassion can free you from anxiety, fear, and panic.* Oakland, CA: New Harbinger Publications.

Bromberg, P. M. (1998). *Standing in the spaces: Essays on clinical process, trauma, and dissociation.* New York: Psychology Press.

Bromberg, P. M. (2006). *Awakening the dreamer: Clinical journeys.* Mahwah, NJ: The Analytic Press.

Carroll, M. (2008). *The mindful leader: Awakening your natural leadership skills through mindfulness meditation.* Boston, MA: Trumpeter.

Chah, A., & Amaro, A. (2002). *Food for the heart: The collected teachings of Ajahn Chah.* Somerville, MA: Wisdom Publications.

Chödrön, P. (1991). *The wisdom of no escape and the path of lovingkindness.* Boston, MA: Shambhala Publications.

Chödrön, P. (2003). *The Pema Chödrön collection.* New York, NY: One Spirit.

Chödrön, P. (2005). *No time to lose: A timely guide to the way of the Bodhisattva.* Boston, MA: Shambala Publications.

Conze, E. (1993). *Buddhism: A short history.* London: One World Publications, Ltd.

Csikszentmihalyi, M. (1990). *Flow: The psychology of optimal experience.* New York: HarperCollins Publishers.

Cushman, A. (2014). *Moving into meditation: A twelve week mindfulness program for yoga practitioners.* Boston, MA: Shambhala Publications.

Cushman, P. (1995). *Constructing the self, constructing America: A cultural history of psychotherapy.* Reading, MA: Addison-Wesley Publishing Company.

Dimeff, L. A., & Koerner, K. (Eds.). (2007). *Dialectical behavior therapy in clinical practice: Applications across disorders and settings.* New York: Guilford Press.

Duncan, B. L., Miller, S. D., Wampold, B. E., & Hubble, M. A. (Eds.). (2010). *The heart & soul of change: Delivering what works in psychotherapy* (2nd ed.). Washington, DC: American Psychological Association.

Epstein, M. (1995). *Thoughts without a thinker: Psychotherapy from a Buddhist perspective.* New York, NY: Basic Books.

Epstein, M. (1998). *Going to pieces without falling apart: A Buddhist perspective on wholeness.* New York, NY: Broadway Books.

Epstein, M. (2005). *Open to desire: Embracing a lust for life, insights from Buddhism and psychotherapy.* New York, NY: Gotham Books.

Epstein, M. (2008). *Psychotherapy without the self.* New Haven, CT: Yale University Press.

Fields, R. (1981). *How the swans came to the lake: A narrative history of Buddhism in America.* Boston, MA: Shambhala Publications.

Gergen, K. J. (1991). *The saturated self: Dilemmas of identity in contemporary life.* New York, NY: Basic Books.

Germer, C. K. (2009). *The mindful path to self-compassion: Freeing yourself from destructive thoughts and emotions.* New York, NY: Guilford Press.

Germer, C. K, & Siegel, R. D. (Eds.). (2013). *Mindfulness and psychotherapy* (2nd ed.). New York, NY: Guilford Press.

Gilbert, P. (2009). *The compassionate mind: A new approach to life's challenges.* Oakland, CA: New Harbinger Publications.

Glassman, B. (1998). *Bearing witness: A Zen master's lessons in making peace.* New York, NY: Bell Tower.

Glassman, B., & Fields, R. (1996). *Instructions to the cook: A Zen master's lessons in living a life that matters.* New York, NY: Bell Tower.

Goldstein, J. (1993). *Insight meditation: The practice of freedom.* Boston, MA: Shambhala Publications.

Goldstein, J. (2002). *One Dharma: The emerging Western Buddhism.* San Francisco: HarperCollins.

Goldstein, J. (2013). *Mindfulness: A practical guide to awakening.* Boulder, CO: Sounds True.

Goldstein, J., & Kornfield, J. (1987). *Seeking the heart of wisdom: The path of insight meditation.* Boston, MA: Shambhala Publications.

Goleman, D. (1988). *The meditative mind: The varieties of meditative experience.* New York, NY: G. P. Putnam's Sons.

Hayes, S. C., Follette, V. M., & Linehan, M. M. (Eds.). (2004). *Mindfulness and acceptance: Expanding the cognitive-behavioral tradition.* New York, NY: Guilford Press.

Hayes, S. C., & Smith, S. (2005). *Get out of your mind and into your life: The new acceptance and commitment therapy.* Oakland, CA: New Harbinger Publications.

Hayes, S. C., Strosahl, K. D., & Wilson, K. G. (2003). *Acceptance and commitment therapy: An experimental approach to behavior change.* New York, NY: Guilford Press.

Heschel, A. J. (1951). *Sabbath: Its meaning for modern man.* New York, NY: Farrar, Strauss & Giroux.

Hölzel, B. K., Carmody, J., Evans, K. C., Hoge, E. A., Dusek, J. A., Morgan, L. et al. (2010). Stress reduction correlates with structural changes in the amygdala. *Social, Cognitive, and Affective Neuroscience, 5*(1), 11–17.

Hölzel, B. K., Carmody, J., Vangel, M., Congleton, C., Yerramsetti, S. M., Gard, T. et al. (2011). Mindfulness practice leads to increases in regional brain gray matter density. *Psychiatry Research: Neuroimaging, 191*(1), 36–43.

Ingram, C. (2003). *Passionate presence: Experiencing the seven qualities of awakened awareness.* New York, NY: Gotham Books.

James, W. (1983). *Principles of psychology* (Vols. 1–2). Cambridge, MA: Harvard University Press.

Jennings, P. A. (2015). *Mindfulness for teachers: Simple skills for peace and productivity in the classroom.* New York, NY: W. W. Norton & Co.

Jinpa, T. (2015). *A fearless heart: How the courage to be compassionate can transform our lives.* New York, NY: Hudson Street Press.

Jones, E. (1963). *The life and work of Sigmund Freud.* New York, NY: Anchor Books.

Jotiko, A. F. (1993). *Awareness itself.* Thailand: P. Samphan Panich Ltd.

Kabat-Zinn, J. (1990). *Full catastrophe living: Using the wisdom of your body and mind to face stress, pain, and illness.* New York, NY: Dell Publishing.

Kabat-Zinn, J. (1994). *Wherever you go, there you are: Mindfulness meditation in everyday life.* New York, NY: Hyperion.

Kabat-Zinn, J. (2005). *Coming to our senses: Healing ourselves and the world through mindfulness.* New York, NY: Hyperion.

Kabat-Zinn, J. (2013). *Full catastrophe living: Using the wisdom of your body and mind to face stress, pain, and illness* (25th anniversary ed.). New York, NY: Bantam Books.

Kafka, F. (2004). *Blue octavo notebooks.* M. Brod (Ed.). Cambridge, MA: Exact Change.

Keeva, S. (2011). *Transforming practices: Finding joy and satisfaction in the legal life.* Washington, DC: American Bar Association.

Khema, A. (1987). *Being nobody, going nowhere: Meditations on the Buddhist path.* Somerville, MA: Wisdom Publications.

Khema, A. (1991). *When the iron eagle flies: Buddhism for the West.* Somerville, MA: Wisdom Publications.

Khempo, K. R. (1997). *Luminous mind: The way of the Buddha.* Boston, MA: Wisdom Publications.

Kohut, H. (2014). *The restoration of the self.* Chicago, IL: University of Chicago Press.

Kornfield, J. (1993). *A path with heart: A guide through the perils and promises of spiritual life.* New York, NY: Bantam Books.

Kornfield, J. (2000). *After the ecstasy, the laundry: How the heart grows wise on the spiritual path.* New York, NY: Bantam Books.

Kutz, I., Borysenko, J. Z., & Benson, H. (1985). Meditation and psychotherapy: A rationale for the integration of dynamic psychotherapy, the relaxation response, and mindfulness meditation. *The American Journal of Psychiatry, 142*(1), 2.

Linehan, M. M. (1993a). *Cognitive-behavioral treatment of borderline personality disorder.* New York, NY: Guilford Press.

Linehan, M. M. (1993b). *Skills training manual for treating borderline personality disorder.* New York, NY: Guilford Press.

Luoma, J. B., Hayes, S. C., & Walser, R. D. (2007). *Learning ACT: An acceptance and commitment therapy skills-training manual for therapists.* Oakland, CA: New Harbinger Publications.

Macy, J. (1991). *World as lover, world as self.* Berkeley, CA: Parallax Press.

Maezumi, T. (2001). *Appreciate your life: The essence of Zen practice*. Boston, MA: Shambhala Publications.

McCown, D., Riebel, D. S., & Micozzi, M. S. (2010). *Teaching mindfulness: A practical guide for clinicians and educators*. New York, NY: Springer.

Miller, A. (1980). *The drama of the gifted child*. New York, NY: HarperCollins.

Minuchin, S. (1974). *Families and family therapy*. Cambridge, MA: Harvard University Press.

Mitchell, S. (Ed.). (1994). *Dropping ashes on the Buddha: The teachings of Zen master Seung Sahn*. New York, NY: Grove Press.

Muller, W. (2000). *Sabbath: Finding rest, renewal and delight in our busy lives*. New York, NY: Bantam Books.

Mumford, G. (2015). *The mindful athlete*. Berkeley, CA: Parallax Press.

Neff, K. (2011). *Self-compassion: Stop beating yourself up and leave insecurity behind*. New York, NY: HarperCollins.

Nhat Hanh, T. (1988a). *The heart of understanding: Commentaries on the Prajnaparamita heart sutra*. Berkeley, CA: Parallax Press.

Nhat Hanh, T. (1988b). *The sutra on the full awareness of breathing*. Berkeley, CA: Parallax Press.

Nhat Hanh, T. (1990). *Present moment, wonderful moment: Mindfulness verses for daily living*. Berkeley, CA: Parallax Press.

Nhat Hanh, T. (1991). *Peace is every step: The path of mindfulness in everyday life*. New York, NY: Bantam Books.

Nhat Hanh, T. (1996). *Being peace*. Berkeley, CA: Parallax Press.

Olendzki, A. (2010). *Unlimiting mind: The radically experiential psychology of Buddhism*. Somerville, MA: Wisdom Publications.

Ornish, D. (1990). *Dr. Dean Ornish's program for reversing heart disease*. New York, NY: Random House.

Pandita, U. (1992). *In this very life: The liberation teachings of the Buddha*. Boston, MA: Wisdom Publications.

Pollack, S. M., Pedulla, T., & Siegel, R. D. (2014). *Sitting together: Essential skills for mindfulness based psychotherapy*. New York, NY: Guilford Press.

Rinpoche, K. (1997). *Luminous mind: The way of the Buddha*. Boston, MA: Wisdom Publications.

Rogers, C. R. (1957). The necessary and sufficient conditions of therapeutic personality change. *Journal of Consulting Psychology, 21*(2), 95–103.

Rogers, C. R. (1966). Client centered therapy. In S. Arieti (Ed.), *Supplement to American handbook of psychiatry* (Vol. 3, pp. 183–200). New York, NY: Basic Books, Inc.

Rogers, C. R. 1980. *A way of being: The founder of the human potential movement looks back on a distinguished career*. New York, NY: Houghton Mifflin Company.

Rosenburg, L. (2000). *Living in the light of death: On the art of being truly alive.* Boston, MA: Shambhala Publications.

Rosenberg, L., & Guy, D. (1998). *Breath by breath: The liberating practice of insight meditation.* Boston, MA: Shambhala Publications.

Rosenkranz, M. A., Davidson, R. J., Maccoon, D. G., Sheridan, J. F., Kalin, N. H., & Lutz, A. A. (2013). Comparison of mindfulness-based stress reduction and an active control in modulation of neurogenic inflammation. *Brain, Behavior, and Immunity, 27*(1), 174–184.

Ryan, T. (2013). *A mindful nation: How a simple practice can help us reduce stress, improve performance, and recapture the American spirit.* Carlsbad, CA: Hay House.

Saint Exupéry, A., & Howard, R. (Trans.). (2000). *The little prince.* New York: Mariner Press.

Santorelli, S. (1999). *Heal thy self: Lessons on mindfulness in medicine.* New York, NY: Bell Tower.

Segal, Z. V., Williams, J. M. G., & Teasdale, J. D. (2002). *Mindfulness-based cognitive therapy for depression: A new approach to preventing relapse.* New York, NY: Guilford Press.

Segal, Z. V., Williams, J. M. G., & Teasdale, J. D. (2012). *Mindfulness-based cognitive therapy for depression: A new approach to preventing relapse* (2nd ed.). New York, NY: Guilford Press.

Shapiro, S. (1995). *Talking with patients: A self-psychological view.* New York, NY: Jason Aronson.

Shapiro, S. L., & Carlson, L. E. (2009). *The art and science of mindfulness: Integrating mindfulness into psychology and the helping professions.* Washington, DC: American Psychological Association.

Siegel, D. J. (2007). *The mindful brain: Reflection and attunement in the cultivation of well-being.* New York, NY: W. W. Norton & Company.

Siegel, D. J. (2010). *The mindful therapist: A clinician's guide to mindsight and neural integration.* New York, NY: W. W. Norton & Company.

Siegel, D. J. (2012). *The developing mind: How relationships and the brain interact to shape who we are* (2nd ed.). New York, NY: W. W. Norton & Company.

Spradlin, S. (2003). *Don't let your emotions run your life: How dialectical behavior therapy can put you in control.* Oakland, CA: New Harbinger Publications.

Stern, D. N. (2004). *The present moment in psychotherapy and everyday life.* New York, NY: W. W. Norton & Company.

Stolorow, R. D., & Atwood, G. E. (1992). *Contexts of being: The intersubjective foundations of psychological life.* Hillsdale, NJ: Analytic Press.

Stolorow, R. D., Atwood, G. E., & Brandchaft, B. (Eds.). (1994). *The intersubjective perspective.* Northvale, NJ: Jason Aronson.

Stolorow, R. D., Brandchaft, B., & Atwood, G. E. (1987). *Psychoanalytic treatment: An intersubjective approach.* Hillsdale, NJ: Analytic Press.

Surya Das, L. (2007). *Buddha is as Buddha does: The ten original practices for enlightened living.* New York, NY: HarperCollins.

Suzuki, S. (1996). *Zen mind, beginner's mind: Informal talks on Zen meditation and practice.* New York, NY: Weatherhill.

Thera, N. (1998). *Abidhamma studies: Buddhist explorations of consciousness and time* (Rev. 4th ed.). Somerville, MA: Wisdom Publications.

Thoreau, H. D. (2006). *Walden.* J. S. Cramer (Ed.). New Haven, CT: Yale University Press.

Thurman, R. (2005). *The jewel tree of Tibet: The enlightenment engine of Tibetan Buddhism.* New York, NY: Free Press, a division of Simon & Schuster.

Trungpa, C. (1984). *Shambhala: The sacred path of the warrior.* Boston, MA: Shambhala Publications.

Varela, F. J., Thompson, E. T., & Rosch, E. (1993). *The embodied mind: Cognitive science and the human experience.* Cambridge, MA: MIT Press.

Wallin, D. J. (2007). *Attachment in psychotherapy.* New York, NY: Guilford Press.

Wilbur, K., Engler, J., & Brown, D. (Eds.). (1986). *Transformations of consciousness: Conventional and contemplative perspectives on development.* Boston, MA: Shambhala Publications.

Wild, J. (1970). *The radical empiricism of William James.* Garden City, NY: Anchor Books.

Williams, M., Teasdale, J., Segal, Z., & Kabat-Zinn, J. (2007). *The mindful way through depression: Freeing yourself from chronic unhappiness.* New York, NY: Guilford Press.

Winnicott, D. W. (1984). *Babies and their mothers.* New York, NY: Perseus Publishing.

Wolf, E. (1988). *Treating the self: Elements of clinical self psychology.* New York, NY: Guilford Press.

Worster, D. (2008). *A passion for nature: The life of John Muir.* Oxford, UK: Oxford University Press.

Yalom, I. D. (1975). *The theory and practice of group psychotherapy* (2nd ed.). New York, NY: Basic Books.

Other Relevant Readings

Altman, D. (1990). *The art of the inner meal: Eating as a spiritual path*. San Francisco, CA: HarperCollins.

Bach, P. A., & Moran, D. J. (2008). *ACT in practice: Case conceptualization in acceptance and commitment therapy*. Oakland, CA: New Harbinger Publications.

Batchelor, S. (1997). *Buddhism without beliefs: A contemporary guide to awakening*. New York, NY: Riverhead Books.

Batchelor, S. (2000). *Verses from the center: A Buddhist vision of the sublime*. New York, NY: Riverhead Books.

Boorstein, S. (1997). *That's funny, you don't look Buddhist: On being a faithful Jew and a passionate Buddhist*. New York: HarperCollins.

Eifert, G. H., & Forsyth, J. P. (2005). *Acceptance and commitment therapy for anxiety disorders: A practitioner's treatment guide to using mindfulness, acceptance, and values-based behavior change strategies*. Oakland, CA: New Harbinger Publications.

Feldman, C., & Kornfield, J. (Eds.). (1991). *Stories of the spirit, stories of the heart: Parables of the spiritual path from around the world*. San Francisco, CA: HarperCollins.

Flickstein, M. (2007). *The meditator's atlas: A roadmap of the inner world*. Somerville, MA: Wisdom Publications.

Frankl, V. (2006). *Man's search for meaning*. Boston, MA: Beacon Press.

Goldstein, E., & Stahl, B. (2015). *MBSR every day: Daily practices from the heart of mindfulness-based stress reduction*. Oakland, CA: New Harbinger Publications.

Gunaratana, B. G. (2011). *Mindfulness in plain English: 20th anniversary edition*. Somerville, MA: Wisdom Publications.

Kabat-Zinn, J., & Santorelli, S. (Eds.). (1988). *Mindfulness-based stress reduction professional training manual*. Worcester, MA: Center for Mindfulness in Medicine, Health Care, and Society.

Kabat-Zinn, J., & Santorelli, S. (Eds.). (1993). *Mindfulness-based stress reduction professional training resource manual*. Worcester, MA: Center for Mindfulness in Medicine, Health Care, and Society.

Khema, A. (1997). *I give you my life: The autobiography of a Western Buddhist nun*. Boston, MA: Shambhala Publications.

Magid, B. (2008). *Ending the pursuit of happiness: A Zen guide*. Somerville, MA: Wisdom Publications.

Marra, T. (2005). *Dialectical behavior therapy in private practice: A practical and comprehensive guide*. Oakland, CA: New Harbinger Publications.

McQuaid, J. R., & Carmona, P. E. (2004). *Peaceful mind: Using mindfulness and cognitive behavioral psychology to overcome depression*. Oakland, CA: New Harbinger Publications.

Muir, J. (2004). *My first summer in the Sierra*. New York, NY: Modern Library.

Remen, R. N. (1996). *Kitchen table wisdom: Stories that heal*. New York, NY: Riverhead Books.

Ricard, M. (2003). *Happiness: A guide to developing life's most important skill*. New York, NY: Little, Brown & Company.

Salzberg, S. (2005). *The force of kindness: Change your life with love and compassion*. Boulder, CO: Sounds True.

Sapolsky, R. M. (1994). *Why zebras don't get ulcers: A guide to stress, stress-related diseases, and coping*. New York, NY: W. H. Freeman & Company.

Sayadaw, M. (1981). *Fundamentals of vipassana meditation*. Berkeley, CA: Dhammachakka Meditation Center.

Smith, E. G. (n. d.). *The four practice principles*. La Alameda Press. Retrieved from http:// www.laalamedapress.com/practiceprinciples.html.

Stahl, B., & Goldstein, E. (2010). *A mindfulness-based stress reduction workbook*. Oakland, CA: New Harbinger Publications.

Stahl, B., Meleo-Myer, F., & Koerbel, L. (2014). *A mindfulness-based stress reduction workbook for anxiety*. Oakland, CA: New Harbinger Publications.

Stahl, B., & Milstine, W. (2013). *Calming the rush of panic: A mindfulness-based stress reduction guide to freeing yourself from panic attacks and living a vital life*. Oakland, CA: New Harbinger Publications.

Tarrant, J. (1998). *The light inside the dark: Zen, soul, and the spiritual life*. New York, NY: HarperCollins.

Tarthang, T. (1977). *Gesture of balance: A guide to awareness, self-healing, meditation*. Berkeley, CA: Dharma Publishing.

Tarthang, T. (1991). *Skillful means: Patterns for success* (2nd ed.). Berkeley, CA: Dharma Publishing.

Teasdale, J. D., Williams, J. M. G., & Segal, Z. V. (2014). *The mindful way workbook: An 8 week program to free yourself from depression and emotional distress*. New York, NY: Guilford Press.

Thynn, T. (1995). *Living meditation, living insight: The path of mindfulness in daily life*. Taipei, Taiwan: Buddha Educational Foundation.

Titmuss, C. (1998). *Light on enlightenment: Revolutionary teachings on the inner life*. Boston, MA: Shambhala Publications.

Young, S. (2004). *Breaking through pain*. Boulder, CO: Sounds True.

Steven A. Alper, MSW, LCSW, is a psychotherapist and mindfulness practitioner who has taught mindfulness-based stress reduction (MBSR) for twenty-four years. He established the first hospital-based MBSR programs in Southern California in 1994 at the University of California, San Diego Department of Psychiatry Outpatient Clinic, and in 1995 at the Scripps Center for Integrative Medicine in La Jolla, CA, where he was MBSR program director and senior instructor from 1995-2005. In addition to his private practice, he has taught mindfulness nationally and internationally since 2005 to mental health and health care professionals, as well as in a range of corporate, non-profit, and professional settings.

Index

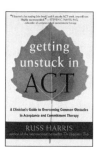
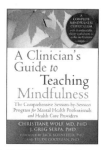
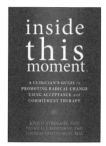
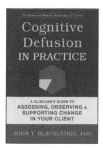

Register your **new harbinger** titles for additional benefits!

When you register your **new harbinger** title—purchased in any format, from any source—you get access to benefits like the following:

- Downloadable accessories like printable worksheets and extra content

- Instructional videos and audio files

- Information about updates, corrections, and new editions

Not every title has accessories, but we're adding new material all the time.

Access free accessories in 3 easy steps:

1. Sign in at NewHarbinger.com (or **register** to create an account).

2. Click on **register a book**. Search for your title and click the **register** button when it appears.

3. Click on the **book cover or title** to go to its details page. Click on **accessories** to view and access files.

That's all there is to it!

If you need help, visit:

NewHarbinger.com/accessories

new harbinger
CELEBRATING
40 YEARS